Jewish-American Fiction, 1917–1987

Sanford Pinsker

Franklin and Marshall College

Twayne Publishers • New York
Maxwell Macmillan Canada • Toronto
Maxwell Macmillan International • New York   Oxford   Singapore   Sydney

Jewish-American Fiction, 1917–1987
Sanford Pinsker

Twayne Publishers   Maxwell Macmillan Canada Inc.
Macmillan Publishing Company   1200 Eglinton Avenue East
866 Third Avenue   Suite 200
New York, New York 10022   Don Mills, Ontario M3C 3N1

Macmillan Publishing Company is a member of the Maxwell Communication Group
of Companies.

10 9 8 7 6 5 4 3 2 1

The paper used in this publication meets the minimum requirements of American
National Standard for Information Sciences—Permanence of Paper for Printed
Library Materials, ANSI Z39.48-1984. ∞™

Printed and bound in the United States of America.

Library of Congress Cataloging-in-Publication Data

Pinsker, Sanford.
   Jewish-American fiction, 1917-1987 / Sanford Pinsker.
      p.   cm. — (Twayne's United States authors series ; TUSAS 606)
   Includes bibliographical references and index
   ISBN 0-8057-3959-9 (alk. paper)
      1. American fiction—Jewish authors—History and criticism.
2. American fiction—20th century—History and criticism. 3. Jewish
fiction—United States—History and criticism. 4. Jews—United
States—Intellectual life. 5. Jews in Literature. I. Title.
II. Series.
PS153.J4P56   1992
813'.5098924—dc20

                                                    92-2948
                                                        CIP

Jewish-American Fiction, 1917–1987

Twayne's United States Authors Series

Warren French, Editor

University College of Swansea, Wales

TUSAS 606

Simply, and always, for Ann

Contents

Preface

Merely to sound their names—Henry Roth, Delmore Schwartz, Isaac Rosenfeld, Bernard Malamud, Philip Roth, Saul Bellow, Cynthia Ozick—is to realize how important, how "established," Jewish-American writers have become. Such was not always the case. Indeed, one can turn the 1,000-plus pages of the first edition of *The Literary History of the United States* (1948) without encountering a single Jewish-American fictionist. How a significant body of Jewish-American novels came to be written and to be widely recognized as an achievement of considerable consequence to American literature is the subject of this book.

There have been several surveys of Jewish-American writing that aspire to comprehensiveness: Sol Liptzin's *The Jew in the American Novel* (1966), Allen Guttmann's *The Jewish Writer in America* (1971), and, perhaps most exhaustive of them all, Louis Harap's twin volumes *The Image of the Jew in American Literature: From Early Republic to Mass Immigration* (1974) and *Creative Awakening: The Jewish Presence in Twentieth-Century American Literature, 1900–1940s* (1987). *Jewish-American Fiction, 1917–1987* both benefits from and builds on these studies but is not designed primarily as a comprehensive literary survey. Rather, by concentrating on a handful of representative fictions, I hope to show the significance of Jewish-American fiction as it moved from obscure beginnings to international importance in the decades following World War II.

As the rabbis of old knew full well, "Of the making of books there is no end." Stories beget more stories, novels beget more novels, and, to nobody's surprise, literary critics beget more literary criticism—and often in ways that suggest the continuities and the *dis*continuities, the shared values and the internecine squabbles, that afflicted those "begettings" recorded in the King James version of Genesis. Jewish-American writers are, of course, a representative case of a general condition, albeit one writ large and in exclamation points.

To be sure, Jewish writing has a long and venerable history. Commentaries on the Torah were less a cottage industry than they were simultaneously an intellectual compulsion and a survival technique that generated commentaries-on-commentaries—and still more commentaries on *those* commentaries—in Babylonia, Spain, and indeed wherever Jews wandered. Only the names of the respective lands changed, and to the Jewish writer swaying over a tractate of Talmud, he was always in *galut,* in "exile," and his task there was always the same—namely, to explicate God's revealed Word, and in specifically "Jewish" languages (Hebrew, Yiddish, Ladino). His purpose—what he would have called his *takhlis*—raised neither Jewish eyebrows nor Jewish questions.

By contrast, phrases like "Jewish literature" or, even more troubling, "*Jewish-American* literature" find themselves surrounded by quotation marks and heated debate.[1] To be a hyphenated American is perplexing enough, but when "Jewish-American" becomes an adjective modifying *writer,* the result takes on the look, the *feel,* of an oxymoron rather than that of a useful designation. And yet for all its inaccuracies, its contradictions, its sheer chutzpah, writers as radically different as Saul Bellow and Bernard Malamud, as I. B. Singer and Philip Roth, found themselves sharing space in anthologies designed to put "Jewish-American literature" between hard covers.

Small wonder, then, that these writers raised vigorous objections from the floor. I. B. Singer put it this way:

I never call myself a Jewish writer, although I'm a Jew and much immersed in Jewishness. I would prefer to call myself a Yiddish writer because a writer is called after his language, not his religion. But you can also call me a Jewish writer. My father would have denied this because, to him, a Jewish writer was only a man who wrote about Jewish religion. But there is a lot of religion and religious content also in my writing and I'm at least as much a religion writer as the other writers [e.g., Philip Roth, Norman Mailer] who are Jewish and write either in Yiddish or English.[2]

Singer, of course, was a diplomat among literary diplomats, a man who knew how to generate good press and to cultivate an adoring pubic. Why bite the busily typing fingers that review his books, write articles and scholarly books on his behalf? If they insist on calling him a Jewish writer, so be it.

Saul Bellow is a very different case. He does not suffer fools, particularly academic fools, gladly:

Suppose you have an uncle in the wooden handle business and the wooden handle business went out of date and was broke. And you got stuck with a big inventory of wooden handles. Well, you would want to go around and attach wooden handles to as many things as possible. I'm just an unfortunate creature who gets a lot of these handles attached to him. The whole Jewish writer business is sheer invention—by the media, by critics and by "scholars." It never even passes my mind. I'm well aware of being Jewish and also of being an American and of being a writer. But I'm also a hockey fan, a fact which nobody ever mentions. (Pinsker, 55)

For Bellow, the whole "Jewish writer business" was a racket, one that kept linking the names Bellow, Malamud, and Roth until they sounded like Hart, Schaffner, and Marx—makers of off-the-rack suiting rather than makers of individual fictions.[3]

No doubt Philip Roth hoped that his "Jewish problem" would simply go away when he announced, in Israel no less, that he was not a Jewish writer but, rather, a writer who happened to be a Jew. Yet as one Zuckerman novel after another indicates, Roth cannot avoid confronting the Jewish ghosts of his Newark childhood. They exacerbate, they infuriate, they haunt; they remain, in a word, his *material*.

How, then, to see Jewish-American writing both steady and whole? For the New York Jewish intellectuals we associate with the heyday of the *Partisan Review*—writers like Philip Rahv and Delmore Schwartz, Irving Howe and Isaac Rosenfeld—"Jewishness" was a condition of being that did not warrant special efforts either to deny or to define. It simply *was*—a fact that, in retrospect, might account for their attraction to radical politics and to literary modernism but that they knew more intimately as the stuff of secret (read: Yiddish) codes and the thousand small cultural moments that constitute an immigrant Jewish childhood. To be formed by such a world, by its grinding poverty and parochial limitations, its seductive warmth and abiding sense of the past, meant that one looked at mass American culture as an outsider, fully credentialed in marginality and finely attuned to alienation. The saga has been with us nearly as long as our century—sometimes powerfully evoked but always threatened by the seeds of its own destruction.

That much said, I begin with Abraham Cahan's *The Rise of David Levinsky* (1917) and end with Cynthia Ozick's *The Messiah of Stockholm* (1987). Both novels can be thought of as chronicles of "quest"—Levinsky chasing material success in America's garment industry; the protagonist of Ozick's novel seeking a lost manuscript that may or may not exist by a man who may or may not be his father—as well as indicators of significant shifts in direction and attitude by Jewish-American fictionists. As Dan Walden points out, "The Eastern European experience, written by the Yiddish writers, gave way to the American Jewish writers and they in turn gave way to the Jewish American writers."[4] In the concluding paragraph of Cahan's novel, David Levinsky confesses that he cannot "escape" from his old self: "David, the poor lad swinging over a Talmud volume at the Preacher's Synagogue, seems to have more in common with my inner identity than David Levinsky, the well-known cloak manufacturer." By contrast, Ozick's protagonists often find themselves moving backward in spiritual time to the very sources of Jewish folklore and Law.

The result is a wide circle, the cyclical development that this study attempts to trace. The earliest Jewish immigrants were the Sephardim, Spanish Jews who were forced to leave Spain in 1492—the same year Columbus set sail for America. They settled in colonial Newport, Rhode Island, and in what was then called New Amsterdam. That there were Jews in America prior to the mass emigration of Russian Jews that followed the assassination of Alexander II (1882)—some of whom, such as Gershom Mendes Seixas (1745–1816) and Haym Solomon (d. 1785), played significant roles in the American Revolution—or that the *image* of the Jew figures prominently in the work of Hawthorne, Melville, and a wide variety of American popular fiction and poetry is true enough. But the task of telling their own story, in a language somewhere between the Yiddish they brought with them and the English they learned, fell to the "huddled [Russian Jewish] masses" of New York City's Lower East Side.

By now, some of the road signs of this protracted journey are familiar: the attractions and resistances to acculturation; the giddy freedoms and opportunities to be found on America's "golden streets"; the tensions—indeed, the guilts—of father-son conflicts; the battle royal between Orthodoxy and secular energies (usually defined in a series of isms, as in socialism, communism, Zionism); the charged words of *marginality, alienation,* and *discontinuity* on the one hand and *redemption, transcendence,* and *messianism* on the other; the meretriciousness of the American-Jewish suburbs; and, finally, the conscious efforts to reclaim an authentically Jewish-American identity. These become the preoccupations, the abiding themes, if you will, of the chapters that follow.

Jewish-American writers are simultaneously blessed and cursed by having readerships that first read their books and then take them seriously. Some (e.g., Philip Roth) remain surprised by the animosity their work creates, especially when their satires hit sensitive nerves. Others insist they are "American" rather than "Jewish" writers (e.g., Malamud and Bellow). Still others, such as Ozick, make neither apology nor compromise for the Jewish sources at work in their imaginations. Some things, I think, are clear: that Jewish-American authors—however secular, however assimilated, however Jewishly committed—continue to value the "word," and as long as this remains the case there will be those who find fiction a congenial place to work out their visions, be they messianic, sociopolitical, or some combination of the two, and that these ongoing efforts suggest that the final chapter of their "achievements" has yet to be written.

Acknowledgments

Parts of this book have been drawn from earlier books of mine, including *The Schlemiel as Metaphor, The Comedy that "Hoits," The Uncompromising Fictions of Cynthia Ozick,* and *Understanding Joseph Heller,* and from articles that appeared originally in *Modern Fiction Studies* and *Anglo-American Studies.* In each case the material has been revised, modified, or expanded to suit the present situation, and I wish to thank my publishers for permission to use the material in this way.

I would also like to thank Franklin and Marshall College for providing generous research support, and my colleagues and students for providing an atmosphere that prompts me to do more—and, one hopes, better—work.

Finally, to my son Matt and daughter Beth, who gave me patient instruction in the mysteries of moving paragraphs and who proofread with sharp, skeptical eyes, many thanks.

Chronology

1860   Abraham Cahan born in Podberezy, Lithuania, on 7 July.

1893   Michael Gold (Irwin Granich) born in New York City on 12 April.

1903   Nathanael West (Nathan Weinstein) born in New York City on 17 October.

1904   Isaac Bashevis Singer born in Leoncin, Poland on 14 July.

1906   Henry Roth born in Tysmenitsa, Galicia, on 8 February.

1913   Delmore Schwartz born in Brooklyn, New York on 8 December.

1914   Bernard Malamud born in Brooklyn, New York, on 26 April.

1915   Saul Bellow born in Lachine, Quebec, on 10 June.

1917   Leslie Fielder born in Newark, New Jersey, on 8 March; Abraham Cahan's *The Rise of David Levinsky*.

1923   Norman Mailer born in Longbranch, New Jersey, on 31 January; Joseph Heller born in Brooklyn, New York, on 1 May.

1926   Edward Lewis Wallant born in New Haven, Connecticut, on 19 October.

1928   Cynthia Ozick born in New York City on 17 April.

1930   Michael Gold's *Jews without Money*.

1933   Philip Roth born in Newark, New Jersey, on 19 March.

1934   Henry Roth's *Call it Sleep*; Nathanael West's *A Cool Million*.

1938   Delmore Schwartz's *In Dreams Begin Responsibilities*.

1939   Nathanael West's *The Day of the Locust*.

1940   Nathanael West dies on 22 December.

1944   Saul Bellow's *Dangling Man*.

1946   Isaac Rosenfeld's *Passage from Home*.

1947   Saul Bellow's *The Victim*.

1948   Norman Mailer's *The Naked and the Dead*.

1951   Abraham Cahan dies on 31 August.

1953   Saul Bellow's *The Adventures of Augie March*.

1956   Saul Bellow's *Seize the Day*; Leslie Fielder's *The Jew in the American Novel*.

1957   Norman Mailer's *The White Negro*; Bernard Malamud's *The Assistant*; Isaac Bashevis Singer's *Gimpel the Fool*.

1958   Bernard Malamud's *The Magic Barrel*.

1959   Saul Bellow's *Henderson the Rain King*; Philip Roth's *Goodbye, Columbus and Five Short Stories*.

1961   Bernard Malamud's *A New Life*; Edward Lewis Wallant's *The Pawnbroker*.

1962   Edward Lewis Wallant dies on 5 December.

1964   Saul Bellow's *Herzog*.

1967   Michael Gold dies on 14 May; Bernard Malamud's *The Fixer*.

1969   Bernard Malamud's *Pictures of Fidelman*; Philip Roth's *Portnoy's Complaint*.

1970   Saul Bellow's *Mr. Sammler's Planet*.

1971   Bernard Malamud's *The Tenants*; Cynthia Ozick's *The Pagan Rabbi and Other Stories*.

1973   Arthur Cohen's *In the Days of Simon Stern*; Bernard Malamud's *Rembrandt's Hat*.

1974   Philip Roth's *My Life as a Man*.

1975   Saul Bellow's *Humboldt's Gift*; Philip Roth's *Reading Myself and Others*.

1976   Saul Bellow wins the Nobel Prize in literature.

1978   Isaac Bashevis Singer wins the Nobel Prize in literature.

1979   Joseph Heller's *Good as Gold*; Bernard Malamud's *Dubin's Lives*; Philip Roth's *The Ghost Writer*.

1981   Philip Roth's *Zuckerman Unbound*.

1982   Saul Bellow's *Dean's December*; Cynthia Ozick's *Levitation: Five Fictions*; Isaac Bashevis Singer's *Collected Stories*.

1983 Cynthia Ozick's *Art and Ardor: Essays* and *The Cannibal Galaxy*; Philip Roth's *The Anatomy Lesson*; Bernard Malamud's *Collected Stories.*

1984 Joseph Heller's *God Knows*; Saul Bellow's *Him with His Foot in His Mouth.*

1985 Tova Reich's *Master of the Return,* which wins Edward Lewis Wallant Prize.

1986 Bernard Malamud dies on 18 March.

1987 Cynthia Ozick's *The Messiah of Stockholm*; Saul Bellow's *More Die of Heartbreak*; Steve Stern's *Lazar Malkin Enters Heaven,* which wins Edward Lewis Wallant Prize.

1988 Philip Roth's *The Facts.*

1989 Saul Bellow's *A Theft* and *The Bellarosa Connection*; Cynthia Ozick's *Metaphor and Memory.*

1990 Philip Roth's *Deception.*

1991 Philip Roth's *Patrimony.*

Chapter One
The Triumphs and Tragedies of Jewish Immigrant Life

By any reckoning 1917 was a year crowded with significant events: General Pershing arrived in Paris to head the American forces in what President Woodrow Wilson had optimistically—and wrongly—called "the war to end all wars"; the Russian Revolution that John Reed so vividly described in *Ten Days That Shook the World* ended one bloody chapter of czarist rule only to replace it with even greater tyrannies; Freud published *Introduction to Psychoanalysis*; and in America, whereas daring young women (soon to be known as "flappers") bobbed their hair, serious readers could choose between the posthumous publication of Henry James's "The Middle Years" or the work of a young modernist experimenter named T. S. Eliot (*Prufrock and Other Observations*). Given such a heady atmosphere, it is small wonder that the world of Abraham Cahan's *The Rise of David Levinsky* might seem constricted and of interest only to those who, like William Dean Howells, were committed to championing the cause of literary realism.

The Rise of David Levinsky

Immigrant Jewry, of course, paid attention to Cahan—he was, after all, the editor of the influential *Jewish Daily Forward* and a towering figure on New York's Lower East Side. Perhaps more than anyone else, Cahan was *the* embodiment of the Jewish immigrant world's aspirations and anxieties. As Irving Howe points out, the *Jewish Daily Forward* (which Cahan helped to found in 1897 and which he edited until his death in 1951) was "like a large enclosing mirror," one that "reflected the whole of the world of Yiddish—its best, its worst, its most ingrown, its most outgoing, its soaring idealism, its crass materialism, everything."[1]

Nonetheless, Cahan's novel must have been a painful read. Levinsky's efforts to tell what he calls the "unvarnished truth" about his life neither justify nor excuse it, and insofar as his dreams of material suc-

1

cess were shared by the larger Jewish immigrant community, the shock of recognition must have been as widespread as it was unsettling.

Moreover, as the conditions separating Levinsky's world from ours increased, contemporary Jewish-American writers tended to regard the novel as a "period piece," full of realistic detail perhaps, but not worth dusting off, much less rereading. In fact, Isaac Rosenfeld begins his 1952 essay on *The Rise of David Levinsky* by making this very point— namely, that he had long avoided the novel because "I imagined it was a badly written account of immigrants and sweatshops in a genre which—though the novel had practically established it—was intolerably stale by now."[2] But that said, Rosenfeld not only goes on to claim that *The Rise of David Levinsky* is "one of the best fictional studies of the Jewish character in English" but also suggests the essential continuities that link Levinsky's psychic condition with his own:

Levinsky is a man who cannot feel at home with his desires. Because hunger is strong in him, he must always strive to relieve it; but precisely because it is strong, it has to be preserved. It owes its strength to the fact that for so many years everything that influenced Levinsky most deeply—say, piety and mother love—was inseparable from it. For hunger, in this broader, rather metaphysical sense of the term that I have been using, is not only the state of tension out of which the desires for relief and betterment spring; precisely because the desires are formed under its sign, they become assimilated to it, and convert it into the prime source of all value, so that the man, in his pursuit of whatever he considers pleasurable and good, seeks to return to his yearning as much as he does to escape it. (Rosenfeld, 155–56)

Unfulfillment is the central theme of Abraham Cahan's realistic portrayal of New York City's Lower East Side, just as *unfulfillment* was the spine that held together the complex appetites and ambitions of Cahan himself. At first glance his credentials strike one as altogether "representative": he had been born in a small village near Vilna, Lithuania, and educated in a small heder (Hebrew school), no different from hundreds of similarly squalid institutions. Later, an exposure to city life brought with it the usual series of cultural upheavals: he discovered the works of Turgenev and Tolstoy; he abandoned his religious faith; he became a radical; and after nearly being arrested in the polical roundups that followed the assassination of Alexander II, he made his way to America. In New York City he became a fixture at meetings, lecturing and writing for various radical groups; he studied English at night school; and by 1897 his spirit and that of the immigrant Jewish Lower East Side were virtually indistinguishable.

But Cahan was more than the sum of his formative parts. If he was a passionate socialist and a writer with a considerable talent for propaganda, he was also very much his own man. Those who were so enthusiastic about the former soon learned about the latter when he was chosen as the *Jewish Daily Forward*'s first editor. Cahan had no interest in running a Yiddish newspaper that would air narrow political quarrels in print. Nor was he especially interested in aiming the *Forward*'s pages toward the highest brows in the community. Rather, what Cahan wanted was "a popular paper, not a party organ—a paper that the average Jew in the street could understand without preliminary courses in dialectics. And in a short time, though it is hard to weigh with what degree of self-awareness, he began to regard himself as a guide, perhaps *the* guide, for the masses of immigrants. His task, as he saw it, was simultaneously to educate them in Yiddish culture and tear them away from it in behalf of American fulfillment."[3]

Perhaps the very contradictions embedded in Cahan's "program" account not only for the mixture of vulgarity and seriousness that characterized the *Jewish Daily Forward*'s pages but also for the ambivalences one detects in Cahan's novel. Divided himself, Cahan creates an equally divided protagonist in David Levinsky. Consider, for example, the novel's opening paragraph:

Sometimes, when I think of my past in a superficial, casual way, the metamorphosis I have gone through strikes me as nothing short of a miracle. I was born and reared in the lowest depths of poverty and I arrived in America—in 1865—with cents in my pocket. I am now worth more than two million dollars and recognized as one of the two or three leading men in the cloak-and-suit trade in the United States. And yet when I take a look at my inner identity it impresses me as being precisely the same as it was thirty or forty years ago. My present station, power, the amount of worldly happiness at my command, and the rest of it, seem to be devoid of significance.[4]

For a man whose wealth and social position presumably confirm Spengler's philosophy of social Darwinism, a man who prides himself on his intellectual curiosity and the precision of his painfully correct English, a man who insists above all else that, as the narrator of his life's chronicle, he is telling us the "unvarnished truth," Levinsky's "and yet" speaks volumes. No doubt some readers found a small measure of comfort in learning that even millionaires cry themselves to sleep or at least that their heads lie uneasily on silken pillowcases, but *The Rise of David Levinsky* is more than an extended case of special pleading or even a cautionary tale about the ashy taste of success. Rather, the candor about which Levinsky protests too much is multifaceted, as much the result of rationalization as the product of self-deception, for what Levinsky seeks to expiate is neither more nor less than the entire record of his life. To insist that there is still a glimmer in his soul of the poor David who once swayed over a Talmud volume is to keep memory alive, to link himself, however sentimentally or mistakenly, with history. It is perhaps most of all to forestall the final "letting go" that would eradicate the Jewish half of his hyphenated Jewish-American identity.

In David's dual nature—simultaneously attracted to and repulsed by the secular world—lies the central tension of Jewish-American novels to come. But that generalization offered, let me hasten to add that in his case the pendulum arcing wildly between the sacred and the profane is complicated by the psychodynamics of his confessional mode. Levinsky labors under the grand illusion that candor is a conscious and therefore controllable business. He pulls it out like a checkbook, paying off guilts both real and imagined.

Genuine candor, of course, is fashioned from sterner stuff; it moves in oblique angles somewhere between a selective memory and the heart's need for consolation. In Levinsky's case the source of his deepest pain lies beyond that pale where making a "clean breast of things" equals success. Granted, he quickly learns that there are moments in business when utter honesty is indeed the best policy, that, for example, when one is completely baffled by the "glint and rattle of knives and forks" in a fancy restaurant, it is best to admit the fact. But there is something disturbing about the way Levinsky announces his discomfort to his socially confident, Anglo-Saxon dinner partner: "Finally my instinct of self-preservation whispered in my ear, 'Make a clean breast of it.' And so, dropping the bill of fare with an air of mock despair, I said jovially: 'I'm afraid you'll have to tell me what to do, Mr. Eaton. . . . I'm scared to death. Take pity'" (*RDL,* 260).

America's literary heroes tend to have their rites of passage in the forest; David Levinsky finds his amid the strange formality, the very *goyishness,* if you will, of upper-class restaurants. And yet even here—or, perhaps more correctly, especially here—at a juncture in Levinsky's career where "confession" leads to a lifelong and highly profitable business relationship with Eaton, one cannot help but notice the odd mixture of desperate honesty and cunning subterfuge. For Levinsky, making a clean breast of things—telling an unvarnished truth—has a theatrical look about it.

Interestingly enough, such outbursts of "honesty" (however unconvincing his "mock depair" might have been) are as effective with business associates as they are disastrous with potential lovers. Leslie Fiedler suggests that "it is easy to forget the sense in which Cahan's book is a love story, or even more precisely a story of the failure of love":

Each failure of David Levinsky at winning a woman (and the book is in effect a tally of such failures) is given a symbolic social meaning. He does not get Matilda, his first love whom he desires while still in Europe, because he is not yet sufficiently emancipated from his Talmudic training; he cannot keep Dora, the wife of a friend with whom he carries on an inconclusive affair, because he has stepped out of the Jewish family and cannot smuggle his way back in; he cannot win Anna Tevkin, young socialist and daughter of an eminent Hebrew poet, because he has learned to sing THE STAR-SPANGLED BANNER with tears in his eyes, because he is a "Good American."[5]

On these fronts Levinsky's confessional zeal turns timid. The best he can offer by way of explanation are testimonies to the abiding influence of religious orthodoxy and its rigid patterns of sexual separation, its stern injunctions against romantic love. Although he assures his readers that he has "a better recollection of many a trifle of my childhood days than I have of some important things that occurred to me recently (*RDL,* 3)," Levinsky has precious little *understanding* of what those childhood moments meant. His "candor," in short, is at once a mask and a strategy, a means of eliciting our sympathies in much the same way that his fawning "confession" about bewilderment worked with Eaton.

Put more baldly, it is one thing to have Levinsky admit that he systematically fleeced his workers or that he was not above taking kickbacks from those presumably receiving union wages, and quite another to have him come clean about his own sexual demons. In this regard it is worth noting that in 1913, four years before Cahan published his novel, D. H. Lawrence had published *Sons and Lovers* and that 1917 also saw the publication of James Joyce's *A Portrait of the Artist as a Young Man*—novels that were to have a tremendous impact on subsequent Jewish-American fiction. By contrast, Cahan's fiction has that guarded pre-Freudian ring we associate with the Victorian age. Nonetheless, the novel contains all the information necessary to construct a psychological profile of sorts: a father who died before David was three years old; a mother whose loving security is no match for the females who follow; even dashes of homosexual attraction in the yeshivas of Europe. But neither author nor character seems willing to make the connections that would reveal the figure deeply embedded in the psychic carpet.

Not surprisingly, as the graph of Levinsky's material success soars, that of his love life plunges downward. In both contrary movements transparent rationalizations play a significant role. And once again, the story is told from oblique angles, as when, with a pragmatism that might have made both Benjamin Franklin *and* Horatio Alger blush, Levinsky sets out to conquer the world of high-class restaurants: "I would enter in my notebook names of dishes on the bills of fare of the better restaurants, with explanations of my own. I would describe the difference between Roquefort cheese and Liderkrantz cheese, between consommé Celestine and consommé princesse; I would make note of the composition of macaroni au gratin, the appearance and taste of potatoes Lyonnaise, of various salad dressings" (*RDL, 292*).

Thus, Levinsky spends much of the novel divided between dreamer and garment-industry warrior. That the latter takes its toll on the former is hardly surprising. For example, as Levinsky moves steadily up the economic ladder he finds himself looking "studiously away" whenever he is in the vicinity of City College. As Levinsky—ever the regretful yeshiva *bocher* (yeshiva student)—puts it, he felt "like a convert Jew passing a synagogue" (*RDL, 207*). Still, it is easier to imagine Levinsky as the college student he never actually became than as the husband he is doomed never to be.

But if Levinsky is anything, he is eminently adaptable. As one incarnation of the American dream sours, he quickly replaces it with another. Religious orthodoxy is obviously no match for the combined weight of Herbert Spencer and Charles Darwin, and one could say the same of liberal education. Levinsky's protestations aside, the voices that argue for the survival of the fittest square most easily with the no-holds-barred "business ethics" he picks up in America. As with his sense of how to dress and what fork to use, Levinsky takes on the mantle of "capitalist" with dedication and something of a vengeance.

The rub, of course, is that Levinsky is never quite willing to admit that business is business and, further, that in his case business is *all*: "I had no creed. I knew of no ideals. The only thing I believed in was the cold, drab theory of the struggle for existence and the survival of the fittest. This could not satisfy a heart that was hungry for enthusiasm, and affection, so dreams of family life become my religion" (*RDL*, 380).

Unfortunately, the connections drawn between physicality and sinfulness (so much a part of his yeshiva sensibility) demand the payment of psychological dues long after one has left the organization. As Reb Sender, David's Talmud teacher, once put it, "'He who looks even at the little finger of a woman is as guilty as though he looked at a woman that is wholly naked.' He quoted the Talmudic maxim in a tone of passionate sternness, beating the desk with his snuff-box at each word" (*RDL*, 39). Indeed, one could argue that David never recovered from such instructions. Add a mother oedipally loved, plus the infamous streetwalkers of Eastern Europe's Abner's Court, and the scenario that leaves one a psychological cripple is complete.

Granted, Levinsky has a nasty habit of chalking up a wide range of emotions to that column called "love." Only the names change—from Matilda to Dora to Anna Tevkin—as if to protect Cahan as an innocently inept lover. But the English so carefully cultivated in night school no longer stands him in good stead; what works in merchandise showrooms waxes artificial in a would-be lover's living room: "Dost thou love me, Dora? Tell me. I want to hear it from thine own lips" (*RDL*, 279).

To be sure, Levinsky's romanticism is twofold: one part directed toward the mystique of checkbooks and business in general; the other, involved with doomed love affairs. But if his story is filled with sharp moves with regard to the former, his disastrous choices with regard to the latter suggest that he is bent on unconsciously proving the truth at the center of Denis De Rougement's *Love in the Western World*—namely, that romantic love must be both adulterous and impossible.

Like Levinsky, Cahan was a man who never felt quite comfortable with his desires. And his novel, brimming as it is with sharply rendered social detail, is distinguished by an ability to split itself between an account of one man's "success" and an account—in effect a savage critique—of its terrible cost. Sentence by sentence, paragraph by paragraph, Cahan is hardly an accomplished writer; his "style" is wooden, his rhythms stilted. But the public world he evokes—with its painful wrenching from Old World traditions to a tentative accommodation with American values—remains a compelling vision.

Call It Sleep: The Childhood of David Schearl

By contrast, Henry Roth's *Call It Sleep* (1934) is a linguistic marvel, one largely made possible as a generation of Jewish-American writers sat in the classrooms of the same City College Levinsky so studiously avoided and, more important, began to think of themselves as serious writers in the modernist tradition of James Joyce's *A Portrait of the Artist as a Young Man* and *Ulysses*. If Cahan saw the Lower East Side through a wide lens, Roth narrowed his vision to the dreams and nightmares of an individual child. For David Schearl, the novel's protagonist, the Jewish immigrant world is what swirls around him in a cacophony of voices and languages as disorienting as they are potentially destructive.

Put another way, *Call It Sleep* remains imaginatively anchored in the Jewish immigrant milieu, rather than in the highly politicized world of its original publication. Rediscovered in 1964, the novel enjoyed an unexpected burst of popularity—ironically enough, at a moment when the Jewish world Roth had described with mixtures of affection and Freudian terror had nearly faded out of collective memory. How to explain such a phenomenon? One way, of course, is to point to those shifts in circumstances which separated those who read *Call It Sleep* in 1934 from those who encountered the paperback reprint 30 years later. The parochial barriers, the crimped possibilities, the grinding poverty, and perhaps above all else the nearly unbelievable squalor of the tenements that a generation of sons was happy enough to put behind them struck readers, Jewish and non-Jewish alike, as fascinating sociocultural material just three decades later.

In short, a hunger for "things Jewish"—sometimes authentic, sometimes merely kitsch, but nearly always overanalyzed and overpraised—quickly established itself. And as ethnicity moved from being perceived as an asset rather than a liability, everything from Roth's thickly textured portrait of the immigrant Lower East Side to Chaim Potok's page-turners about Hasidic life in contemporary Brooklyn found its way onto the best-seller lists.

But that said, what finally distinguishes Roth's novel is less its curious sociological history than its high standard of literary achievement. The charged word in *Call It Sleep* is *power,* as embodied in its complicated strands of Freudian imagery, in its Joycean lyricism, and, most important, in its movement to what the novel's final lines call David Schearl's "strangest triumph, strangest acquiescence." That David is but a child when such portentous language is ascribed to his consciousness raises a number of questions. After all, how much *triumph* can be read into the epiphanic moment when he plunges a milk ladle into the lips of the electrified third rail and narrowly escapes death? Unlike other literary protagonists—say, Lawrence's Paul Morel, Joyce's Stephen Dedalus, or Sherwood Anderson's George Willard—David cannot leave hearth and home for larger cities, unalloyed independence, or the implied assurance of becoming a successful artist. At the same time, however, one is convinced that David's domestic situation has changed markedly: "In the kitchen, he could hear the policeman interrogating his father, and his father was answering in a dazed unsteady voice. That sense of triumph that David had felt on first being brought in, welled up within him again as he listened to his father and knew him shaken."[6]

Roth's novel, of course, *begins* with a very different father, one whose rhythms are impatient, angry, and energized by paranoia. No scene gives evidence to these conditions more poignantly or with a greater sense of foreboding than the moment at Ellis Island when Albert Schearl greets his wife, Genya, and the son he secretly fears may not be his. That "others" are laughing at him—because his wife seems so befuddled, because his son is so oddly dressed, and indeed because they see him as a cuckold—leads to a moment of rage so pure, so "symbolic," that it is hardly surprising critics have read it in Freudian terms: "[Albert's] long fingers scooped the hat from the child's head. The next instant it was sailing over the ship's side to the green waters below" (*CIS,* 15).

Roth's "account of a hat" (unlike, say, Sholom Aleichem's more conventional Yiddish story with this title) has the thoroughly modern look of the Kafkaesque about it. But that said, I labor the point about the first traumatic meeting of a psychotic father and a terrorized son less to emphasize Albert's paranoia or David's castration anxieties than to see the moment as a synecdoche of the tensions that propel Roth's sensitive protagonist toward a self-styled mysticism. Power, after all, clusters around more than the parade of phallic images—hammers, whips, bullhorns—associated with Albert; it is also palpably connected to David's vivid imagination and his capacity for transcendent vision.

Interestingly enough, Roth dodges the opportunities interviewers have extended to talk about the novel's Freudian dimensions (that such notions were "in the air" and were most certainly in the rarefied atmosphere he breathed during the years he lived with Edna Lou Walton is beyond dispute). He is, however, eager to talk about the liberating influence of James Joyce; for among the lessons a young

Jewish-American might learn, perhaps most important is that the raw material of art is always to be found at the end of one's nose. Not that *A Portrait of the Artist as a Young Man* is "pure" autobiography (whatever that might be) or that *Call It Sleep* accurately reflects life in the Roth household. Quite the contrary: whereas Joyce demonstrated that the felt conditions of one's environment—what Eudora Welty means by her lovely phrase "the heart's field"—could be transmogrified into myth, Henry Roth showed how Joycean models could be applied to a Jewish immigrant condition.

Joyce, of course, constructed his mythologies from the distance and safety of self-exile, knowing full well that to stay in Dublin would be to fritter away his days (as his father had done) in drink, song, and self-serving anecdotes. Roth's "exiles"—first to Maine and later to Albuquerque, New Mexico—reflect his severe displacement from the Lower East Side of his childhood. No chronicle of "life and art" tells more about the inherent contradictions of immigrant life, about its tragedies and triumphs. And yet for all its scrupulous attention to quotidian detail, to the grit of urban squalor and the cacophony of "voices" that swirl around young David's ears, *Call It Sleep* is as dependent on mythologizing as was Joyce's *Portrait*.

Consider, for example, the contrasts between the fictional Albert Schearl and the actual Herman Roth. Although there were significant similarities (e.g., Herman, like Albert, came to America first and, more important, became estranged from his wife, Leah, over issues of Henry's paternity that are reflected in the novel), Herman Roth was neither as embittered nor as angry, as oedipally ferocious nor as "huge," as the Albert Schearl one meets in the pages of *Call It Sleep*. Nor, for that matter, was David's mother as loving, as maternally protective, as Genya. In truth, Roth's mother was a composite of Genya and her high-spirited, wisecracking sister. Finally, the young Henry Roth was hardly the sensitive plant whose lyrical ruminations give the novel its distinctive combination of mystical vision and Freudian terror.

At this point, a representative passage, one that demonstrates David's youthful consciousness at concrete work, may be helpful:

Standing before the kitchen sink and regarding the bright faucets that gleamed so far away, each with a bead of water at its nose, slowly swelling, falling, David again became aware that this world had been created without thought of him. He was thirsty, but the iron hip of the sink rested on legs tall almost as his own body, and by no stretch of arm, no leap, could he ever reach the distant tap. Where did the water come from that lurked so secretly in the curve of the basin? Where did it go, gurgling down the drain? What a strange world must be hidden behind the walls of a house! But he was thirsty.

"Mama!" he called. . . . "Mama, I want a drink."

The unseen broom stopped to listen. "I'll be there in a moment." (*CIS,* 17)

Roth renders the particulars of David's world from a child's perspective (in this case the oversized, adult dimensions of a kitchen sink) and in ways that echo the opening section of Joyce's *A Portrait of the Artist as a Young Man.* Nor do the Joycean influences end there, for in David's questions one also hears intimations of *Ulysses,* especially the hyperrealistic questions and answers of its penultimate chapter. Granted, Roth's adaptation gives his Joycean model a particularly "Jewish" twist—namely, in David's instinctive sense that "this world had been created without thought of him." Moreover, as the narrative unfolds, the tensions that matter most will pit David's alienation—his deep sense of being uncomfortable in the harsh, quotidian world—against metaphysical urges that are simultaneously mystical and profoundly messianic.

Small wonder, then, that Roth told Harold Ribalow, the man most responsible for the extraordinary resurrection of *Call It Sleep* as a 1964 paperback, that "redemption is my favorite literary theme."[7] Finally, let me point out that nothing so reflects the multifaceted tensions of which I've been speaking than the novel's language. In the safety of the Schearl apartment, David speaks to his mother in the clarity and warmth of Yiddish—a language Roth represents on the page as uninflected, "pure" Yiddish. Outside its walls, however, he is exposed to and often confused by the Yiddishized English that washes around him on the mean immigrant streets. Puns (yet another point of connection/influence between Roth and Joyce) abound in the resulting patois. Thus, *Christmas* becomes transliterated into the Yiddish for "scratch me"; *cocaine* is misheard as the Yiddish for "bowel movement"; and, most frightening, David's efforts to tell well-meaning strangers that he is "losted" end in confusion: "'Bodder Street?' [The stranger] screwed a tip of his mustache to a tighter pitch and regarded David with an oblique, critical eye. 'Bodder Street. Can't say that I've ever—Oh! Heh! Heh!' He exploded good-natured again. 'You mean Potter Street'" (*CIS,* 97). Later—at the police station—other possibilities are added to the mix: Pother Street? Barhdee Street? Like the larger question of David's paternity, Roth shrouds the truth in layers of language, each effectively canceling the other out. In short, readers are as uncertain about the Schearls' actual street address as they are about Genya's "condition" when she married Albert. The story Genya tells her sister—significantly enough, lapsing into Polish just as an eavesdropping David is about to learn the truth—remains unresolved.

The result is a novel bathed in a studied ambivalence. David remains simultaneously attracted to and repulsed by the larger world's claims, just as he is ambivalent about the smaller orbit—alternately protective and terrifying—of the Schearl apartment. For example, he associates the "red days" on the family calendar with his father ("Red days were Sundays, days his father was home. It always gave David a little qualm of dread to watch them draw near"; *CIS,* 19), but alarm clocks—especially those which have been systematically taken apart—are lessons you learn on the street.

Yussie had stripped off the outer shell of an alarm-clock. Exposed, the brassy, geometric vitals ticked when prodded, whirred and jingled falteringly.

"It still c'n go," Yussie gravely enlightened him. . . . Id's coz id's a machine."

"Oh!"

"It wakes op mine fodder in de mawning."

"It tells yuh w'en yuh sh'd eat an' w'en yuh have tuh go tuh sleep. It shows yuh w'ea, but I tooked it off." (*CIS,* 20–21)

A generation earlier, Abraham Cahan would have studiously avoided such passages, no doubt feeling that English should be written as it appears in grammar books—that is, with *i*'s dotted and *t*'s crossed, with rules scrupulously followed, and with just enough *notwithstanding*'s sprinkled in to indicate "proficiency." That the result was wooden, "starchy" prose is hardly surprising, given everything that encouraged Cahan to write in such a fashion. By contrast, Roth would reflect a very different grasp of language, one supple enough to become a tool he mastered rather than one that mastered *him.*

And yet for all the shaping of experience, the rendering of the child caught between crumbling Old World values and an accommodation not yet formed, there is a sense that *Call It Sleep* is a book that wrote its author rather than the other way around. As Irving Howe points out, "The whole experience is here, rendered with a luxuriant fulness: quarrels and precocious sex, dark tenements with rat infested cellars, the oppressive comedy of Hebrew school where children learn to torment an enraged rabbi, and, above all, the beauty of his mother, tall and pale, glowing with feminine grace and chastened sexuality, that sexuality always present in the Jewish world but rarely acknowledged" (Howe, 1976, 583). Roth's protracted "sleep" since 1934 (when *Call It Sleep* was first published) would seem to corroborate Howe's view; not only did his subsequent efforts at fiction writing turn sour (e.g., a conventional 1930s proletarian novel), but, more important, Roth himself felt he had, in his own words, "failed at adulthood." His truest art, as well as his truest "self," remained forever anchored to the Lower East Side of his childhood and to the imaginative transformation he gave it in *Call It Sleep*.

But is it the immigrant experience in general or the Jewish-American experience in its defining, nontransferable dimensions that is at the root of both Roth's artistic triumph and his personal tragedy? Some have argued (most prominently, Robert Alter) that *Call It Sleep* is less a "Jewish" book than a novel about the universality of the immigrant experience, and that with minor changes in detail, the story of David Schearl could as well have been the story of an Italian, Irish, or Polish immigrant family. Thus, for him, *Call It Sleep* is best and most authentically seen as a quintessentially "American" story. Others, of course, argue in behalf of the novel's essential Jewishness—in tone, in nuance, and, most of all, in *vision*—and there have even been those who deny that non-Jews can "read" the novel at all and that the "universalists" are simply deluding themselves and, perhaps more important, deluding non-Jewish readers.

My own experience would suggest that the last position is simply not true; even so, I have trouble numbering myself in Alter's camp. Too much of *Call It Sleep*'s power—as well as the novel's very theme of power—resides in Jewish values and what I would call "Jewish conflict," though labels per se interest me less than those who have chosen sides over the issue. It is entirely possible, for example, that *Call It Sleep* is both particular and universal, and that depending on which passages are being discussed, one might choose to emphasize the socioeconomic conditions of immigrant life or the Jewish particulars that provide a major part of David's messianic vision.

One thing, however, is clear: Roth works hard to convey a world in which Albert's temper does not necessarily hamper his ability to land another job. Indeed, as David discovers when sent to the printing shop to pick up his father's severance pay, he had "near brained" a fellow employee with a hammer. And while the encounter causes David a spate of bad dreams ("[H]e no longer could tell where his father was

flesh and where dream. Who would believe him if he said, I saw my
father lift a hammer"; *CIS*, 28), the event does not dog Albert's work
records, much less ruin his chance for subsequent jobs.

Granted, Albert is a dangerous customer—short of fuse, violent,
altogether undependable. But in more conventional novels of the period
(e.g., Michael Gold's *Jews without Money*, published in 1930), capitalist
exploitation would not only account for Albert's proletarian rage but
also justify his righteous indignation. No such formula dominates the
world of *Call It Sleep*; instead, Albert simply changes jobs, this time to
one that allows him to deliver milk, to work outdoors and, best of all,
with a horse. In short, neither bad recommendations nor a "blacklist"
haunt Albert's prospects (how different all this will become in the anxious world of Saul Bellow's *The Victim*!) and nobody—with the notable
exception of David—ever finds out about the hammer Albert so vio-
lently wielded.

But, of course, David knows, and for Roth's oedipal pattern that is
quite enough. Moreover, what David "overhears" is part vision, part
dream. That Albert's hammer is imaginatively associated with the hammer of Thor turns "father" into a figure of godlike vengeance and
power. Add David's account of a naked torso and a gleaming razor—as
the "broad spindle and mounds of muscles along [Albert's] arms and
shoulders knotted powerfully" (*CIS*, 176)—and the result is not unlike
the way a frightened Franz will describe Herr Kafka.

Albert's hammer, his gleaming razor, and, later, the whip and bullhorns he brings home as talisman and tableau—these are the phallic
images defining his oppressive masculinity and his deepest fears about
cukoldry, for if those deep images are not fully explained until late in
the novel (when we learn that a young Albert had watched—in combined fear and delight—his own father being gored to death by a bull),
we feel their unconscious power as David does.

That sons replace fathers, only to be replaced by their own sons,
is the pattern David tries to break as he gathers images of light: from
his mother's story about peasant superstitions in the Old Country, from
the blinding rays of the sun as they bounce off the East River, from his
Christian friend Leo's picture of Jesus of the "burning heart," from the
electric force unleashed from the train's third rail, and, most important,
from the story of Isaiah and the cleansing coal David overhears in heder.
In a novel that can boast nearly as many "languages" as *Ulysses*, Roth
uses half-overheard and partly understood information to suggest how
David forms his self-styled, mystical "reality." Such a world divides

itself—perhaps too neatly, too "symbolically"—between the dark sinfulness of the cellar, with its rats, coal, and intimations of sexuality, and the roof, with its promises of transcendent flight.

And yet for all the thematic connections that give the novel its sense of unity and imagistic power, what energizes David's quest is his equation of God with power. Caught breaking into (rather than out of) the Hebrew school over which an embittered, sadistic Reb Pankower presides, a startled David puts it this way: "I came for the book. The blue book with the coal in it! The man and the coal!" (*CIS,* 256). And as David goes on to explain, he has connected the biblical Isaiah who is miraculously cleansed by a white-hot coal with the searing electric heat he felt when older boys taunted him into placing a zinc sword into the lip of the electric car's third rail: "I remember, and I—I wanted to read it . . . because I went and saw a coal like—like Isaiah" (*CIS,* 257).

Pankower's initial reaction is exasperation: "Fool! . . . Go beat your head on a wall! God's light is not between car-tracks" (*CIS,* 257). Moreover, Roth makes it abundantly clear that Pankower belongs to a long tradition of frustrated, sadistic *melamidim* (Hebrew teachers who taught beginning students the alphabet by less-than-subtle combinations of humiliation and terror). Unsuccessful by American standards, these itinerant teachers railed against the widespread evidence of acculturation and cursed the bad luck that had reduced them to their lowly fate.

Indeed, Roth's savage portrait spares nothing: Pankower is a disheveled, tobacco-stained tyrant. As one student puts it, "He's a louser. He hits (*CIS,* 213)." More germane to the novel's tapestry of images, his infamous "pointers" (popsicle sticks sharpened at the tip and used to keep one's place in a Hebrew text, as bribes against his outbursts, and for disciplinary purposes) suggest yet another set of phallic images in a novel fairly riddled with them. But this much said, Pankower also knows specialness when he sees it, and David is a rare student: he reads Hebrew with blinding speed (despite the fact that he has virtually no idea what he is reciting) and, even spookier, his unconscious "takes in" the lessons older boys recite. Indeed, it is these talents that have brought David and Isaiah into strange conjunction.

Roth insists that he stumbled by accident on the passage in which Isaiah proclaims that he, a common man, has "seen the Almighty. I, unclean one, have seen him! Behold, my lips are unclean and I live in a land unclean" (*CIS,* 227), that he was hardly a student of the Hebrew Bible, either as a young man or as a fledgling author. Rather, discovering the story of Isaiah and the fiery coal was simply a stroke of luck. But if so, it was good luck indeed, for it provides one of the novel's most powerful objective correlatives—that is, a way of merging David's abiding sense of sinfulness (the coal reminding him of his traumatic sexual encounter with the crippled Annie) with his nascent messianic yearnings. That David is powerfully drawn to the story—indeed, that he is obsessed with God in ways that his more prankish, fun-loving classmates are not—deeply moves Reb Pankower.

Moreover, as it turns out, Pankower is not *quite* the cartoon monster that many critics have made of him, for his concern for his student's well-being is genuine, as is his tragic sense that America will be Yiddishkeit's graveyard. As he walks toward David's home (in a scene heavily indebted to the rhythms of the "Scylla and Charibdis" chapter of *Ulysses*), his stream-of-consciousness associations paint a richer, more poignant portrait:

> Threading his way among the hordes of children, hurdles of baby carriages, darting tricycles and skatewheel skooters that cluttered the sidewalks of Avenue B, the squat, untidy Jew waddled northward on weak and flabby hams. . . . What would become of this new breed? These Americans? This sidewalk-and-gutter generation? . . . On ball playing their minds dwelt, on skates, on kites, on marbles, on gambling for the cardboard pictures, and the older ones, on dancing, and the ferocious jangle of horns and strings and jiggling with their feet. And God? Forgotten, forgotten wholly. Ask one of them who Mendel Beiliss is? Ask one, did he shed goyish blood for the Passover? Would they know? Could they answer? (*CIS,* 372–73)

With a small change here, an alteration of reference there, the speech might well have been made by Father Conmee as he makes his way across Dublin in Joyce's *Ulysses.* And with a different set of changes, the diatribe might well be that of an Allan Bloom or an E. D. Hirsch, contemporary educators who also believe that idleness has brought the Golden Age of Education to ruin. Granted, neither Bloom nor Hirsch shares Pankower's religious-cultural agenda, but they know a good, bracing jeremiad when they see one.

Nor, of course, do the ironies stop there—for if Pankower imagines that David is a "special case," utterly unlike others of his "sidewalk-and-gutter generation," he is dead wrong. David may find himself inexplicably drawn to the figure of Isaiah, but he is equally attracted by kites, zinc swords, and, most of all, the skates of his friend Leo Du-govka. In the fashionable parlance of the day, Leo is the "other," a Christian presence among the welter of immigrant Jews David knows more familiarly. But Leo also represents an index of freedom. He is not only a latchkey child who fends for himself, gives himself "to eat," but, even more impressive, his skates allow for mobility, for expanding one's horizons—in a word, for *flight*.

To be sure, Leo's skates are "skates"—that is, an appropriately real-istic detail in a novel out to sustain our illusion that David is, after all, a nine-year-old boy rather than a literary symbol. But since so much of the novel hangs on David's efforts to run away, to escape, they also suggest that "other world" which ties his respective quests into a the-matic whole.

That the two conditions—*di velt* (his immigrant world) and *di yenah velt* (the other, *higher* world) are constantly fusing is, of course, what *Call It Sleep* is largely about. David experiences something of this du-ality during an epiphanic moment beside the East River. Not surpris-ingly, *light* is the passage's charged word—one that knits together the *chumitz* (leavened bread, forbidden during the Passover season) recently burned with the "white matzohs" that remain, the fiery coal that mys-tically cleanses, the pure snow that a grimy urban world dirties, and, most important of all, the contradictory impulses within David him-self: "Brighter than day. . . . Brighter . . . sin melted into light" (*CIS*, 248).

Granted, David's pattern of associations is part of the novel's heavy Joycean debt. But Joyce's characters seldom muse in such mystical di-mensions, such highly charged moments when the physical world gives way (in David's word, "melts") to pure vision. Not that either David or his author means to direct our attention to cabala and the compli-cated algebra that accounts for the creation of the world, the existence of sinfulness, and the redemptive sparks that lie hidden within the world's shells, awaiting release. Henry Roth is, in short, hardly a scholar of the Gersholm Scholem sort; nor is *Call It Sleep* a working out, in fictional terms, of a study like *Major Trends in Jewish Mysticism*.

Roughly the same things are true for David's fascination with the symbolic power packed into the Dugovka family's emblem of Jesus and the Burning Heart. As Leo puts it, "Dat's Christian light—it's way bigger. Bigger den Jew light" (*CIS*, 322). Moreover, Leo's "scappiler" is a powerful amulet, one that allows a person to dive into a river without fear. As Leopold Bloom, Joyce's curious, open-minded outsider, might put it, "There's a big idea" behind such religious trappings, and David is both fixated by and drawn toward their power.

Ultimately, David's fascination is the stuff with which deals on the Lower East Side are struck: Leo's broken rosary for David's arranging a "meeting" between Leo and one of his cousins. That the result both reconstitutes David's traumatic memory of playing "bad" in the cellar with Annie and reduces him to a pint-sized pimp for the sexually precocious Leo suggests just how fateful David's interior fusion of God, light, and power has become. Even more important, David's ill-acquired rosary later serves to confirm Albert's worst suspicions—namely, that David is indeed the illegitimate son of a gentile organist. The moment pits Albert's phallic power against his son's growing realization that he can summon up even greater powers by tapping into the mysteries of the third rail.

Those critics who have labored the associations to Siegfried, the Grail Knights, and heroes in general are surely not wrong, for David meets his "test"—by plunging a milk ladle into the lip of the electic rail—in ways that bring the classical world to Avenue D. His is a rite of passage into "mystery," a dangerous yet fatally attractive realm where power and sexuality are inextricably intertwined. The moment both defines and forever changes him.

David has an appointment with destiny, one as surrounded by the intimations of tragedy (he, like Oedipus, will be simultaneously wounded and transformed) as it is rendered in a sustained section of modernist experimentation. Thus, chapter 20—in which David races toward the electric rail and the fiery cleansing it alone can provide—is designed as a tour de force, weaving David's interior consciousness with the larger, public world surrounding it. The effect—illustrated by the small sample that follows—is a complicated, interlacing style, one that raises language itself to a level bordering on the transcendent:

"An' I picks up a rivet in de tongs an' I sez—"
   and there was the last crossing of
   Tenth Street, the last cross—
"Heazuh a flowuh fer ye, yeller-belly, shove it up yer
ass!"
   ing, and beyond, beyond the elevateds,
"How many times'll your red cock crow, Peter, befaw y'

gives up? T'ree?"
   as in the pit of the west, the last (CIS, 418)

Here Roth means not only to widen the novel's sociocultural panorama
(adding even more ethnic voices to its heady brew) but also to include hints
of a political activism and unrest (e.g., the "red cock crowing") he has so
assiduously avoided by concentrating on the world of childhood.

   Nonetheless, the major theme of the section—as of the novel itself—
continues to be "power" as it shapes and defines David Schearl:

   Power
   Power! Power like a paw, titanic power,
   ripped through the earth and slammed
   against his body and shackled him
   where he stood. Power! Incredible,
   barbaric power! (CIS, 419)

Language as highly charged as these representative lines, as integral to the
novel's imagery and impetus, lies beyond analysis. One reads the last pages
of *Call It Sleep* and simply nods, breathless: this is the Genuine Article.

   Since its "rediscovery," *Call It Sleep* is no longer the neglected novel
it was when Alfred Kazin and Leslie Fiedler made a case for its importance in a 1956 issue of the *American Scholar*. Few American novels are
as successfully Freudian or as richly modernist in their execution, and
none provides a more telling account of the psychological dimensions of
a Jewish immigrant childhood. David's *triumph* may have been
"strange," his "acquiescence" ambivalent, but the quotation marks do
not apply to Roth's novel. Its triumph and its power are now a matter
of historical record.

   There were, of course, other novels that concentrated on the sociocultural conditions of the immigrant Lower East Side (indeed, in
chapter 2 I will talk at some length about *Jews without Money*), but none
were as distinguished or significant as the fictions by Abraham Cahan
and Henry Roth. Their novels established the central tensions that
would remain during the decades when Jewish-American writers explored what had been gained, as well as what had been lost, in their
fateful encounter with "the Golden Land."

Chapter Two
Novels of Wide Cultural Panorama

In their respective ways both *The Rise of David Levinsky* and *Call It Sleep* are novels that balance gain against loss, the assets of American possibility against its liabilities. Indeed, Sol Liptzin has argued that Jewish-American literature falls into three roughly distinct periods: immigrant assimilation, acculturation, and rediscovery.[1] Levinsky's regrets and David's torments belong to the first category and, for all their value of sociological statements about first-generation adjustment, are primarily psychological profiles of individual types—Levinsky, the man who embraces materialism at the expense of his Jewish soul; David, the sensitive child who seeks godlike power in mystical reveries. And while the next important grouping of Jewish-American novels continues to explore these themes (how could they not?), one feels a sense of broader expanse, of widening the scope of the novel to its traditional concerns—namely, statements about the wider cultural panorama.

Toward the Proletarian Novel

Indeed, there were those for whom America itself was the wider panorama, and who responded to its possibilities with everything from giddy excitement to more balanced assessments. Some writers—Mary Antin, for example—gushed about the America they saw through lace curtains and did so without embarrassment, without irony, and certainly without humor. A book like Antin's *The Promised Land* (1912), an account of the life she left and the life she found, is long on patriotism (three cheers for the red, white, and blue would hardly have struck Antin as sufficient) and very short indeed on collective memory. As Antin would have it, one can—nay, must—shed the skin of the Old World in order to march off—properly in step and to the right drumbeat—into the American future. It made for uplifting stuff, simultaneously as antique as Crèvecoeur's 1782 speculations about this "new

[American] man" and as fresh as the newest arrival on Ellis Island. In any event, here was "optimism" with all-capital letters and no room left for the self-deprecating quips about beating death by opening a funeral parlor:

This is my latest home, and it invites me to a glad new life. The endless ages have indeed throbbed through my blood, but a new rhythm dances in my veins. . . . The past was only my cradle, and now it cannot hold me, because I am grown too big. . . . No! it is not I that belong to the past, but the past that belongs to me. America is the youngest of the nations, and inherits all that went before in history. And I am the youngest of America's children, and into my hands is given all her priceless heritage, to the last white star espied through the telescope, to the last great thought of the philosopher. Mine is the whole majestic past, and mine is the shining future.[2]

By contrast, other writers—tougher, more hard-boiled than Antin—focused on the arithmetic of poverty and pluck that made for picaresque antiheroes, such as the Meyer Hirsch of Samuel Ornitz's *Haunch, Paunch, and Jowl* (1923). As Ornitz's shocking exposé would have it, adaptability—rather than Antin's brand of idealism—is what Jewish immigrant youngsters learned best, first in the street gangs of their crowded tenement neighborhoods and then in the labyrinthian corruption of the court system. Learning to live by one's wits meant not only survival but also—at least in the case of Meyer Hirsch—a steady stream of promotions.

Antin and Ornitz provide interesting points for comparison, not only of the diametrically opposed visions they held as young writers but also of the respective ways their subsequent lives unfolded. Antin graduated from Barnard College and later married the son of a Lutheran minister. Granted, she often wondered "if the conversion of the Jew to any alien belief or disbelief is ever thoroughly accomplished" (and in a certain sense, the very impulse to write *The Promised Land* reflects this ambivalence), yet it wasn't until the rise of Adolf Hitler that Antin was moved to acknowledge her kinship with the people of Israel. She died in 1949, having lived through the great wave of Russian Jewish immigration, the Holocaust, and the establishment of the state of Israel. Her testimonial to America, however, remained essentially the same as it was in 1912, when she first announced her "rebirth" and went on, in *The Promised Land,* to chronicle it. By contrast, Samuel Ornitz made his way to Hollywood, where a scriptwriter, if he were clever, might make a wage that eluded most novelists. In large measure, Hollywood turned out to be congenial both to Ornitz's talent and to his temperament—that is, until the chilly political climate of the 1950s, with its cold war and Red scares, when the House Un-American Activities Committee and Senator Joseph McCarthy forced him to trade a modest reputation as a journeyman screenwriter for the martyrdom and notoriety that came with being one of the Hollywood Ten.

But that is to jump ahead of our story. During the years when the David Levinskys and the Meyer Hirsches were trying so desperately to move from greenhorn to "alrightnik," from presser to cutter, from runner to political "aide," a group of young American writers—among them T. S. Eliot, Ernest Hemingway, John Dos Passos, and Archibald MacLeish—made their collective way across an ocean the Jewish immigrants had recently crossed. Give or take a few years and they might well have waved to each other as they crossed the ocean—the restless and disillusioned on one side, the eager and ambitious on the other.

By any measure, the American expatriates of the 1920s were a talented, impatient bunch. Many of them were in flight from the Midwest and the middle-class values it so smugly and unquestionably stood for. When Ernest Hemingway reputedly described the well-heeled Oak Park, Illinois, of his childhood as a place of "wide lawns and narrow minds," he might well have been speaking for all those eager to give Main Street the Bronx cheer and the Champs Elysées a respectful *bon jour.*

Nevertheless, given their situation as expatriates, as "outsiders," as members of what Gertrude Stein called the Lost Generation, it is hardly surprising that their art would in effect turn the established order upside down by focusing on codes of behavior and significant gestures that either made somebody "one of us" or, conversely, consigned him or her to a life beyond the pale. Robert Cohn, the Jew-as-outsider in Hemingway's *The Sun Also Rises,* stands as a mean-spirited, textbook case of the phenomenon: a sloppy romantic, a whiner par excellence, and, worst of all, a man who acts badly under pressure. Cohn, in short, spoils his chances, and to the Lost Generation crowd—who knew how to slosh down a drink or appreciate a bullfight or treat a "broad" like Brett Ashley—he could be written down in a single, unpleasant word: Jew.

Like much that separates Hemingway from T. S. Eliot, the way they responded to Jewish characters or to a growing Jewish "influence" in the arts suggests much about their respective backgrounds. Hemingway's cultural anti-Semitism was an inheritance, something one simply acquired in those times and places. It was in large measure the result of neither experience nor systematic thought. To be sure, immigrant energy may well have threatened the orderly world toward which Hemingway felt so ambivalent, but he was more interested in the inappropriate uses to which a spoiled Cohn put Princeton boxing lessons than in why he took them in the first place. By contrast, the anti-Semitic brushstrokes in Eliot's poetry (e.g., "Bleistein with a Baedeaker") and essays reflect a view in which English culture—its Christian moral values, its essential conservatism, and its literary tradition—must be protected from the undue, unsavory influence of the Jews. For Eliot, the self-appointed Anglophile "protector," Jews were, in a word, despoilers—that is, Eliot could easily imagine their corrupting modernity adulterating *everything,* as he put it in "Gerontion," with its Jewish landlord.

Indeed, among the major modernists only James Joyce—as a Dubliner in exile from his family, church, and state—was himself sufficiently "marginal" to imagine fully a comic protagonist like Leopold Bloom, for while Bloom may be many things—including the anti-heroic, modern equivalent of Odysseus as well as the representative modern man—he is also the quintessential "little man," the flop as beautiful loser, the figure immortalized by Chaplin and Woody Allen. And, of course, one hastens to add that he is also the man whose humanity ultimately triumphs over his troubles—over the small-minded Dublin world he travels through on 16 June 1904; over the phallic power of a Blazes Boylan; over the elemental Molly Bloom.

It is easy to see, however, how a humor of failure—whether it revolves around a Tevye or a Bloom—would seem out of place to those newly arrived in in the "land of opportunity." To the immigrant sensibility, stories about comic failure seemed un-American, and for those who wanted to avoid the tag of "greenhorn," this was a serious charge indeed. Moreover, as Freudian psychology began to shape the very atmosphere of twentieth-century life, it became increasingly difficult to believe that anybody could really be a victim of bad luck.

Mike Gold: *Jews without Money*

In the 1930s the proletarian novel gave a number of Jewish-American authors the chance to talk about the ways a "golden dream" had turned dark after only a brief decade or two. Consider, for example,

Michael Gold's *Jews without Money* (1930), a novel about growing up amid the blighted conditions of New York's Lower East Side. Had this book been included in the preceding chapter, few eyebrows would have been raised, since Gold's turf is essentially the same as Abraham Cahan's and Henry Roth's. But I would argue that the differences outweigh the similarities and, more important, that Gold's book seeks out those "wider panoramas" this chapter means to explore. As Gold put it in his introduction,

I have told in my book a tale of Jewish poverty in one ghetto, that of New York. The same story can be told of a hundred other ghettoes scattered over all the world. For centuries the Jew has lived in this universal ghetto. Yiddish literature is saturated with the ghetto melancholy and poverty.

And Jewish bankers are fascists everywhere. Hitler has received their support, both with money and ideas. Some of his most important secret conferences were held in the home of a Jewish banker. They gave large sums to his party before he came to power.

Hitler's whole program is to save the banking and profiteering capitalist system. The attack on the Jews is merely a piece of demagogy, to throw the hungry German masses off the trail of their real enemy.

No, every Jew is not a millionaire. The majority of Jews belong to the working-class and to the bankrupt lower middle class. It is natural that in the present hour so many of them are to be found in the Socialist, Communist and trade union ranks. Jewish bankers are fascists; Jewish workers are radicals; the historical class division is true among the Jews as with any other race.[3]

As editor of the *New Masses,* a magazine dedicated to the ideals and aspirations of radical workers, Gold was well acquainted with the language of class consciousness. Indeed, his sense that the plight of the Lower East Side Jews was inextricably linked to the fate of all exploited workers suffering under the yoke of capitalism is what broadens the panorama of *Jews without Money,* is what keeps it from being, to Gold's mind, a "parochial" book.

In fact, nothing more clearly distinguishes *Call It Sleep* from *Jews without Money* than the former's intense concentration on David Schearl's psychological states and the latter's insistence that sociopolitical conditions determine character and delineate fate. As the anonymous reviewer for the *New Masses* (most probably Gold himself) put the case, "It is a pity that so many young writers [e.g., Henry Roth] drawn from the proletariat can make no better use of their working-class experience than as material for introspective and febrile novels [e.g., *Call It Sleep*].[4]

To be sure, this is the case for an activist literature writ large, and while history has clearly vindicated the introspective Roth from hostile reviewers' accusations, the times and their pressures took their toll on Roth, the card-carrying proletarian. His next novel—never completed, as it turned out—would no doubt have warmed the cockles of Mr. Gold's political heart but probably also have ended up on the ash heap of "proletarian fiction"—as, indeed, so many of Gold's stories did.

Jews without Money persists, however, not only as a splendid "period piece" but also as a Jewish-American novel out to appeal to workers everywhere. In this sense it is self-consciously "universal" in ways that foreshadow the "cosmopolitanism" that would become a defining characteristic of the New York intellectuals a generation later. That said, however, one must admit there was something altogether crude and transparent about the way Gold raided his memory bank to construct his autobiographical sketches.

That there were Jewish prostitutes, for example, is common knowledge (though their exact numbers continue to defy the best efforts of scholars; a community eager to tout its successes was equally scrupulous about hiding its failures). But Gold would have us believe that, say, Allen Street, the center of the Lower East Side red-light district, was absolutely awash with strolling hookers: "There were hundreds of prostitutes on my street. They occupied vacant stores, they crowded into flats and apartments in all the tenements. . . . On sunshiny days the whores sat on chairs along the sidewalks. They sprawled indolently, their legs taking up half the pavements. People stumbled over a gauntlet of whores' meaty legs" (*JWM,* 15). Gold's point, of course, is entirely doctrinaire: prostitution is a visible index of capitalist/political exploitation, but it is a point he cannot make without an exaggeration that often verges on the ludicrous. On this score his writing is both formed and smothered by self-righteousness.

Or consider the matter of finding a job on the Lower East Side. Granted, there was exploitation, there were sweatshops, there was everything required to drive workers to political consciousness and the union movement. But it is also true that immigrants moved out of the worst tenements—and to slightly better jobs and modestly improved living conditions—in relatively short order. Granted, census figures and other official city records are notoriously inaccurate (like the poor everywhere, the immigrant Jews were fearful and suspicious—often with good reason—and who can say what gap existed between the actual occupants of a given railroad-style apartment and the figure duly recorded by a civil servant?). Yet one suspects that Gold's account of job seeking is of a piece with his estimates of Jewish prostitution:

> It was not easy to find my first job. I hunted for months, in a New York summer of furnace skies and fogs of humidity. I bought the *World* each morning, and ran through the want ads:
>
> Agents Wanted—Addresser Wanted—Barbers Wanted—Bushelmen Wanted—Butchers Wanted—Boys Wanted—
>
> That fateful ad page bringing news of life and death each morning to hundreds of thousands. How often have I read it with gloomy heart. Even to-day the sight of it brings back the ache and hopelessness of my youth. . . .
>
> No one can go through the shame and humiliation of the job-hunt without being marked for life. I hated my first experience at it, and have hated every other since. There can be no freedom in the world while men must beg for jobs. (*JWM*, 305)

That the Albert Schearl of *Call It Sleep* moves so effortlessly from one job to another must surely have wrankled Gold, and no doubt accounts for his feeling that Roth had ignored the significant for the merely oedipal. Indeed, the whole point that *Jews without Money* drives toward is initiation, albeit of a rather special sort—that is, into the glimmers of a new political consciousness and the new Eden that revolution promises. In David Schearl's messianic vision, redemption comes in mystical vision; in Mikey Gold's case, the new messiah's name is Marx:

> A man on an East Side soap-box, one night, proclaimed that out of the despair, melancholy and helpless rage of millions, a world movement had been born to abolish poverty.
>
> I listened to him.
>
> O workers' Revolution, you brought hope to me, a lonely, suicidal boy. You are the true Messiah. You will destroy the East Side when you come, and build there a garden for the human spirit.
>
> O Revolution, that forced me to think, to struggle and to live.
>
> O great Beginning! (*JWM*, 309)

Whatever else can be said of conventional proletarian literature—and *Jews without Money* is squarely in the genre—it loved the upbeat, hopeful ending. Nor was there embarrassment about the litany of O's that a later generation of New Critical readers would find offensive. For true believers, it was sufficient that the sentiments were politically "correct" and, more important, that workers could read them and realize they had nothing to lose but their chains.

In short, Michael Gold was a spectacular but hardly isolated case. Disappointment with America's promise surely afflicted many other writers, Jewish and non-Jewish alike, as they reckoned the gap between expectation and exploitation. One thinks, for example, of Max Eastman's *Venture* (1927), of Edward Dalhberg's *Bottom Dogs* (1930), of Josephine Hebst's *Pity Is Not Enough* (1933), and of Clifford Odets's play *Waiting for Lefty* (1935)—and of such non-Jewish "proletarians" as Jack Conroy (*The Disinherited*, 1933), James T. Farrell (*Studs Lonigan*, 1935), John Dos Passos (*U.S.A.*, 1937), and John Steinbeck (*The Grapes of Wrath*, 1939).

Nathanael West and Other Dystopians

Curiously enough, the same Great Depression that gave rise to a string of grim, essentially humorless novels also occasioned Nathanael West's *A Cool Million* (1934), a novel that set about dismantling myths about the American dream by dismantling a naive protagonist named Lemuel Pitkin. As his first name suggests, this Lemuel is a distant cousin of Swift's gullible protagonist, one who leaves his home with $30 and an unshakable belief that "this is the land of opportunity." The result, of course, is a bitter reversal of the typical Horatio Alger scenario: rather than finding his fortune, Pitkin moves from one disaster to another. His teeth are pulled, his right eye is removed, his leg is amputated. He is scalped, and finally killed—all in the name of "the right of every American boy to go out into the world and there receive fair play and a chance to make his fortune in industry and probity without being laughed at or conspired against by sophisticated aliens."[5]

In his more famous novels—say, *Miss Lonelyhearts* (1933) or *The Day of the Locust* (1939)—West couples accident and failure with tougher-minded assessments of the American condition. In *The Day of the Locust*, for example, Hollywood is portrayed as a land filled to overflowing with schlemiels of every sort. Indeed, Hollywood is the great mythical West to which people gravitate with their dreams. But sunshine and navel oranges only deepen the despair, and in a final tableau of terror toward which the novel points from its opening page the mobs rush you, the locusts devour the pharaoh's land, and the Apocalypse unleashes its full, psychic fury.

Miss Lonelyhearts has much the same message, although here the grotesqueries of suffering come via airmail. Like Pitkin, "Miss Lonely-hearts"—the reluctant male writer of a sob-sister column for a newspaper—is a knight in a rigged cause. The more he relates to the suffering of his readers, the more he suffers "accidents" of his own: he is knocked down in taverns, mocked unmercifully by his boss (whose name, Shrike, suggests the butcher-bird that impales its victims on thorns), and finally killed (mistakenly, ironically) by a jealous husband who misconstrues his intentions.

West died prematurely, the victim of a car accident, in 1940. At the time, he was 37 and had written four novels. During his lifetime he was numbered among those writers who have an affection for the grotesque, for the savagely satiric—in short, for the surrealistic. In the decades that followed his death, however, West emerged as an important "influence" for many Jewish-American fictionists—this, despite the fact that he took considerable pains to distance himself from Jewishness. Nonetheless, in a novel like Edward Lewis Wallant's *The Pawn-broker* (1962) the affinities with *Miss Lonelyhearts* are unmistakable. What West may have lacked in terms of a relation to traditional Jewish materials or to a distinctively Jewish vision postwar writers were quick to fill in. Perhaps West signals an end to that period of assimilation among Jewish-American writers in which joining non-Jewish fraternities at Brown University loomed as more important than confronting the implications of one's identity closer to home. In any event, Jewishness must have struck West as impossibly parochial, as delimiting both the scope and the bite of the fiction he wanted to write. For him, Nathanael Wallenstein Weinstein was a name that cried out for changing, and, remembering the advice of Horace Greeley, he "went West" with a vengeance.

But to talk about how critics and fellow writers went about reconsidering West during the heyday of the American Jewish renaissance is to leap ahead of the chronological story. During the 1930s, such novelists as Meyer Levin and Daniel Fuchs were still writing about their respective neighborhoods—Chicago for Levin, Williamsburg for Fuchs—and trying to figure out if one's world was Jewish, American, or a tenuous combination of the two. For example, a novel like Levin's *The Old Bunch* (1937) allows us to follow the diverse paths that a group of some 20 boys and girls from Chicago's West Side (the "old bunch") take on their respective odysseys through American culture. For Levin, the individual in the family unit (e.g., David Schearl) was no longer the benchmark by which society is measured; rather, it was "the surrounding group, the bunch, as perhaps even more important than the family in the formative years. Particularly in the children of immigrants, the life-values were determined largely through these group relationships."[6]

Thus, the old bunch's 964-page movement from 1921 to 1934 provides a sociological account of those times and places. That the portrait is filled with the sheer stuff of the prevailing American culture is hardly surprising. Here, for example, is a description of the up-to-date, thoroughly Americanized house of the Moscowitzes: "The apartment was swell, too, with a full-width sunparlor and French doors. Near the gas log fireplace was a grand piano—not a baby grand. A great red and yellow Spanish shawl was slung over its propped-up top. There were at least a dozen lamps, floor lamps and table lamps, and Celia's mother was always buying marvelous new lamp shades at Field's. Yellow silk shades with domes growing out of domes, and pagoda shapes with gorgeous long bead fringes. There was a big oriental vase that was always full of flowers" (*OB*, 361).

More revealing still is Levin's description of the seder that Sam Eisen "arranges," complete with place cards of biblical characters with "devilish little short skirts over the long gowns of the women characters, and . . . derby hats on the men (*OB*, 259)." And as if that were not enough, Ev has cut out pictures of movie stars and pasted their faces on the biblical figures—Adolphe Menjou as an Egyptian taskmaster, Groucho Marx as Adam, Lillian Gish as Queen Esther. To call such a mishmash "irreverent" is true enough, but it speaks to both the cultural liberation and the advanced stages of acculturalization that are at the heart of *The Old Bunch*. At such a raucous seder all the old stops have been systematically pulled out, and when the maid "brought in an immense, sugar-cured ham" (*OB*, 259), there were squeals and titters but nothing that would suggest the wrath of God operates in Chicago.

By contrast, Fuchs's *The Williamsburg Trilogy* (1934–37) is largely restricted to the bustling, colorful, often-eccentric life that immigrant Jews found in Brooklyn. Indeed, as Allen Guttmann argues, "Daniel Fuchs was the first to take apart the world of Sholom Aleichem's Kasrilevka and to reconstruct it on the sidewalks of New York."[7] Here is a representative sample:

"You and your ideas!" Ruth said, her eyes glistening with tears. "You've got a million ideas and you ain't even got a job. You wanted the subways to put in radio sets so that the people they shouldn't get bored riding in the trains. You wanted to open a nation-wide chain of soft-drink stands from coast to coast, only they should sell hot chicken soup. In cups. You wanted to invent a self-sustaining parachute for people to stay up in the air as long as they felt like. Every idea you got is going to make a million dollars apiece, but you ain't got a job, you ain't got a penny, all you got is a million ideas."[8]

And such dreamy ideas, it hardly needs pointing out, belonged in the Old Country or on the Yiddish stage—indeed, anywhere but in one's living room.

Nonetheless, both the dreamy "ideas" and the tensions they created continued. What had been acculturation moved, by slow degrees, to assimilation and then to gloomy pronouncements about the decline of the Jewish-American experience and the fall of Jewish-American literature. These directions will be explored in the next chapters.

Chapter Three

Reflections of the New York Jewish Intellectuals

If fictionists such as Michael Gold or Daniel Fuchs were both shaped and limited by the Depression, the generation of Jewish-American writers and essayists who followed them added heavy doses of cosmopolitanism to the more parochial aspects of a Jewish immigrant experience.

For better or worse, the phrases "*Partisan Review* crowd" and "New York Jewish intellectuals" have become nearly interchangeable—the former indicating those associated with the *Partisan Review,* a journal that stood for an anti-Stalinist politics, an avant-garde aesthetic, and perhaps most of all for independent thought; the latter, a convenient way of yoking general tendencies and disparate writers/critics under a single, admittedly squeezed umbrella.

Given the circumstances, impatient grumbling was to be expected (critics, it turns out, dislike "labels" just as much as their subjects do). But not to be expected was the ensuing spate of books out to set the record straight—not only about life "behind the scenes" at the *Partisan Review* (and especially as that testy, mean-spirited, and, yes, brilliant life was reflected in its editor, Philip Rahv) but also about who was or was not a *real* New York intellectual. There are, for example, Alexander Bloom's *Prodigal Sons* (1986), Terry A. Cooney's *The Rise of the New York Intellectuals* (1987), and, most recently, Alan Wald's *The New York Intellectuals* (1987).

What these scholarly studies—valuable as they are—tend to overlook is the sheer volume of fear that was an inheritance from Jewish immigrant fathers and that often masqueraded as chutzpah in the most utopian schemes of their sons. As Irving Howe observes, in retrospect and with an understanding he could not have summoned in the mid-1930s, "Immigrant Jewish life left us with a large weight of fear. Fear had seeped into Jewish bones over the centuries, fear had become the intuitive Jewish response to authority, fear seemed the strongest emotion to the very world itself, earth, sky, and sun, brought out in Jews.

To be Jewish meant—not this alone, but this always—to live with fear, on the edge of foreseen catastrophe. 'A Jew's joy,' says the Yiddish proverb, 'is not without fright.'"[1] Later, when Howe writes about the titanic struggle between Left and Right as it was so advertised during the Spanish Civil War, he depicts somberly the nightmare of our century against a backdrop of catastrophe: "Nothing else reveals so graphically the tragic character of those years than that the yearning for some better world should repeatedly end in muck, foul play, murder" (Howe 1983, 215). If history has taught us anything it is to distrust those with a programmatic reading of "history"— whether it comes as garden-variety utopianism or with a full head of ideological steam.

Small wonder, then, that the New York intellectuals themselves have had cause to reassess what the old battles meant—some by way of setting the record straight (e.g., Lionel Abel's *The Intellectual Follies,* 1984) and others by way of justifying their drift toward neoconservatism (e.g., William Barrett's *The Truants,* 1982). The magazines around which writers cluster are, of course, one way to gauge the changes in our mental landscape, for what are intellectual quarterlies if not the shapers of "taste"—whether it be the *Hudson Review, Salmagundi,* or the *Raritan Review?* And from this perspective, the gradual decline of *Partisan Review* as *the* preeminent vehicle for the New York intellectuals and the concomitant rise of *Commentary* (from 1960, under the editorship of Norman Podhoretz) put the issue of where we stand in bold relief. Those who embraced, or at least accommodated themselves to, the affluence and conformity of the 1950s (most notably, the influential Columbia University critic Lionel Trilling) drew sharp rebukes from the likes of Irving Howe and Norman Mailer. At stake was nothing less than "dissent" itself, and, as such, it is hardly surprising that Howe would feel compelled to start a journal of his own and to name it *Dissent.*

But if the days of what Trilling called "the adversary culture" were numbered in the 1950s, they returned—with something of a vengeance—in the countercultural, antiwar days of the late 1960s and 1970s. Howe, again not surprisingly, had his quarrels with the New Left (as did many of the older New York intellectuals), but a number of former Marxists, such as Irving Kristol and Sidney Hook, found themselves growing increasingly disenchanted with liberalism itself. As Norman Podhoretz outlines the case in *Breaking Ranks* (1979), everything from the excesses of student radicalism to black anti-Semitism contributed to his disaffection with the Left and to the making of what became known as neoconservatism.

The evolution of *Commentary* from a magazine that once championed fiction writers like Bernard Malamud to one best known for its conservative ideology says much about the shifting values of certain New York Jewish intellectuals. Because so many fiction writers still cling stubbornly to the politics of the liberal Left—one thinks, for example, of E. L. Doctorow—*Commentary*'s position seems to be that neither they nor their fiction merit anything but brickbats. Indeed, much of its energy has gone into corraling figures from the past (notably Trilling and George Orwell) for the neoconservative camp. Predictably enough, those New York Jewish intellectuals who stand against revisionism in general feel a special urgency to oppose these revisions in particular.

No doubt the New York Jewish intellectuals were *never* the close-knit band of like minds portrayed in the latest crop of literary histories; nor were they especially shy about turning their polemical guns inward. But during the years when the likes of Alfred Kazin and Irving Howe, Norman Podhoretz and Sidney Hook, were writing the books and articles that made them famous, it did not occur to them to parade insider gossip through public print. That virtually every member of what is loosely known as the New York Jewish intellectuals has now written his or her account of those times and places says much about their deep divisions and bitter animosities. And the very fact that these exercises in selective memory have attracted such wide public attention reveals much about the contemporary literary marketplace.

Indeed, only the Bloomsbury group of London—including such hardy perennials as Virginia Woolf, Lytton Strachey, and Bertrand Russell—produces more commentary about itself, but this can be explained partly by the enormous investment feminists have in Virginia Woolf and partly by the rarefied atmosphere and sexual titillation that Bloomsbury exposés unfailingly provide. By contrast, the story of the New York Jewish intellectuals may seem a tamer tale ("ideas" always are), but I would argue that their quarrels were, and are, infinitely more important.

For whatever else may be said of those New York Jews who scratched their way through City College in the mid-1930s and, to their enormous surprise, ended up holding down jobs as academics and, later, as wielders of considerable intellectual power, they thought of themselves as engaged in the defining cultural-political battles of the modern pe-

riod: the totalitarian threat of Stalin as well as Hitler; the moral bank-
ruptcy of capitalism and the large promises of socialism; the explosion
of cultural modernism in all its dizzying variety of complicated forms;
and, perhaps most of all, the exhilaration of argument in essays that
were simultaneously polemical, brilliant, and, in the new sense of the
term, "literary."

Harold Rosenberg once argued that "for two thousand years the main
energies of Jewish communities in various parts of the world have gone
into the mass production of intellectuals."[2] Rosenberg means, of course,
to harken up the image of the Talmud *hakhem,* but there are "eternal
students" and *eternal students,* those who sway, like the young David
Levinsky, over a Talmud volume and those who cut their teeth on
Marx, Freud, and James Joyce. The New York Jewish intellectuals were
clearly of the latter group. In *World of Our Fathers* Irving Howe defines
their central characteristics this way:

> The New York intellectuals comprised the first group of Jewish writers to
> come out of the immigrant milieu who did not crucially define themselves
> through a relationship to memories of Jewishness. They were the first genera-
> tion of Jewish writers for whom the recall of an immigrant childhood seems
> not to have been unshakable. They sought to declare themselves through a
> stringency of will, breaking clean from the immediate past and becoming
> autonomous men of the mind. If this severance from immigrant experiences
> and Jewish roots would later come to seem a little suspect, the point needs
> nevertheless to be emphasized that when the New York intellectuals began to
> cohere as a political-literary tendency around *Partisan Review* in the thirties,
> Jewishness as idea or sentiment played only a minor, barely acknowledged role
> in their thought. (Apart, that is, from a bitter awareness that no matter what
> their cultural or political program, the sheer fact that they had recently
> emerged from immigrant families meant that their group still *had* to be seen
> within the context of American Jewish life.) (Howe 1976, 595)

Those usually numbered in this admittedly loose group include
Philip Rahv, Meyer Shapiro, Sidney Hook, Daniel Bell, Delmore
Schwartz, Lionel Trilling, Alfred Kazin, and Irving Howe—each, in
his fashion, a New York Jew and an "intellectual" in the sense of rang-
ing widely among cultural matters, of being a specialist, if you will, at
being a nonspecialist. But there were others—say, Saul Bellow and
Isaac Rosenfeld—who were formed by Chicago rather than New York,
and still others, such as Leslie Fiedler, who spent the bulk of his most
productive years in, of all places, Montana. And finally, there were

powerful New York "Jewish" intellectuals who were not Jewish at all: Mary McCarthy, Dwight Macdonald, and, perhaps most spectacularly, Edmund Wilson.

Still, with all that separated them and all that broke out in periodic spats, those writers and critics who identified themselves with the *Partisan Review* knew full well what they were *not*. They were not, for example, members of the Ivy League establishment; nor were they ever likely to be—although that, too, came to pass as their prestige and power reached its crest in the 1950s. Nor were they numbered among the southern agrarians who huddled at Vanderbilt University and perfected the New Criticism that was ultimately to change the way literature was taught in American colleges and universities—although here too (and despite the considerable cultural/political differences) they found themselves making common cause with the likes of John Crowe Ransom and Allen Tate, their articles appearing in such New Critical journals as the *Kenyon* and the *Southern Review*. Indeed, as Marian Janssen's recent critical history of the *Kenyon Review* points out,

> The New York intellectuals and the New Critics shared a deep concern for literature as literature and a belief in the value and necessity of literary criticism. This formed a strong if uneasy bond between them, a measure of agreement often obscured by the disproportionate attention paid to their disagreements and differences. The antipathies that existed were mainly political and rather one-sided to boot: the New York intellectuals found grave fault with the alleged conservatism of the New Critics; most of the time, the New Critics could not care less about the political beliefs of the New Yorkers. In general, there was more that drew these two groups together than kept them apart.[3]

In this regard, Irving Howe provides an instructive example. Whatever his politics, he long held the now-unfashionable view that critical reading required little more than a focused concentration and a pencil. Others in the bad, old days were less sanguine, not because Howe eschewed "theory" (academia's current obsession) but because he sprang from immigrant stock. And what the raised eyebrows and whispers of the 1940s came down to was this: could such a person be trusted to teach and write about American literature?

In this sense such books as Alfred Kazin's *On Native Grounds* and Irving Howe's critical studies of Sherwood Anderson and William Faulkner were out to "prove" that the sons of immigrants could take on mainstream American literature. In the case of the book on Faulkner, other factors also muddied the branch water, for whole worlds of difference—in politics, in demeanor, in "style"—separated southern Faulkner critics, such as Cleanth Brooks and Robert Penn Warren, from a New York intellectual like Howe. But as mentioned earlier, what the New Yorkers and the southerners shared was an enthusiasm for literature in general and for Faulkner in particular, as well as a history of publishing across the lines of critical difference. Indeed, as Howe told me recently, their quarrels about literature had the advantage of being conducted "in English"—that is, both groups reacted to books rather than to "texts," and both talked about them in understandable language rather than in heavy-water jargon.

Still, there must have been a sense that some folks had squatter's rights to Faulkner, whereas others had to learn about grits in the library stacks. Howe grew up among people who drank celery tonic, not Dr Pepper, and while there certainly must have been other "Irvings" in his neighborhood, I suspect there was not a single Joe Bob. In short, there must have been some hangers-on in Nashville who regarded Howe as a literary carpetbagger.

Granted, none of this should matter, and for the best of the New York intellectuals and for the most impressive of the New Critics it did not. Both groups agreed wholeheartedly with T. S. Eliot's position that all a critic really needs is "intelligence." Howe might miss a southern nuance here, a whiff of verbena there, but even his most grudging critics would concede that he was a perceptive reader and a persuasive writer. After all, if the central question for apologist southern writers was, How could God allow us to lose the war? and the agony that modernist southern writers struggled with was, Why do you hate the South? Howe had been pondering similar questions—albeit in another country—all his life.

Not surprisingly, then, the Faulkner who most interested Howe was the one who shared his passion for elegy, for missions of retrieval and rescue, for what are such novels as *The Sound and the Fury* and *Absalom, Absalom!* if not exercises in lamentation, written at the moment when the residue of a culture faced, for better or worse, extinction? And for that matter, what is Eliot's *The Waste Land,* literary modernism's quintessential epic, but an extended lament for the redemptive rhythms that haunt industrial societies in the ambivalent space between "memory and desire"?

My point is simply that the energies Howe plowed into ambitious and pointedly Jewish-American projects such as *World of Our Fathers* were not unlike the energies he expended in behalf of Faulkner, or what he called "the idea of the modern." But here again Howe found himself attracted—or, perhaps more correctly, *chosen*—by subjects he came to late. It was a tendency he shared with other New York Jewish intellectuals, one that he explains this way: "The great battles for Joyce, Proust, and Eliot had been fought in the twenties and mostly won; now, while clashes with entrenched philistinism might still occur, these were mostly mopping-up operations. The New York intellectuals came toward the end of the modernist experience, just as they came at what yet has to be judged the end of the radical experience, and as they certainly came at the end of the immigrant Jewish experience. One quick way of describing their situation, a cause of both their feverish brilliance and recurrent instability, is to say that *they came late*" (Howe 1976, 508).

Marxism and Alternatives

I have thus far been concentrating on the *literary* aspects of the New York intellectuals, and that will remain my focus as this chapter unfolds. At the same time, however, I am well aware that there are those who see the *Partisan Review* crowd as being primarily involved in building a Marxist alternative to the offical Communist movement. Among the works stressing this side of the story, none stands taller, or more heavily documented, than Alan Wald's *The New York Intellectuals.* As he says,

Simply put, without Trotskyism there would have never appeared an anti-Stalinist left among intellectuals in the mid-1930s; there would only have been the anticommunist movement already existing, one associated with the essential Menshevik politics of various social democratic organizations, with David Dubinsky and Sidney Hillman in the needle trades unions, and with publications such as the *New Leader* and the *Jewish Daily Forward.* But it is inconceivable that Menshevism had the power to inspire such young writers as Sidney Hook and Philip Rahv, who were drawn to the Russian Revolution, because Menshevism denied the validity of that revolution while Trotskyism, despite its opposition to Stalin's politics, celebrated its significance and achievements. Trotskyism made it possible for these rebellious intellectuals to declare themselves on the side of the revolution (as opposed to the side of the social democrats who had just then succumbed to the Nazis without resistance), and yet also to denounce Stalin from the left as the arch betrayer of Lenin's heritage.

In a certain sense their position anticipated the one promoted three decades later by the Soviet dissident Roy Medvedev: that one can be a Leninist and for democracy at the same time.[4]

Wald, I should point out, writes as a latter-day Trotskyite, one who believes that this is the movement most likely to renew itself on our college campuses and among our brightest young intellectuals. On this score I think he is wildly off the mark, but for those interested in keeping the personalities and politics of a wide array of splinter groups, schisms, and internecine warfares straight, *The New York Intellectuals* is an indispensable reference.

My own view, however, is that the best fiction came from those writers who became disillusioned with narrow ideologies early, who suffered as much from the breakdown of the radical Left as they had from the parochialism of a Jewish immigrant world, and who released these disparate energies and frustrations in bursts of creativity during the 1940s. One need only think of Lionel Trilling's *In the Middle of the Journey,* of Saul Bellow's *The Victim,* of Norman Mailer's *The Naked and the Dead*—indeed, to read the pages of the *Partisan Review* in the 1940s—to understand why a wag once quipped that their typewriters must have had keys marked "alienation" and "disillusionment." In one sense, of course, Howe is dead right: the defining characteristic of the New York intellectuals is that they came late—late to literary modernism, late to the vibrancy of the immigrant experience, late to revolutionary ardor, late to nearly everything that had created the unsettled, unsettling world of the 1940s. The result makes for a restless, impatient brilliance, as an entire group of intellectuals came of age, although one could also argue that they were "like that" from childhood.

Consider, for example, the opening lines of "Zetland: By a Character Witness (1974)," a fictionalized portrait of Isaac Rosenfeld, Saul Bellow's boyhood friend:

Yes, I knew the guy. We were boys in Chicago. He was wonderful. At fourteen, when we became friends, he had things already worked out and would willingly tell you how everything had come about. It went like this: First the earth was molten elements and glowed in space. Then hot rains fell. Steaming seas were formed. For half the earth's history, the seas were azoic, and then life began. In other words, first there was astronomy, and then geology, and by and by there was biology, and biology was followed by evolution.

Next came prehistory and then history—epics and epic heroes, great ages, great men; then smaller ages with smaller men; then classical antiquity, the Hebrews, Rome, feudalism, papacy, renaissance, rationalism, the industrial revolution, science, democracy, and so on. All this Zetland got out of books in the late twenties. He was a clever kid. His bookishness pleased everyone. Over pale-blue eyes, which at times looked strained, he wore big goggles.[5]

Like other bookish immigrant children, Rosenfeld/Zetland was sickly, pampered, and most of all prodded by his family to be the best "intellectual" he could be. And as the story's narrator reckons the results, his perspective blends considerable awe and wry amusement: "He was encouraged to be a little intellectual. So, in short pants, he was a junior Immanuel Kant. Musical (like Frederick the Great or the Esterhazys), witty (like Voltaire), a sentimental radical (like Rousseau), bereft of gods (like Nietzsche), devoted to the heart and to the law of love (like Tolstoy)" (*HWHF*, 196).

To be sure, Zetland is at least as much comic archetype as factual portraiture. But if the words exaggerate, if they gild the intellectual lily, the essential "music" is on target. And it is but a short jump from Zetland's early efforts at surrealism—"foaming rabbis rub electrical fish"—to the Isaac Rosenfeld who cracked up the *Partisan Review* crowd with his Yiddish version of T. S. Eliot's "The Love Song of J. Alfred Prufrock" or who outraged the rabbis with "Adam and Eve on Delancey Street" (1949)—ostensibly an extended reaction to Kosher Beef Fry, a bacon substitute—that moved, by comic degrees and outrageous analogies, to a piece of memorable cultural analysis: "The complex centering in *kashruth* is not the only one that works on sex. There is also *milchigs* and *fleishigs*; and this, I feel, is the arch taboo. My own Orthodox grandparents would tremble, as though some catastrophe had occurred, if *milchigs* and *fleishigs* ever came into contact with one another, and with good reason. This is the sexual taboo not only of exogamy, but of the tribe itself. It is the taboo of sex as such. *Milchigs,* having to do with milk, is feminine; *fleishigs,* meat, is masculine. Their juncture in one meal, or within one vessel, is forbidden, for their union is the sexual act."[6]

In short, Rosenfeld could be a card, as well as a scamp—and one can see both elements in "King Solomon (1956)," a story that poignantly balances biblical resonances with contemporary detail, a sense of tragic nobility with comic undercutting. As Rosenfeld's version would have it, Solomon is a demystified, thoroughly domesticated character, one who struck readers as alternately a biblical giant and a contemporary Jewish-American uncle:

> None [of the counselors] has seen the King's nakedness; yet all have seen him in shirt sleeves or suspenders, paunchy, loose-jowled, in need of a trim. . . . When he appears in this fashion with, say, a cigar in his mouth and circles under his eyes; his armpits showing yellowish and hairy under the arm holes of his undershirt; his wrinkles deep and his skin slack; a wallet protruding from one hip pocket and a kerchief from the other—at such moments, whether he be concerned with issues of government or merely the condition of the plumbing, he does show himself in human nakedness after all, he is much like any man, he even resembles a policeman on his day off or a small time gambler. And sometimes, unexpectedly, he summons the cabinet to a game of pinochle.[7]

Joseph Heller's *God Knows* (1984) applies much the same technique to the story of King David's military conquests, love affairs, domestic tragedies, and, most of all, insistence that his writing has been undervalued: "Moses has the Ten Commandments, it's true, but I've got much better lines. I've got the poetry and passion, savage violence and the plain raw civilizing grief of human heartbreak."[8] The rub, of course, is that Heller stuffs every Borscht Belt gag, every Yiddish stage cliché, every "bit" from television's Golden Age into King David's 350-plus-page monologue. By contrast, "King Solomon" has not only the advantage of freshness but also the brevity of genuine wit.

That Rosenfeld was a "minor" writer—his promising career cut short by a heart attack at age 38—is true enough. His characteristic stance, both in his fiction and in his life, was one of alienation, although as Mark Shechner argues, "Few of his stories stir his conflicts into life; most do little more than announce them."[9] Still, Rosenfeld remains an important, even defining element within the context of the New York intellectuals. And *Passage from Home* (1946), his autobiographical account of a family in shambles and of a young artist searching for congenial surroundings, is likely to survive the limitations of its plot circumstances. For in this work Rosenfeld altered the usual formula of domestic squabbling that had characterized, say, Anzia Yezierska in *Bread Givers* (1925); the Jewish-American family was in considerable disarray by the time *Passage from Home* appeared. Its protagonist, 14-year-old Bernard Miller, flees his home one summer for the bohemian promises of adventure and knowledge he associates with his Aunt Minna. That such illusions turn sour (at one point Bernard goes to his aunt's sink and "[sees] a roach scurrying across the drainboard and [draws] back nauseated")[10] is hardly surprising. Bernard is too delicate, too fastidious—too pampered, in a word—for the rawer aspects of Minna's life. One by one his great romantic expectations are punctured.

His options thus closed, Bernard returns home—surely a change from the normal pattern of the bildungsroman but one that takes on new meaning when talking about the New York intellectuals and their complicated responses to Jewish-American life. As Bernard puts it at the conclusion of his formative, ill-fated summer, "Perhaps I longed to return; perhaps I strove each day, through some maneuver of which I remained unaware, to bring my reconciliation nearer. . . . Had I only the courage for it I would have acknowledged that my actual longing looked neither here nor there, neither to home nor exile, but to a life foreign to both in which some beauty and freedom prevailed" (*PFH*, 240–42).

One can, of course, compare Bernard's dream with that of the slightly older protagonist of Delmore Schwartz's "In Dreams Begin Responsibilities," and at a later point in this chapter, I will do precisely that. But for the moment, let me suggest that Irving Howe's memoirs provide an instructive gloss, as both instance and model. In 1953 Howe began collaborating with Eliezer Greenberg on a series of Yiddish translations. As Howe relates the story in *A Margin of Hope*, he had reviewed a collection of Sholom Aleichem's stories for the *Partisan Review* and Greenberg sent him a note saying, first, that he liked the piece and, second, that they should become "partners." Normally one keeps such "offers" at a healthy arm's length, but this one struck pyschic paydirt. Howe went to see Greenberg, unsure as to what this "partnership" might consist of, and the rest is the history of such anthologies as the enormously influential *A Treasury of Yiddish Poetry*.

But there is a prehistory as well—and for that one must imagine a young Irving Howe just beginning to establish himself with the New York intellectual crowd and eager to review books for, say, the *Partisan Review*. Enter Philip Rahv, the legendary gruff-neck who ran the *Partisan Review* with an iron fist and an icy wit. That insiders often joked about the magazine's initials being the same as Rahv's suggests something of the control he wielded and the nervous admiration his megalomania inspired. In any event, there sat Rahv in the crowded office of the *Partisan Review*, at once the quintessential cosmopolitan and a man whose stinging Jewish wit betrayed more plebian origins. Irving Howe was ushered into the Great Man's office and then asked to scan a shelf of review copies in the event a book might strike his fancy. Here is a case where possibilities really *are* dazzling, where the moment's choice might spell the difference between success and disaster. Howe chose a book by Sholom Aleichem, Rahv smiled his approval, and the wheels that would grind slowly toward *World of Our Fathers* were set into motion.

Irving Howe's "The Lost Young Intellectual: A Marginal Man, Twice Alienated"

Good luck? A fortuitous accident? Hardly. Indeed, one could argue that the story really started much, much earlier: in Howe's painful, ambivalent memories of his Yiddish-speaking childhood, and the extraordinary piece he wrote about it for *Commentary* called "The Lost Young Intellectual: A Marginal Man, Twice Alienated." In seeking to describe "a new social type"—the author who has published a few stories, perhaps even a novel, and who reviews books for obscure magazines; the painter whose pictures do not reach public view; the leader of a revolutionary movement with few followers; and most of all "the unattached intellectual who can function neither as creator nor politician because he is either frustrated and barren in his cultural pursuits or disillusioned with politics"[11]—Howe was at once giving expression to a general condition and offering a self-portrait.

As the essay's subtitle would have it, such a man is both "marginal" and "twice alienated": "Usually born into an immigrant Jewish family, he teeters between an origin he can no longer accept and a desired status he cannot attain. He has largely lost his sense of Jewishness, of belonging to a people with a meaningful tradition, and he has not succeeded in finding a place for himself in the American scene or the American tradition" (Howe 1946, 362).

To be sure, Howe invented neither the condition nor the term we call "alienation," and, to his credit, did not crusade—as Rosenfeld often seemed to—in its behalf. But it was perhaps Howe who best understood how this peculiar condition affected the heart, how its "ambiguous compound of rejection and nostalgia" led not only to blockage and grief but also to the possibility of an elegaic mode that could encompass both the pangs of history and the pain of self. In this regard, a vignette from *A Margin of Hope* is especially revealing:

> When I was a few years older, about eight or nine, my parents had a grocery store in an "Americanized" Jewish neighborhood, the West Bronx. I used to play in an abandoned lot about a block away from the store, and when I'd neglect to come home at supper time, my father would come to call for me. He would shout my name from afar, giving it a Yiddish twist: "Oivee!" I would always feel a sense of shame at hearing my name so mutilated in the presence of amused onlookers, and though I would come home—supper was supper—I would always run ahead of my father as if to emphasize the existence of a certain distance between us. In later years I often wondered how I would react if my father were again to call "Oivee" at the top of his lungs in, say, Washington Square. (Howe 1983, 173)

One cites these painfully confessional lines without being quite sure how to describe this mixture of bravado and self-laceration, this subtle blending of irony and indignation, this laying bare of the conflicts that raged—admittedly, on less discerning, less articulate levels—between an entire generation of Jewish-American sons and their immigrant fathers. Never shy about turning his analytical skills inward, Howe wrote himself down as "*a victim of his own complexity of vision*: even the most harrowing of his feelings, the most intolerable aspects of his alienation, he must still examine with the same mordant irony he applies to everything else" (Howe 1946, 144). Which is perhaps to say that although it might, in Hemingway's famous formula, "be pretty to think so," nice Jewish boys are not likely to rebel by floating down the East River on a raft. Supper *is* supper—how that sentiment could apply to a wide range of Jewish-American characters, from Roth's David Schearl to Rosenfeld's Bernard Miller—and postures (including alienation) are postures. Thus, one does what one can—and in this case Howe writes "The Lost Young Intellectual." But one must also learn to live on in the full knowledge of one's age and its defining burdens. In this manner Howe's composite intellectual "can find consolation and dignity, however, in the consciousness of his vision, in the awareness of his complexity, and the rejection of self-pity. To each age its own burdens" (Howe 1946, 146).

"The Lost Young Intellectual: A Marginal Man, Twice Alienated" has the ring of manifesto about it, albeit one less fueled by revolutionary zeal than by a sense of impasse and cultural despair. But how dif-

ferent it is from the strident, even chilling manifestos that would char-
acterize Jewish-American writing just a decade later. Norman Mailer's
"The White Negro" and his other pieces exalting the hipster-psycho-
path are perhaps the most vivid examples, but these are hardly the only
instances. On a variety of fronts—sometimes invoking Wilhelm Reich,
sometimes Norman O. Brown—such New York intellectuals as Leslie
Fiedler and Paul Goodman celebrated license as if to overturn the old
Jewish predilection for Law. But for Howe, despite the handwringing
about "alienation"—one suspects he was *always* far more "rooted" in
Jewishness than he let on—this early essay introduced the themes, or,
perhaps more correctly, the cause for lament, that he would continue
to explore throughout his long career.

Consider, for example, the strains as well as the estrangement that
Yiddish caused for those who spoke *mamaloshen* in their parents' kitchen
and the King's English in the public kindergarten. As Howe relates a
particularly chilling moment—one he repeats in *World of Our Fathers*—
it is easy, perhaps *too* easy, for us to imagine the humiliated five-year-
old consigning Yiddish forever to the ash can of history:

Like many other Jewish children, I had been brought up in a constricted family
environment, especially since I was an only child, and at the age of five really
knew Yiddish better than English. I attended my first day of kindergarten as
if it were a visit to a new country. The teacher asked the children to identify
various common objects. When my turn came he held up a fork and without
hesitation I called it by its Yiddish name: *"a goopel."* The whole class burst out
laughing at me with that special cruelty of children. That afternoon I told my
parents that I had made up my mind never to speak Yiddish to them again.
(Howe 1976, 141)

Rather like Howe's memory of racing home past his embarrassing
immigrant father, his vow to forsake Yiddish was forged more in
ambivalence than in theater; the truth is that the longest journeys often end
where they began. And the same paradox also applies to the denials that
have a way of turning into versions of affirmation.

Delmore Schwartz's "In Dreams Begin Responsibilities"

Impressive though Howe's "The Lost Young Intellectual: A Marginal Man, Twice Alienated" and Rosenfeld's *Passage from Home* might

be, they are not, however, always successful as art. Granted, Howe's essay is precisely that—an essay—and as such need not raise aesthetic questions. Rosenfeld's autobiographical account, on the other hand, is a novel and as such is marred by too much exposition, by "telling" rather than *showing*. Which brings me to Delmore Schwartz's "In Dreams Begin Responsibilities," a story that first appeared in the Autumn 1937 issue of the *Partisan Review,* brought the 24-year-old Schwartz instant attention, and still stands as one of the richest, most artistically achieved renditions of the contradictory impulses, the attractions and repulsions, that characterized the New York intellectuals.

Schwartz's title comes from a line from the Irish poet William Butler Yeats and moves toward its consideration of adulthood and its special burdens of consequences and responsibilities by way of what at the time was a daring use of narrative technique. The story is framed in sleep, as its uneasy protagonist "dreams" his way toward a twenty-first birthday. The setting is a motion picture theater in which increasingly significant, often-nightmarish images flicker across the screen. "I think it is the year 1909. I feel as if I were in a motion picture theatre, the long arm of light crossing the darkness and spinning, my eyes fixed on the screen. This is a silent picture as if an old Biograph one, in which the actors are dressed in ridiculously old-fashioned clothes, and one flash succeeds another with sudden jumps. The actors too seem to jump about and walk too fast. The shots themselves are full of dots and rays, as if it were raining when the picture was photographed. The light is bad."[12] In this imagined world, the story's protagonist watches as his father makes his way down the quiet streets of Brooklyn for a date with the woman who will become the narrator's mother. Granted, there is a certain awkwardness as the young man greets the woman's family, but nothing especially out of the ordinary, much less ominously foreshadowing. After all, the narrator's imaginatively projected parents are to spend what looks for all the world to be an ordinary day at Coney Island. But something is drastically amiss, both on the "screen" and in the narrator's unconsciousness:

My father tells my mother how much money he has made in the past week, exaggerating an amount which need not have been exaggerated. But my father has always felt that actualities somehow fall short. Suddenly I begin to weep. The determined old lady who sits next to me in the theatre is annoyed and looks at me with an angry face, and being intimidated, I stop. I drag out my handkerchief and dry my face, licking the drop which has fallen near my lips.

Meanwhile I have missed something, for here are my mother and father alighting at the last stop, Coney Island. ("Dreams," 188–89)

On one level, "In Dreams Begin Responsibilities" chronicles the fateful afternoon in 1909 that ends in the parents' engagement, foreshadows their tumultuous marriage, and most of all produces an offspring—the narrator. But on a level filled with "deep images," the story is a poetic rendering that blends landscape with psyche, the small, nearly imperceptible nuance heavy with grief. Consider, for example, this description of the ocean as the narrator's parents see it from Coney Island's boardwalk:

The ocean is becoming rough; the waves come in slowly, tugging strength from far back. The moment before they somersault, the moment when they arch their backs so beautifully, showing green and white veins amid the black, that moment is intolerable. They finally crack, dashing fiercely upon the sand, actually driving, full force downward, against the sand, bouncing upward and forward, and at last petering out into a small stream which races up the beach and then is recalled. My parents gaze absentmindedly at the ocean, scarcely interested in its harshness. The sun overhead does not disturb them. But I stare at the terrible sun which breaks up sight, and the fatal, merciless, passionate ocean. ("Dreams," 189–90)

The passage generates so much romantic intensity, such absorption in the symbolic, quasi-mystical character of the natural universe, that the heart cracks. Here is exquisite feeling rendered with the full force of poetry that it deserves, and here too is everything that need be said about the gulf that separates immigrant parents from their sensitive, intellectual sons.

The tensions of "Dreams" reach their climax when the camera moves in for a close-up of the father's awkward proposal and the mother's equally awkward acceptance. It is not, the father thinks, as he thought it would be "on his long walks over Brooklyn Bridge in the revery of a fine cigar." This was life in all its messiness, confusion, crossed purposes, and portents for an unfortunate future. Granted, all this the narrator's father only dimly realizes; by contrast, the narrator sees all too clearly what is destined to unroll in the theater of life: "Don't do it. It's not too late to change your minds, both of you. Nothing good will come of it, only remorse, hatred, scandal, and two children whose characters are monstrous" ("Dreams," 191).

But, of course, the film that is the narrator's imaginative reconstruction and his deepest nightmare cannot be stopped; indeed, his parents' day at Coney Island can only continue, its images growing ever more ominous. For example, here is a description of the photograph at the center of the "film" that functions as an image-within-an-image:

> The photographer is instructing my parents how to pose. My father has his arm over my mother's shoulder, and both of them smile emphatically. The photographer brings my mother a bouquet of flowers to hold in her hand but she holds it at the wrong angle. . . . My father is becoming impatient. They try a seated pose. The photographer explains that he has pride, he is not interested in all of this for the money, he wants to make beautiful pictures. My father says: "Hurry up, will you? We haven't got all night." But the photographer only scurries about apologetically, and issues new directions. The photographer charms me. I approve of him with all my heart, for I know just how he feels, and as he criticizes each revised pose according to some unknown idea of rightness, I become quite hopeful. But then my father says angrily: "Come on, you've had enough time, we're not going to wait any longer." And the photographer, sighing unhappily, goes back under his black covering, holds out his hand, says: "One, two, three, Now!", and the picture is taken, with my father's smile turned to a grimace and my mother's bright and false. It takes a few minutes for the picture to be developed and as my parents sit in the curious light they become quite depressed. ("Dreams," 192)

One need not labor the scene's symbolic significance—the ways in which the photographer is a surrogate for the narrator, or the ways in which the sadness of the picture is redoubled on the movie screen. Later, when his parents pay an equally traumatic visit to a boardwalk fortune-teller, the narrator breaks down and finds himself shouting uncontrollably, "What are they doing? Don't they know what they are doing?" ("Dreams," 193). But nothing in the "dream" that will be their collective lives can be stopped. As the usher puts it, "You will find that . . . everything you do matters too much." And with that ambivalent, prophetic "wisdom," the story ends as the narrator wakens "into the bleak winter morning of [his] 21st birthday, the window sill shining with its lip of snow, and the morning already begun ("Dreams," 194).

In a reversal of our normal expectations about the seasons, the narrator's long dark night of the soul has led to a renewal in winter, while the hot summer's night dream that set consequences and responsibilities into motion has the look of death. That there are strong affinities between Schwartz and his narrator seems clear enough; indeed, James Atlas's fine biography, *Delmore Schwartz: The Life of an American Poet* (1977), outlines the disastrous marriage of Delmore's parents in excruciating detail. Moreover, Saul Bellow's *Humboldt's Gift*—discussed later in this volume—adds to our understanding of the complicated artist Schwartz became: a poet (e.g., "In the Naked Bed, in Plato's Cave" and "The Heavy Bear Goes with Me"); an assistant editor of the *Partisan Review*, a fictionist whose short stories often centered on a protagonist with the outrageous, thoroughly *un*-Jewish name of Shenandoah Fish; and a critic and essayist of considerable power and influence. In short, Schwartz was both a man of letters in terms of his sheer literary range and a prototypical New York intellectual with respect to his brilliance, frenetic energy, and deep-seated ambivalences. As Bellow observes about Schwartz/Humboldt von Fleisher, he was a "Mozart of conversation"—as was Rosenfeld / Zetland and as were nearly all the combative, feisty types who traveled under the moniker of New York Jewish intellectuals.

Chapter Four
Saintly Fools/Sensitive Flops

Jewish literature has always had a special fondness for the humorous, whether focusing on schlemiels and *schlimazls,* arrogant beggars and would-be wise men, or saintly fools and sensitive flops. And it is hardly surprising that such characters would breed Jewish-American equivalents, or that their collective memory would remain long after most immigrants had moved beyond the ghetto and the grip of its poverty. Indeed, one could argue that humor, albeit of a rather special sort (earthy, skeptical, and above all deeply ironic), is the most important and certainly most durable contribution of Jewish-American culture to the national tradition. Moreover, even those inclined to be skeptical about Jewish humor would have to concede its central importance in much of the most accomplished, most interesting Jewish-American fiction.

I. B. Singer's "Gimpel the Fool"

Perhaps no single story illustrates these principles better than Isaac Bashevis Singer's "Gimpel the Fool." Although Singer is a prolific and wide-ranging author, the tale of the much-deceived and comically suffering Gimpel remains his most frequently anthologized, best-known, and, arguably, most loved story. Both Irving Howe (who helped arrange its translation by Saul Bellow and its publication in the *Partisan Review*) and Alfred Kazin have pointed out the similarities to "Bontsha the Silent," by the Polish-Yiddish writer Y. L. Peretz, but neither critic has elaborated on the connections.

For many American readers, the story of Bontsha is a heavy dose of Yiddish sentimentalism, the sort of unadulterated play to the emotions that makes for a parochial, second-rate product. As they might put it, Bontsha's signature—his leitmotif, if you will—is silent suffering: "He lived unknown, in silence, and in silence he died. He passed through our world, like a shadow. When Bontsha was born no one took a drink of wine; there was no sound of glasses clinking. When he was confirmed he made no speech of celebration. He existed like a grain of sand at the rim of a vast ocean, amid millions of other grains of sand exactly similar, and when the wind at last lifted him up and carried him across to the other shore of that ocean, no one noticed, no one at all."[1]

As a Yiddish Everyman, Bontsha thus crystallized the experiences and aspirations of a people who saw themselves reflected all too clearly in the mirror of his life. This is not to suggest, however, that Bontsha's readers were as isolated as he was; rather, it was Bontsha—orphaned and alone, silent and long-suffering—who became a convenient index for the *tsoris* (trouble) of a people, if not of individual persons. Sholom Aleichem's humor cast an ironic yet loving eye on this world; Peretz tried to accomplish much the same result by projecting a sentimental gaze toward the next one—or so it might seem to those not prone to reading the fable of Bontsha through a Yiddishist's eyes, for Bontsha's "silence," his extreme passivity, is less a cause for sentimental celebration than it is a call to action. Granted, life *is* crowded with others, and the human condition imposes sobering limitations; nonetheless, Peretz's story, for all its folkloric character, remains committed to the activities, to the *words,* that would insist "this world" can become more attractive. In this sense Bontsha's life is less an emblem of suffering rewarded than it is a cautionary tale.

For contemporary writers (e.g., Saul Bellow), the sheer weight of numbers—whether they are crowding into a subway train or competing for space in academic journals—is cause enough for despair. Bontsha, however, sees "others" as a necessary condition of life, one best dealt with in silence: "When Bontsha was brought to the hospital ten people were waiting for him to die and leave his narrow little cot; when he was brought from the hospital to the morgue twenty were waiting to occupy his pall; when he was taken out of the morgue forty were waiting to lie where he would lie forever. Who knows how many are now waiting to snatch from him that bit of earth?" ("Bontsha," 224).

Granted, the point of Peretz's story is made in heaven rather than on earth. There Bontsha's bottomless humility embarrasses even the angels when he answers their order to "Choose! Take whatever you want!" with a timid request for a hot roll and butter every morning. And as with the Rabbi of Nemerov (in Peretz's famous story "If Not Higher"), the resulting tableau of Bontsha among the angels causes them to "bend their heads in shame at this "unending meekness they have created on earth." Because the story presumably endorses versions of holiness beyond even those sponsored by the official religion, it encourages its sentimental readings. Still, Bontsha's suffering was never meant to be equated with the symbolic sufferers one finds in the fiction of Jewish-American writers like Bernard Malamud (*The Assistant*) and Edward Louis Wallant (*The Pawnbroker*). If Bontsha is the saint-as-mensch, if he is an extension of the shtetl's belief in the transitory nature of his life and the eternal justice of Gan-Eyden (literally, the Garden of Eden, and used to indicate a heavenly afterlife), he is also a study of passivity grown grotesque.

By contrast, Singer's Gimpel is simultaneously saint and fool. *His* "foolishness" is directly related to his naïveté, his willingness to believe even the most preposterous of *bobbemysehs* (literally, grandmother's stories): "They said, 'Gimpel, you know the rabbi's wife has been brought to childbed?' So I skipped school. Well, it turned out to be a lie. How was I supposed to know?"[2] Unlike Bontsha, Gimpel responds to peer pressure in ways that follow the standard psychoanalytic line about sadomasochism to the letter. For his victimizers, the cruel sport is spoiled only by the fact that Gimpel makes such an easy target. On Gimpel's side, his endless rationalizations and verbal outbursts (no creature of silence, he) cannot disguise what we and his analysts recognize all too clearly.

And yet Gimpel also seems to be a man more sinned against than sinning. Granted, he later marries a woman whose virtue is less than doubtful, alternating between the roles of cuckold and father to her growing brood of illegitimate children. But for all this, Gimpel does not contribute to his failures in the time-honored way that cuckolds became the butt of jokes. Instead, Gimpel is the saint-as-holy-fool, the satiric persona whose innocence becomes an indicator of the depravity that surrounds him. Critics—particularly those well grounded in the traditional modes of Yiddish satire—have had difficulty with what they feel is an undue concentration on the grotesque and physically disgusting in Singer's stories: "His characters still seem always indecently carnal; man is caught in his animal functions of eating, drinking, lusting, displaying his body, copulating, evacuating, scratching. He is riddled with hideous and deforming diseases, most often venereal: the bone-ache, falling hair, a decayed nose, ulcerous teeth, boils, scruff . . . and any trace of the beautiful or the spiritual is always in danger of being destroyed by the weight of this mere 'stuff.'"[3] Although the passage just quoted tells us more about Gimpel's world than much of what passes as Singer criticism does, it was not written about Gimpel specifically or even about Singer in general. Indeed, the quotation is taken from Alvin B. Kernan's seminal study of satiric technique, *The Cankered Muse*—the "his" referring to the fictive world of the satirist.

To be sure, Gimpel stubbornly maintains his belief in much the same way Bontsha keeps his silence. As Gimpel puts it, "What's the good of *not* believing? Today it's your wife you don't believe; tomorrow it's God himself you won't take stock in" ("Gimpel," 10). And here, despite the bleakness, the sheer dreck, that surrounds Gimpel, is where Singer and the traditional satirist part company. Unwilling to remain the mere butt of sadistic jokes, Gimpel turns his attention to the next world. Although "the schoolboys threw burrs" at his wedding and the House of Prayer "rang with laughter" at the circumcision of his illegitimate son (standard enough treatment for stereotypical schlemiel-cuckolds), Gimpel remains characteristically saintlike: "I was no weakling. If I slapped someone, he'd see all the way to Cracow. But I'm really not a slugger by nature. I think to myself, let it pass. So they take advantage of me" ("Gimpel," 11).

Whereas the traditional Yiddish fools were blissfully unaware of their comic difficulties, Gimpel prefers to leave the doors of imagination and metaphysical possibility wide open. And it is here that Singer most differs from his Yiddish predecessors. At every turn of comic misfortune, every outlandish explanation given to justify deception, Gimpel steadfastly reaffirms that "everything is possible." When the town teases him, he counters with the notion that "a whole town can't go altogether crazy"; when he catches his wife in the act of adultery, he refuses to shout because "he might wake the children"; and when his marriage produces six illegitimate children, he remembers the rabbi's words that "belief itself is beneficial."

But that said, if Gimpel is immune to the cruel vicissitudes of this world, he is more than impressed by the supernatural possibilities of the next one. And it is this dimension of devils and their ability to deceive that makes Singer's story more than a "Bontsha the Silent" in modern dress. For Peretz, the next world is a bastion of unbounded reward and an occasion for easy sentimentality; by contrast, Singer's vision is riddled with doubt. When the Spirit of Evil suggests that Gimpel "ought to deceive the world" by contaminating the bread of Frampol with filth, the prospect of revenge is tempting indeed.

Only the fear of judgment in the world to come stops Gimpel, and even this is systematically broken down by a devil who is infinitely better at hitting nerves than Gimpel's earthly tormentors are. Thus, when the devil finally convinces him that "there is no world to come," the notion of falsehood, of deception, takes a quarter-turn, introducing new complexities at the very moment it destroys old fears: "They've sold you a bill of goods and talked you into believing you carried a cat in your belly. What nonsense!" ("Gimpel," 18). For the Gimpel who had characterized himself as "the type that bears it and says nothing," the insight is shattering. After all, the falsehoods of this world—its pranks and perennial deceptions—are one thing, but those of the next are another matter altogether.

Thus, Gimpel's exchange with the devil resembles a negative catechism, the rude instruction that characters of initiation—say, Nick Adams in Hemingway's "The Killers" or Ike McCaslin in Faulkner's "The Bear"—receive as part of their growth into the ways of the modern world. Gimpel's learning differs only in its metaphysical directions and in the bizarre nature of his antagonist; otherwise, the scene has immediate parallels as its question-and-answer format moves toward a vision in which, as the devil would have it, a "thick mire" presumably replaces God.

But if the devil prompts Gimpel to vengeful action, the ghost of his dead wife urges him toward repudiation. As he waits for Frampol's urine-laden bread to rise, he is interrupted by visions of his wife Elka. At the moment of her death Gimpel had imagined that "dead as she was, she was saying, 'I deceived Gimpel. That was the meaning of my brief life.'" Now Elka returns from the world of Gehenna to trick him no longer: "You fool!" she says. "You fool. Because I was false is everything else false too? I never deceived anyone but myself" ("Gimpel," 22).

Deception, then, is the leitmotif of Gimpel's story—from the devil's thesis ("the whole world deceives you") to its antithesis in Elka ("I never deceived anyone but myself"). Gimpel, however, is less the synthesis that my Hegelian terminology might imply than he is an artist that shtetl life hurt into story, for as Gimpel comes to discover, there "were really no lies": whatever doesn't really happen happens in the world of dreams and if not today, then tomorrow; if not tomorrow, then "a century hence if not next year" ("Gimpel," 25).

The result is a portrait of Gimpel as the wandering wiseman/storyteller, the artist-as-Lamed Vovnik (one of the 36 Righteous Men whose humble and secret piety sustains the world), the saintly fool who props up the world with fantastic stories instead of humble deeds. As Gimpel puts it, in sentiments that seem to speak as much to his author as to

himself, "Going from place to place, eating at strange tables, often
happens that I spin yarns—improbable things that could never have
happened—about devils, magicians, windmills, and the like" ("Gimpel," 25). Indeed, these are the elements we have come to expect in I.
B. Singer's fiction. His persistent questions—Why are we born? Why
do we suffer? Why do we die?—are those of the child and the great
artist alike, and Singer's "answers" are a fictive comedy at once univer-
sally human and distinctively Jewish.

Bernard Malamud's "The Magic Barrel"

No doubt there are those who will balk at my claim that "Gimpel
the Fool" is Singer's signature story, but I suspect few will quarrel with
a similar argument in behalf of Malamud's "The Magic Barrel," for the
story has long been regarded as quintessential Malamud—in form, in
content, and most of all in vision. Considered as a whole, "The Magic
Barrel" is an initiation story, although the exact dimensions of its "initiation" are hard to pin down. It opens innocently enough—"Not long
ago there lived in uptown New York, in a small, almost meager room,
though crowded with books, Leo Finkle, a rabbinical student in the
Yeshiva University"[4]—as if to answer the objections of critics who continually demand that Jewish-American literature be more Jewish and
less like "literature." But for all its Lower East Side touches—the Yiddishized diction and the realistic local detail—Jewishness is as much a
literary illusion in "The Magic Barrel" as black dialects are in *The Adventures of Huckleberry Finn*. As with most of Malamud's protagonists,
Leo Finkle's problem is an inability to love, a failure to link his isolation
with others'. As a consequence, Finkle is initiated into "suffering" almost by accident. Because he "[has] been advised by an acquaintance
that he might find it easier to win himself a congregation if he were
married," Finkle opens himself to Eros, *shadchens* (marriage brokers),
and his fate as a sainty fool. Initially, the rabbinical student is radically
different from the mercurial matchmaker—Finkle represents the force
of Law, while Salzman stands for the power of flesh. And yet Salzman,
for all his vulgarisms, betrays a "depth of sadness" that Finkle uses as
a convenient mirror for his own.

The progress of the typical Malamud protagonist nearly always involves identification with suffering and some strategy for taking on the
burdens of others. In Malamud's most earnestly serious novels, similar

movements are chronicled with both a straighter face and a tongue more prone to lashing out at social injustice than lodging ironically in its cheek. Nonetheless, comic misfortunes dog his protagonists' collective heels. In Finkle's case, sympathy is as much his leitmotif as Salzman's is fish. Each of the "much-handled cards" in Salzman's magic barrel represents a person whose aloneness is a counterpart of his own.

Granted, Salzman is more pimp than "commercial cupid"—regardless of Finkle's elaborate rationalizations about the honorable tradition of the *schadchen*. In fact, what Finkle really imagines is a world in which hundreds of cards—each one longing for marriage—are churned about and finally brought together by the indefatigable matchmaker's machinations. Finkle's comic misfortune is a function of his willingness to believe in such highly romantic visions and, moreover, to replace them with new combinations as quickly as old ones turn sour.

That Salzman plays the con man to such a willing dupe is hardly surprising. After all, Finkle has the words *live one* written all over his face. At a used-car lot he'd be looking anxiously for an automobile; at a marriage broker's, he's desperately seeking a wife. So far as Salzman's sales pitches are concerned, the two commodities are virtually the same: "Sophie P. Twenty-four years. Widow one year. No children. Educated high school and two years college. Father promises eight thousand dollars. Has wonderful wholesale business. Also real estate. On the mother's side comes teachers, also one actor. Well known on Second Avenue" ("Magic," 196). In this way the juxtapositions of Finkle's hesitation about "buying" and Salzman's aggressive brand of "selling" create what might have been a purely comic situation; however, Finkle gradually begins to see Salzman's portfolio as a microcosm of the world's suffering and his shoulders as the proper place on which it might rest. What breaks down, of course, are the very pillars of Finkle's world—the justifications of Tradition, the pragmatic need for a wife, the commonsensical arguments for using a matchmaker in the first place.

Moreover, if the "much-handled cards" of Salzman's portfolio make it clear that others suffer the loneliness and indignation of being damaged, passed-over goods, Finkle's traumatic meeting with Lily Hirschorn forces him to realize, for the first time, "the true nature of his relationship to God, and from that it had come to him, with shocking force, that apart from his parents, he had never loved anyone" ("Magic," 205). "The Magic Barrel" is, then, a love story, one that operates simultaneously on the levels of Eros and agape. That Finkle's "learning" leads him to admit his essentially loveless condition, his particular death of the heart, is a necessary precondition for the comic victimhood that will follow.

And yet Lily Hirschorn, important though she might be as a catalyst, is simply another frantic figure yoo-hooing after a life that has already passed her by; there are dozens of similar stories in Salzman's "magic barrel." Moreover, if Finkle has been conned by Salzman, so has Lily. After all, she expected to meet a biblical prophet, a man "enamored with God," and instead found herself walking with a man incapable of passion in either the physical or the spiritual senses of the term. In the Finkle-Salzman-Hirschorn triangle, then, the end result is initiation; Finkle finds out how and what he is, and in the context of the story this information provides the tension, the essential ground condition, of which moral bunglers are made.

Stella, of course, provides the occasion. Unlike the typical Salzman portrait, Stella's dime-store photo suggests she "had *lived,* or wanted to—more than just wanted, perhaps regretted how she had lived—had somehow deeply suffered" ("Magic," 209). In a world where "suffering" is the standard for one-upmanship, she is the hands-down winner. A Lily Hirschorn may have wanted to live, Finkle himself has the urge to try, but it is Stella who has actually been there. And it is through the figure of Stella (her name suggesting the ironic star that guides Finkle's destiny) that the prospective rabbi hopes to "convert her to goodness, himself to God."

Thus, a new triangle is created: Finkle represents a tortured attempt to achieve spiritual resurrection; Salzman (variously characterized as Pan, Cupid, and other fertility figures) emerges as a Yiddish version of Creon; while Stella vacillates between the scarlet of her prostitution and the whiteness of her purity.

Indeed, it is Finkle's highly stylized movement toward Stella that turns him into a saintly fool, at least in the sense that his goal of spiritual regeneration is incommensurate with his activity. The story's concluding tableau crystallizes the matter of Finkle's "salvation" and/or "destruction" without providing the luxury of a clear reading direction. On the one hand, Finkle runs toward Stella, seeking "in her, his own redemption" in ways that make this now-passionate rabbi akin to the biblical Hosea. On the other hand, Salzman remains just "around the corner . . . chanting prayers for the dead." Is this kaddish for Finkle? for Stella? or perhaps for Salzman himself? In much of Malamud's early fiction, ironic affirmations become an essential part of his aesthetic—as if movements toward moral change were not enough, but total regeneration is not possible. In Malamud's greatest stories—"The Angel Levine," "Take Pity!" and "The Jew Bird"—moral allegories slip easily from the gritty surfaces of realistic detail to surrealistic fancy, and back again, so that his most artistically consummate short fictions have the feel of Marc Chagall paintings.

The Assistant

Malamud's *The Assistant* (1957) is cut from the same bolt of sackcloth (marked "Judaic suffering") that gave us the moral qualms and saintly comedy of a Leo Finkle. In this case, however, Morris Bober's circumstances strike us as grounded in the quotidian detail of his failing grocery store, rather than in the luxury of Finkle's self-consciousness. Unlike Finkle, Bober is neither the protagonist nor the moral filter of his tale. Rather, his suffering merely *is,* and it is the task of Frankie Alpine, his assistant, to learn what such suffering means and how it might apply to his own situation.

Granted, Frankie has what can only be called some curious notions about Judaism, but then again, Bober—for all his heartfelt sighs—may not be the best instructor. For example, at one point in the novel Bober claims that he suffers "for the Law," although it is hard to see precisely how Law—in the sense of the Torah's 613 Divine Commandments— operates in Morris's life. Rather, Bober is portrayed as a secular *tsaddick,* a righteous man who once "ran two blocks in the snow to give back five cents a customer forgot."[5] His cachet is good deeds: the roll he provides to the sour, gray-haired, vaguely anti-Semitic Polish woman who wakes him up each morning; the endless credit he extends to the "drunk women"; and his insistence that he shovel his sidewalks on Sunday mornings because the snow "don't look so nice for the goyim that go to church."

And yet the bulk of Bober's suffering is not circumscribed by economics or even by the harsh reality that "in a store you were entombed." Rather, it is the unspoken, often-elusive failures of fatherhood that torment Bober's soul. In Malamud's world people always seem out of breath from carrying too many bundles, both physical and psychological; when they finally *do* rest for a glass of tea, we tend to believe in their long, soulful sighs and to feel that the suffering is both earned and appropriate.

Jonathan Baumbach characterizes the novel as the intertwining biographies of surrogate fathers and surrogate sons. As he puts it, "*The Assistant* has two central biographies: the life and death of Morris Bober, unwitting saint, and the guilt and retribution of Frank Alpine, saint-elect, the first life creating the pattern and possibility of the second. At the end, as if by metamorphosis, the young Italian thief replaces the old Jewish storekeeper, the reborn son replacing the father."[6] In important ways Bober's situation echoes that of *Ulysses*'s Leopold Bloom, though Ephraim is not Rudy, and Frankie Alpine is not Stephen Dedalus. What strikes us as similar, however, is the manner in which the respective "adoptions" take place.

Bober's suffering, of course, remains constant; it is a condition of his life and the necessary result of Ephraim's death. Frankie, on the other hand, vacillates between visions of absolute goodness and the reality of compulsive evil. What he needs are standards for moral behavior, of which the life of St. Francis is one and the life of Morris Bober is another. About St. Francis he says: "For instance he gave everything away that he owned, every cent, all his clothes off his back. He enjoyed to be poor. He said poverty was a queen and he loved her like a beautiful woman" (*TA*, 31). Frankie might well have been speaking about Bober, and indeed, as he grows into his role as "assistant," the distinction between the two figures gradually blurs.

There is a sense in *The Assistant* that at least a part of Malamud is playing it straight, believing both in Bober's essential goodness and in Frankie's ability to learn from it. Things crystallize in the funeral scene, at the point where tensions begin to shift from the father/owner to his assistant/son. The rabbi—unfamiliar with Bober and called in for the occasion—delivers the following eulogy at his graveside:

My dear friends, I never had the pleasure to meet the good grocery man that he now lays in his coffin. He lived in a neighborhood where I didn't come in. Still and all I talked this morning to people that knew him and I am now sorry that I didn't know him also. . . . All told me the same, that Morris Bober, who passed away so untimely—he caught double pneumonia from shoveling snow in front of his place of business so people could pass by on the sidewalk—was a man who couldn't be more honest. . . . He was also a very hard worker, a man that never stopped working. How many mornings he got up in the dark and dressed himself in the cold, I can't count. . . . So besides being honest he was a good provider.

When a Jew dies, who asks if he is a Jew? He is a Jew, we don't ask. There are many ways to be a Jew. So if somebody comes to me and says, "Rabbi, shall we call such a man Jewish who lived and worked among gentiles and sold them pig meat, trayfe, that we don't eat, and not once in twenty years comes inside a synagogue, is such a man a Jew, rabbi?" To him I will say, "Yes, Morris Bober was to me a true Jew because he lived in the Jewish experience, which he remembered and with the Jewish heart." (*TA*, 229–30)

I suspect that Bober might well be considered a prize schlemiel by those prone to give the passage a hard-boiled, ironic reading. After all, when the rabbi asks, "Who runs in wintertime without a hat or coat?" the answer that springs to such minds is "A schlemiel, that's who!" Those more inclined to let the text formulate their responses will point out that while Bober might care about his customers, the fact is that they continually desert him for fancier food and lower prices. Indeed, at nearly every point in the rabbi's makeshift remarks the truth of the matter undercuts his well-meaning sentiments. For example, it is easier to number Bober among the Lamed Vov than it is to think of him as a "good provider." His daughter reads *Don Quixote* and dreams of worlds beyond the confines of the grocery store, at the same time blaming Bober for spoiling her chances. His wife simply complains—about business, about Helen's boyfriends, and finally about Bober himself.

Moreover, there is the sticky matter of Bober's "Jewishness." Although the rabbi's words of consolation may have cheered a good many Jewish-American hearts who share much the same definition, those words hardly answer the question in a novel in which "who" or "what" is a Jew looms as centrally important. For Bober, Jewishness is inextricably connected with suffering, with a common humanity, of which Jews—bound by the Law—carry an inordinately large share. As mentioned earlier, whatever Bober might mean by "the Law," it is clearly not Halakha. As he puts it, "Nobody will tell me that I am not Jewish because I put in my mouth once in a while, when my tongue is dry, a piece of ham" (*TA*, 126). The issue, he insists, boils down to who has the "Jewish heart," and when Frankie asks why Jews "suffer so damned much," Bober can only reply, "They suffer because they are Jews. If you live, you suffer. Some people suffer more, but not because they want. But I think if a Jew don't suffer for the Law, he will suffer for nothing" (*TA*, 125).

Part of Bober's "mystery"—particularly to a disciple like Frankie—is the ambivalent quality of his instruction. All men suffer, but some Jews suffer in ways that are special and that smack of redemption. Moreover, the champion sufferers—those Frankie once described as having the ability to hold the pain in their gut the longest—apparently also come equipped with Jewish hearts. Granted, neither Frankie nor Morris is schooled in the theological niceties, but their ruminations raise certain questions nonetheless: Do Jews alone possess Jewish hearts? If not, can a non-Jew acquire one? And if so, how?

For Frankie, the answer seems clear enough: Morris "suffered," and to be like him one must suffer in the same manner. "All men," Malamud is reputed to have once exclaimed, "are Jews," and one could offer up *The Assistant* as exhibit A. Still, for all his seeming folly, for all the personal goodness wasted and the unnecessary sufferings endured, Bober's life seems more a tragic commentary on the American dream than an ironic joke about self-destruction. No matter how wrongheaded he might have been about his customers, family, or friends, Bober's life contained an essential dignity, a certain bittersweetness that justified his sighs and convinced us they were significant.

The fate of his assistant is, however, quite another matter. In Frankie's first outing after Bober's death he continues his lifelong role as the sensitive flop—literally, tragicomically, irrevocably: "Then the diggers began to push in the loose earth around the grave and as it fell on the coffin the mourners wept aloud. Helen tossed in a rose. Frank, standing close to the edge of the grave, leaned forward to see where the flower fell. He lost his balance, and though flailing his arms, landed feet first on the coffin" (*TA*, 231).

Spectacular though it might be, Frankie's pratfall at the gravesite is merely one incident in a long series of self-created accidents. And one fears that his efforts to create a new, Bober-like life for himself will simply be more of the same. For example, his decision to become a convert—a striking reversal of the usual direction in Jewish-American fiction—is riddled with ambiguity and undercutting ironies. For Frankie, conversion points to plot developments that exist beyond the novel's final page. We accept the tableau frozen in the concluding paragraph of "The Magic Barrel" as part and parcel of the short story, but it is harder to know what to do with Frankie. Are we to presume he will emulate Bober by taking over the grocery store? Will he now be the one to supply the gray-haired Polish woman with her six o'clock roll and the "drunken women" with endless credit? And, of course, will he marry Helen and turn her slowly into an Ida? What we *do* know is that a newly circumcised Frankie drags himself around "with a pain between his legs," one that both "enraged and inspired him"—and, we might add, a pain that attracted as much as it repulsed.

At least part of the appeal must be chalked up to Frankie's longstanding masochism. The old guilts must be punished, and what better, more ritualistic way than by circumcision? Implicit in the act are the complicated strands of sexual punishment (for his attempted rape of Helen), castration anxiety (for Bober as oedipal father), and religious conversion (for a covenant he does not understand). In this disparate quest for moral perfection, Frankie Alpine emerges more as flop than as authentic Jew, and more as victim of his desire for sainthood than as "saint." At the end, he sees himself transmogrified into a surrealistic version of St. Francis, reaching into a garbage can to give Helen a wooden rose: "He [i.e., St. Francis] tossed it into the air and it turned into a real flower that he caught in his hand. With a bow he gave it to Helen, who had just come out of the house. 'Little sister, here is your little sister the rose.' From him she took it, although it was with the love and best wishes of Frank Alpine" (*TA*, 245–46). Finkle too had clutched flowers to his anxious breast and raced toward his disastrous/redemptive meeting with Stella. In a similar fashion, Frank Alpine speeds toward an equally ambivalent destiny, duping himself with the belief that he is no longer an "assistant" and that Bober's humanity will soon be his.

A New Life

The progress of sensitive flops and holy saints continued with *A New Life* (1961), but this time Malamud added large doses of the slapstick humor traditionally associated with such figures. However much Bober and Alpine merit inclusion among Malamud's moral bunglers, it is hard to think of *The Assistant* as a comic novel; in Malamud's world a mom-and-pop grocery store not only severely restricts economic possibilities but also sharply curtails what we might think of as bounce, as good cheer. In such stores people are entombed.

S. Levin, "formerly a drunkard,"[7] hails from the same zeitgeist, one that Philip Roth once described as a "timeless depression and placeless lower East Side" and that Malamud, as the Brooklyn son of a hardworking, down-on-his-luck grocer, knew firsthand. In *A New Life*, however, Malamud transports his luckless protagonist to the American West and the groves of academia. That Levin should be a sad sack is as much an a priori assumption as is Bober's "suffering." After all, the traditions of academic satire—like those which clustered around academic treatments of the West as "virgin land"—were established conventions long before S. Levin headed across the Hudson.

Still, it could be argued that one might move a Malamud protagonist out of the city but not move the city out of the character. In this sense *A New Life* shares the same concerns and tensions that energized Malamud's earlier fiction and—despite Levin's repeated comic pratfalls—shares much the same interest in moral allegory. Levin's notebook gives perhaps the best clues of the tensions that will ultimately define the novel: "One section of the notebook was for 'insights,' and a few pages in the middle detailed 'plans'. . . . Among Levin's 'insights' were 'the new life hangs on an old soul,' and 'I am one who creates his own peril.' Also, 'the danger of the times is the betrayal of man'" (*NL*, 58).

We have come to expect that Levin's vision of "a new life" based on geographic change is destined to fail. As Mark Goldman points out, Levin is the "tenderfoot Easterner . . . (always invoking nature like a tenement Rousseau). 'Now he took in miles of countryside, a marvelous invention.'"[8] But whatever the "new life" might be or how ironic such slogans ultimately turn out, it hangs, as it must, on Levin's "old soul." Moreover, if Levin's notebook is a repository of private understanding, it is often at odds with the facts of his public behavior.

In a similar fashion the novel's academic satire has been misunderstood by a number of critics who were quick to point out that they were equally indignant about schools like Cascadia and teachers like Gilley. After all, "the danger of the times" *is* "the betrayal of man," and it is not hard to see how this statement was interpreted as having something to do with the preservation of the liberal arts, with the humanities in general, and with English departments in particular. Ruth Mandel, for example, sees Cascadia College in these terms: "Here is a stereotyped, mediocre, service-oriented English department. The instructors are organization men of the worst kind, men who should know better, men educated in the humanities. The school is a Cascadian Madison Avenue, a school where the emphasis is on practical learning, prestige, school-board approval, and the well-rounded, shallow man who must be an athlete if he wishes to be accepted. The attack is devastating. Malamud's intentions are clear."[9] But are they? If Levin is to function as the traditional satiric persona, his credentials are hardly in order. After all, S. Levin does not come "from a world of pastoral innocence." Nor is he "the prophet come down from the hills to the cities of the plain; the gawky farmboy, shepherd or plowman come to the big city" (Kernan, 18). Rather, Levin arrives in this untainted (?) West from New York City, the very seat of eastern corruption. He is in this sense a reverse Nick Carraway, one who follows his dream of a liberal arts college westward—only to find, instead, the drudgery of required freshman composition and the treachery of departmental politics.

But that said, Levin often seems more akin to the Kurtz of Conrad's "Heart of Darkness" than he does an ironic variant of the Carraway from Fitzgerald's *The Great Gatsby*. Far from being the innocent one simultaneously attracted to and repulsed by corruption (Nick), Levin, like Kurtz, enters the heart of Cascadia College's darkness with high hopes of humanizing the system. Granted, he is as surrounded by absurdities as was Kurtz: one colleague continually revises his *Elements of Composition,* thirteenth edition, the required text for Levin's courses; another labors fitfully on a Laurence Sterne dissertation that nobody will publish; and still another cuts out pictures from old *Life* magazines for a proposed "picture book" of American literature. But Levin, as it turns out, is neither appalled nor paralyzed by the curious directions that publish-or-perish takes at Cascadia; after all, he has some plans of his own:

He could begin to collect material for a critical study of Melville's whale: "White Whale as Burden of Dark World," "Moby Dick as Closet Drama." . . . Levin began to read and make notes but gave up the whale when he discovered it in too many critical hats. He wrote down other possible titles for a short critical essay: "The Forest as Battleground of the Spirit in Some American Novels." "The Stranger as Fallen Angel in Western Fiction." "The American Ideal as Self-Created Tradition." Levin wrote, "The idea of America will always create freedom"; but it was impossible to prove faith. After considering "The Guilt-ridden Revolutionary of the Visionary American Ideal," he settled on "American Self-Criticism in Several Novels." Limiting himself, to start, to six books, Levin read and re-read them, making profuse notes. (*NL,* 267)

The proposed articles—one has the sinking feeling one has encountered them before, either in print or around the table of a graduate seminar—serve a number of functions. First, they suggest the ironic dimensions of Levin's purity, a matter not nearly so important in the groves of academia as it will be in the regeneration of his moral fiber. It is, after all, not Levin but the "others" who have sold out, turning their talents from humanity to commercialism. *Levin's* projected articles are awash with speculations about American guilt and Edenic innocence—all in the best traditions of Cotton Mather, Henry Adams, and the Modern Language Association. Levin might differ from these august presences in degree, but certainly not in kind.

Malamud surely means this hatful of titles to be ironic, although I also suspect that more than a few readers secretly thought that "The Stranger as Fallen Angel in Western Fiction" had the makings of a publishable piece. My point, however, is simply this: Levin's overriding concern is for moral preservation, both in the collective sense of America and in the individual sense of self. If his academic fantasies are those of a *luftmensch,* (a person of no substance, one who lives on air) they must be seen in the larger context of Levin's moral structure. In this sense the pettiness of Cascadia College is only a backdrop for Levin's more pressing concerns: his inability to love, his lack of commitment, his perennial death of the spirit.

In short, whatever comic spirit derives from the incongruity of a Levin plunged knee-deep into Nature, learning how to drive a car, or being initiated into the internecine political warfare of Cascadia College fizzles out almost completely when he moves toward Pauline and the larger complications she will suggest. For a time it looks as if Levin will revivify the legend and the legacy of Leo Duffy. After all, Levin arrives with a Duffy-like beard, begins his career in Duffy's abandoned office, and ends the novel as Pauline's lover-husband.

That said, however, Malamud has more in mind for S. Levin than one more tale of academic martyrdom. Whereas a Duffy commits suicide (the final "protest" and one that is certain to have "meaning"), Levin gradually switches roles from academic complainer and/or critic to moral bungler. At one point in the novel Levin tells Pauline about his first "awakening," his initial encounter with the new life:

For two years I lived in self-hatred, willing to part with life. I won't tell you what I had come to. But one morning in somebody's filthy cellar, I awoke under burlap bags and saw my rotting shoes on a broken chair. They were lit in dim sunlight from a shaft or window. I stared at the chair, it looked like a painting, a thing with a value of its own. I squeezed what was left of my brain to understand why this should move me so deeply, why I was crying. Then I thought, Levin, if you were dead there would be no light on your shoes in this cellar. I came to believe what I had often wanted to, that life is holy. I then became a man of principle. (*NL,* 204)

And it is from this mushrooming sense of "principle" that Levin's link to other characters in the Malamud canon is established. Granted, Levin's concerns take in the vast range of contemporary problems (unlike the more isolated, more claustrophobic ones of, say, Frankie Alpine), but the mechanisms are virtually identical. For Malamud, the important thing may not be that a Gilley or a Fabrikant are exposed but, rather, that a Levin finally acts. Nevertheless, moral action is almost always a qualified commodity in Malamud's world, an occasion more for ironic failures than for spiritual successes. Moreover, if Levin's academic fantasies had a ring of moral urgency about them, consider the following slice of Levin's wishful thinking:

He must *on principle* not be afraid. "The little you do may encourage the next man to do more. It doesn't take a violent revolution to change a policy or institution. All it takes is a good idea and a man with guts. Someone who knows that America's historically successful ideas have been liberal and radical, continuing revolt in the cause of freedom. 'Disaster occurs if a country finally abandons its radical creative past'—R. Chase. Don't be afraid of the mean-spirited. Remember that a man who scorns the idealist scorns the secret image of himself." (Levin's notebook: "Insights") Don't be afraid of names. Your purpose as self-improved man is to help the human lot, notwithstanding universal peril, anxiety, continued betrayal of freedom and oppression of man. He would, as a teacher, do everything he could to help bring forth those gifted few who would do more than their teachers had taught, in the name of democracy and humanity. (Whistles, cheers, prolonged applause.) The instructor took a bow at the urinal. (*NL,* 230)

Meditations of this sort occur often in the john, as any disciple of Norman O. Brown or Martin Luther would attest. In addition, however, Levin's fantasies have an elastic quality about them; they stretch until the savior of the humanities in general and of Cascadia College's English department in particular becomes the Christ-like savior of the entire planet: "He [Levin] healed the sick, crippled, blind, especially children. . . . He lived everywhere. Every country he came to was his own, a matter of understanding history. In Africa he grafted hands on the handless and gave bread and knowledge to the poor. In India he touched the untouchables. In America he opened the granaries and freed the slaves" (*NL,* 273). For Malamud, the giving of bread is a particularly telling symbolic act. As suggested earlier, it encompasses such moments as Bober giving an early-morning roll to the Polish woman and, later, in *The Fixer,* Yakov Bok providing matzo for a wounded Hasid. During a symposium held at the University of Connecticut, Malamud kept stressing the connection, placing a strong emphasis on Levin's dream of giving bread and knowledge to the world's poor as evidence of both the novel's moral growth and its positive ending.

Malamud was, of course, not the only one who had thoughts about how the bread motif worked in his fiction. Much has already been written about the protean character of Levin's name—from the overly formal S. Levin to the more relaxed Sam. Mark Goldman sees the line "Sam, they used to call me home" as especially important because these "concluding words end the search for Levin, happily surrendering S. for Seymour, Sy for sigh, even Pauline's Lev for love, simply to identify with the real past" (Goldman, 109). Evidently, part of the contemporary critic's equipment is the ability to play name games with ingenuity and patience. And while the shifting quality of "S. Levin" may not be as challenging and fraught with meaning as, say, the possibilities built into Moses Elkannah Herzog or nearly any character from a John Barth novel, I suspect the crucial pun is centered on the protagonist's last name rather than on the varieties of his first. As the "leaven" of *A New Life,* he makes "bread"—that is, life itself—possible.

To be sure, most reviewers saw *A New Life* as an extended exercise in irony, one far less life-affirming than either Malamud's protestations or my wordplay on *Levin/leaven* would suggest. These reviewers were, for example, annoyed that the novel ended with Levin forced to give up a college teaching career that had barely begun, and his grandiose fantasies about doing an even greater good outside the profession did not help. For them, the crux of the matter was freedom: in his imaginary articles Levin muses that the "idea of America will always create freedom"; in his reveries on the john he suggests that the betrayal of freedom is the very thing a self-improved man (i.e., himself) must combat; and, perhaps most significant, in his final showdown with Gilley he insists that Pauline is a "free agent." But the novel per se makes the dramatic point that what Levin calls "freedom" others would label "entrapment." As Robert Alter puts it, "Levin suffers the *schlemiel's* fate—ousted from the profession of his choice, burdened with a family he didn't bargain for and a woman he loves only as a matter of principle, rolling westward in his overheated jalopy toward a horizon full of pitfalls."[10] Perhaps this reluctance to see Levin leave the profession (as opposed to just Cascadia College) has something to do with the complicated reasons Oregon State—the ostensible model for Cascadia—

kept asking Malamud back to lecture. Granted, a part of the impulse is purely pragmatic. When Malamud's fictionalized account of academic life in Corvallis was first published, it must have been painful reading indeed, and no doubt there were those who unfurled the banners marked "UNFAIR!" or "UNREPRESENTATIVE!" But in time, even bad press has a marketable value—after all, *A New Life* put the school "on the map"—and Oregon State (which has hosted its share of Malamud conferences and had a hand in making sure that the proceedings were published) can take a certain amount of pride in the fact that he once taught there.

Moreover, the mechanics of Levin's last, fateful decisions also work on the most personal level. As a hard-boiled Jake Barnes might sneer through his clenched teeth, it is "pretty to think" that academic life might be better at some other, more enlightened school, and indeed Malamud's subsequent career at Bennington College suggests that perhaps it can. But I would hasten to add that this tells us more about Levin's critics than about Levin himself. The reason he accepts Gilley's absurd condition that he never teach on the college level again is that his ambitions are more oriented toward becoming a "savior" than a mere professor.

Nonetheless, Levin rushes toward a salvation that strikes more objective observers as hellish. At one point Gilley gives Levin a dose of what Saul Bellow calls "reality instruction": "An older woman than yourself and not dependable, plus two adopted kids, no choice of yours, no job or promise of one and assorted headaches. Why take that load on yourself?" (*NL*, 360). With only slight changes, the lines might have dropped from Pinye Salzman's lips and the world of "The Magic Barrel." Like Salzman, Gilley has a talent for persuasion, and his arguments are so commonsensical that Levin is reduced to gestures that combine comic victimhood with moral revolt. "Because I can, you son of a bitch" simultaneously answers Gilley's final question and seals Levin's fate. Like Finkle, Levin possesses a zeal to affect a moral change, to create "a new life" that has unwittingly willed his destruction. And like the final scene of "The Magic Barrel," the last lines of *A New Life* are packed with ambiguity: "Two tin-hatted workmen with chain saws were in the maple tree in front of Humanities Hall, cutting it down limb by leafy limb, to make room for a heat tunnel. On the Student Union side of the street, Gilley was aiming a camera at the operation. When he saw Levin's Hudson approach he swung the camera around

and snapped. As they drove by he tore a rectangle of paper from
the back of the camera and waved it aloft. 'Got your picture!'" (*NL*,
366–67).

On the one hand, there is the terrifying "picture" of Levin's departure—the battered Hudson on the verge of breaking down and the
human relationships inside very likely to follow suit. On the other
hand, there is the "limb by leafy limb" destruction of both Nature and
Humanity. Gilley might have got one picture, but it is doubtful if he
"got" the other. After all, "pictures" rather than words are the stuff
Gilley's sensibility is made of; one thinks immediately of the photo-
graphic "evidence" he collected against poor Duffy and of the stacks of
old *Life* magazines composing the raw materials of his scholarly research. No doubt this concentration of the visual pleased McCluhanites
in their day and semioticians in our own, but in the context of the novel
Gilley's camera and his pictures suggest an unwillingness to demonstrate either human emotion (for Duffy) or moral concern (for Levin).
Gilley's projected *Picture Book of American Literature* will be as much a
failure as the sordid pictures of his personal life are. Although Malamud
once remarked that Gilley's last "picture" will leave a permanent im-
pression on his mind, I have an easier time imagining him plotting to
replace the *Elements* with his own "pictorial history"—a situation that
should not be too difficult at Cascadia.

The Fixer

From the stories of *The Magic Barrel* collection to *A New Life,* Malamud creates one ironic triangle after another, all by way of suggesting
that moral bungling is at least as likely a possibility as moral regeneration. With a novel like *The Fixer* (1966), however, Malamud alters the
formula in a number of significant ways. Rather than drawing from
personal experience (i.e., *A New Life* as a fictionalized account of his
unhappy days teaching freshman composition at Oregon State) or spinning yet another moral fable about a metaphorical Lower East Side,
with *The Fixer* Malamud turned to the mythic potential of the Mendele
Beiliss case. In a strange, probably inexplicable turn of literary events,
Maurice Samuel's *Blood Accusation,* a highly readable, thoroughly re-
searched account of the same event, appeared the same year. Malamud
may or may not have counted this as good luck, but the coincidence
does suggest that the moral overtones of this most famous of all ritual

murder trials was very much a part of the contemporary sensibility. And too, the sales both of Malamud's "fiction" and of Samuel's "fact" hint that these concerns were shared by those in the marketplace as well as by those who write for it.

That said, let me hasten to point out that *The Fixer* is only loosely based on the Beiliss case. As Robert Alter suggests, "One feels in *The Fixer* that for Malamud 1911 is 1943 in small compass and sharp focus, and 1966 writ very large. The Beiliss case gives him, to begin with, a way of approaching the European holocaust on a scale that is imaginable, susceptible of fictional representation" (Alter, 74). As I see it, there are two issues here: the first involves Malamud's choice of subject matter (although aspects of moral growth had always been part of his fictional landscape, never before had response and occasion been so intimately joined in ways that intimated the Holocaust), while the second revolves around his choice of an essentially comic protagonist.

Yakov Bok is the quintessential flop. Cuckolded and then deserted by his wife, he seems to have come from a long line of those who were the innocent victims of absurd accident: "His own father had been killed in an incident not more than a year after Yakov's birth—something less than a pogrom and less than useless: two drunken soldiers shot the first three Jews in their path, his father had been the second"[11] Yet neither the death of his father nor the impoverished condition of his own life are enough to make a handwringer out of Yakov. As the name *Bok* suggests, Yakov remains obstinate, the Yiddish translation meaning either a goat or an unbendable piece of iron, while the English *balk* characterizes his reluctance to move forward. For the more ingenious, it is only a short distance (linguistically, at least) from *Bok* to *Bog,* the Russian word for Christ. Yakov may begin the novel as the would-be cynic who drinks his tea unsweetened ("It tasted bitter and he blamed existence"), but his speeches are filled with hints of the knowing sighs that will come later:

In my dreams I ate and I ate my dreams. Torah I had little of, Talmud less, though I learned Hebrew because I've got an ear for language. Anyway, I knew the Psalms. They taught me a trade and apprenticed me five minutes after age ten—not that I regret it. So I work. . . . I fix what's broken—except in the heart. In this shtetl everything is falling apart—who bothers with leaks in his roof if he's peeking through the cracks to spy on God? And who can pay to have it fixed let's say he wants it, which he doesn't. If he does, half the time

I work for nothing. If I'm lucky, a dish of noodles. Opportunity here is born dead. (TF, 6–7)

Opportunity may be born dead in the shtetl, but perhaps things will go better in Kiev. Unfortunately, Yakov finds himself beleaguered by the accidents that befall him along the way—none of which (ironically enough) he is able to "fix." Moreover, it is his penchant for doing good deeds that contributes to his misfortune and seals his kinship with other moral bunglers in the Malamud canon. For example, spotting a peasant woman "wearing a man's shoes and carrying a knapsack, a thick shawl wrapped around her head," he

drew over to the side to pass her but as he did Yakov called out, "A ride, granny?"
    "May Jesus bless you." She had three gray teeth.
    Jesus he did not need. . . . Then as the road turned, the right wheel struck a rock and broke with a crunch. . . . But with hatchet, saw, plane, tinsmith's shears, tri-square, putty, wire, pointed knife and two awls, the fixer couldn't fix what was broken. (TF, 22)

The scene is a foreshadowing of greater trouble to come. When he finally arrives at Kiev—ostensibly only a stopover on his way to Amsterdam— Yakov "went looking for luck" but instead finds a drunken member of the anti-Semitic Black Hundreds. What follows is an ironic parody of the Joseph story. In this case Yakov, or "Jacob," functions as a version of the biblical Joseph who finds himself in a foreign land and soon rises to the position of overseer. Of course, Yakov's station is not nearly so grand. He is in truth merely the supervisor of a brick factory owned by the drunken man he once rescued from the snow. For a brief moment it looks as if the fixer has beaten the odds, has opportunity aplenty. He moves into a non-Jewish neighborhood and, like Joseph, goes about the business of assimilation.

    Yet if the drunken Aaron Latke is the mock-Potiphar of the piece, his daughter, Zinaida Nikolaevna, plays the role of temptress, her frustration at Yakov's "morality" aiding his final imprisonment. At this point Yakov makes much of the fact that he is "not a political person. . . . The world's full of it but it's not for me. Politics is not my nature." Nonetheless, 20 pages later Yakov will find himself arrested for the ritual murder of a Russian boy and on trial for his very life. And, again, his moral bungling contributes to his troubles. In a scene that closely parallels the rescue of his anti-Semitic boss, Yakov saves a Hasid from the torments of an angry mob and even offers him a piece of bread. Ironically enough, Yakov—ever the flop—makes his offer during Passover, a religious holiday during which the eating of leavened bread is strictly prohibited. The Hasid will eat only matzo: "Pouring a little [water] over his fingers over a bowl, he then withdrew a small packet from his caftan pocket, some matzo pieces wrapped in a handkerchief. He said the blessing for matzos, and sighing, munched a piece. It came as a surprise to the fixer that it was Passover" (*TF*, 65). The matzos are, of course, the basis of the ritual murder charge that has been brought against Yakov. The State claims that Yakov killed a Russian boy and drained his blood to make the ritual cakes. At first Yakov, who is hardly an observant Jew and who in fact did not even realize it was the Passover season until his encounter with the Hasid, refuses to take the questions of his Russian captors seriously. In short, the accusation is not only false but also absurd:

"Are you certain you did not yourself bake this matzo? A half bag of flour was found in your habitat."
"With respect, your honor, it's the wrong flour. Also I'm not a baker. I once tried to bake bread to save a kopek or two but it didn't rise and came out like a rock. The flour was wasted. Baking isn't one of my skills. I work as a carpenter or painter most of the time—I hope nothing has happened to my tools, they're all I've got in the world—but generally I'm a fixer, never a matzo baker." (*TF*, 102)

It takes Yakov only a short time, however, to realize that "I'm a fixer but all my life I've broken more than I fix." As the time he spends in prison begins to monopolize the novel, Yakov becomes more conscious of his own role in his calamity: "If there's a mistake to make, I'll make it." The long and agonizing prison scenes (which have caused at least one reviewer to complain about needless repetition) make Yakov's sufferings realistic as opposed to merely metaphoric. Whatever else Yakov may be, his chains and the inhuman treatment he receives are real. Unlike Morris Bober, who suffered "for the Law," or even S. Levin, who had "suffering" built into his psyche, Yakov has no a priori assumptions for readers to suspend their disbeliefs about.

Further, Yakov earns his rights as an Everyman. Caught in a web of bureaucratic absurdity, he suggests that "somebody has made a serious mistake," only to find that the case against him is growing stronger every day. If a novel like Kafka's *The Trial* makes the point that K's crime is merely "living"—and that message had a certain appeal for handwringing existentialists who saw most of life as an absurd waste of time anyhow—Malamud's *The Fixer* takes a significantly different tack: Yakov "feared the prison would go badly for him and it went badly at once. It's my luck, he thought bitterly. What do they say—'If I dealt in candles the sun wouldn't set.' Instead, I'm Yakov the Fixer and it sets each hour on the stroke. I'm the kind of man who finds it perilous to be alive. One thing I must learn is to say less—much less, or I'll ruin myself. As it is I'm ruined already" (*TF*, 143).

Yakov's learning comes slowly, interspersed by scenes in which momentary bits of self-deprecation are offset by his systematic torture. One by one, former friends betray him—victims of bribery, for the most part—until Yakov is left totally alone. Even his one Russian ally, Bibikov (a Russian version of Eugene Debs who spouts such lines as "If the law doesn't protect you, it will not, in the end, protect me"), is murdered, or, what seems more likely, forced to commit suicide. Yakov, on the other hand, wears his prayer shawl under his suit ("to keep warm"), employing strategies of pragmatism to stay alive.

If the first stage in Yakov's development is a period in which he sees himself as the unlucky victim of external accident (the material things that break and somehow cannot be "fixed"), his second stage involves an internalized self-knowledge. Rather than in the frenzied movement normally associated with pratfall, it is in complete stasis (represented both realistically and symbolically by his chains) that he begins to understand. The third stage turns this self-knowledge into transcendental wisdom. For example, Yakov now realizes that he "was the accidental choice for the sacrifice. He would be tried because the accusation had been made, there didn't have to be any other reason. Being born a Jew meant being vulnerable to history, including its worst errors" (*TF*, 143).

And too, in the matter of his cuckoldry Yakov seals his fate as the sensitive flop at the same moment he rises above it. In their tireless efforts to extract his confession, the authorities finally allow Yakov's wife a short visit. At first Yakov is annoyed ("to betray me again"), but he soon learns that Raisl is more interested in the fate of her illegitimate child than in complying with the Russians: she had returned to their shtetl when the child was a year and a half old, only to find out that "they blame me for your fate. I tried to take up my little dairy business but I might as well be selling pork. The rabbi calls me to my face, pariah. The child will think his name is bastard" (*TF*, 289). And so Yakov is forced to make a "confession" of a very different sort from the one Raisl had proposed: "On the envelope, pausing between words to remember the letters for the next, he wrote in Yiddish, 'I declare myself to be the father of Chaim, the infant son of my wife Raisl Bok. He was conceived before she left me. Please help the mother and child, for this, amid my troubles, I'll be grateful.' Yakov Bok" (*TF*, 292).

After many years Mendele Beiliss was finally released, the charges of "ritual murder" brought against him dropped. He immigrated to New York's Lower East Side, where he sold his story to the Yiddish newspapers, but otherwise lived his final years in increasing obscurity; the Dreyfus case far overshadowed his. In Malamud's fictional account, however, Yakov ends the novel driven through a teeming crowd on the way, at long last, to his "trial" and an almost-certain death. There are overtones here of Camus's *The Stranger*, but with some important differences. Gone are the artful ambiguities that had characterized Malamud's earlier work. Yakov Bok may be moving toward a literal death, but one does not feel the invisible hand of irony at work. His last moments share little with those of Leo Finkle or S. Levin. Rather, we see Bok as a character who began his life as accident-prone and morally neutral, the bitter and obstinate "Bok," but who exits with tragic dignity and a speech designed to warm the most political heart in Malamud's audience: "One thing I've learned, he thought, there's no such thing as an unpolitical man, especially a Jew. You can't be one without the other, that's clear enough. You can't sit still and see yourself destroyed" (*TF*, 335). To be sure, Malamud had intimations of the American civil rights movement in mind as he crafted the terms and rhythms of Yakov's final speech. In *The Fixer* childhood memories of hearing about the Mendele Beiliss case from his father mixed with contemporary headlines. The result is a moral fable with a political coating.

Dubin's Lives

At the end of his career Malamud would return to a variant of this form, but with considerably less success. *God's Grace* (1982) sacrifices the dramatically convincing to the didactically insistent; in a word, this is a case in which the "allegorical" overwhelms. On the other hand, in collections like *Pictures of Fidelman* (1969) and *Dubin's Lives* (1979), versions of the saintly fool and the sensitive flop stood Malamud in good stead. The six episodes that constitute the former are in a sense a requiem—often zany, occasionally steeped in the formality of a high mass—for Arthur Fidelman, antihero, would-be artist, and inveterate bungler. What he must learn, through a series of painful lessons administered by an unrelenting Susskind, is that taking full stock of one's failures is the first step toward becoming fully human, toward becoming a mensch. As Ruth Wisse observes,

No matter how intimate his knowledge of life or how edifying his many adventures of body and soul, his art never improves. He works among compromises, with dictated subjects, tools, circumstances. This is a generalized portrait of the artist as *schlemiel,* a man drawn on the same scale as other men, small and silly, but involved in a recognizably human enterprise. . . . To live within the comedy of human limitations, while striving to create the aesthetic verities in some eternal form—that is the artistic equivalent to the *schlemiel's* suspension between despair and hope. [12]

By contrast, the William Dubin of *Dubin's Lives* is a disciplined, even earnestly dogged biographer and not, inconsequently, a very productive one. As the novel opens he has a handful of successful biographies behind him and one—on D. H. Lawrence—in the works. Jogging, he meditates (or perhaps vice versa) about what it means to be William Dubin, "formerly of Newark, New Jersey," a 56-year-old man who gives pattern and significance to dead men's lives. In a word, something essential is missing in the Dubin who jogs through the Vermont countryside, who moves through Nature itself, like a stranger:

In sum, William Dubin, visitor to nature, had introduced himself along the way but did not intrude. He gazed from the road, kept his distance even when nature halloowed. Unlikely biographer of Henry David Thoreau—I more or less dared. Even in thought nature is moving. Hunger for Thoreau's experience asserted itself. . . . Thoreau gave an otherwise hidden passion and drew from woods and water the love affair with earth and sky he's recorded in his journals. "All nature is my bride." His biographer-to-be had been knocked off his feet on first serious encounter with nature, a trip to the Adirondacks with a school friend when they were sixteen. . . . [It] had turned him on in the manner of the Wordsworthian youth in "Tintern Abbey": "The sounding cataract haunted like a passion." Dubin, haunted, had been roused to awareness of self extended in nature, highest pitch of consciousness. He felt what made the self richer: who observes beauty contains it. . . . He wanted nature to teach him—not sure what—perhaps to bring forth the self he sought—defined self, best self?[13]

Sensibility, rather than "suffering," makes Dubin's character memorable. As Malamud's novel would have it, biographers become the lives they write about. Dubin is the condition writ large and comic.

But that said, let me hasten to add that *some* things about *Dubin's Lives* look very familiar indeed: a protracted winter follows Dubin's infatuation with the 22-year-old Fanny Bick like the Shakespearean night the day. In such a world the heart swoons and the snowflakes fly; Dubin's book, *The Passion of D. H. Lawrence: A Life,* is symmetrically balanced with Dubin's personal life in ways that smack of formalism's last hurrah. And yet again, moral impulses lead, ironically, to botched results.

By the usual measures, of course, Dubin, the biographer, has made it. He is by now a permanent, successful fixture of Center Campobello life, a "biographer" rather than, say, an impoverished grocer or itinerant matchmaker. Which is to say, Dubin would find little company in the constricted world of Malamud's most representative short stories. Nonetheless, shadows of the Great Depression still fall across his life. In short, he is a typical Malamud character under the skin, however untypical his situation might be. It is hard for men like Dubin to feel entirely comfortable in the world.

Malamud, of course, used to think of this as a peculiarly "Jewish" condition. Now it seems more a function of male menopause or middle-age crisis or whatever the fashionable phrase for this low-level, gnawing angst one prefers. Here, for example, is the cerebral Dubin alternately musing and panting about the nubile Fanny: "It annoyed him a bit that he had felt her sexuality so keenly. It rose from her bare feet. She thus projects herself?—the feminine body, the beautifully formed hefty hips, full bosom, nipples visible—can one see less with two eyes? Or simply his personal view of her?—male chauvinism: reacting reductively? What also ran through his mind was whether he had responded to her as usual self, or as one presently steeped in Lawrence's sexual theories, odd as they were. He had thought much on the subject as he read the man's work" (*DL,* 23).

Fortunately, *Dubin's Lives* is more complex, more interesting, and certainly more indebted to the comic spirit than most contemporary versions of the December–May syndrome tend to be. Part of the credit goes to Dubin's wife, Kitty. Her "crime," as it were, is that after 25 years of marriage, raw sexuality no longer steams upward from her bare toes. My hunch is that this will matter less to mature readers than it obviously does to the comically rendered Dubin. Moreover, those willing to pull Dubin up short, to hector him about the dangers of becoming an ersatz Lawrence are hardly in short supply. Add Malamud's own flair for undercutting irony and the result takes the edge off Dubin's extensive and allusion-filled rationalizations.

In fact, Malamud remains far better on comic failure than he is on amorous success. Dubin's assignation with Fanny in romantic Venice is filled with comic interruptions and assorted pratfalls. Indeed, not since *A New Life* has Malamud been so funny about a would-be lover's parched forehead and cloying tongue. But contemporary novels demand more than a Dubin who trips over his feet while chasing Fanny Bick. He must, eventually, slip her between the sheets, or, in this case, tangle her among the (Lawrentian?) flowers. Alas, on this score neither Malamud nor Dubin is D. H. Lawrence. They are not even John Updike.

Granted, Dubin wriggles out of the dilemma by being as much "father" as lover and more biographer than either. Then too, his liaison with Fanny becomes more serious as she (a) grows as a person and (b) becomes more wife than mistress. In short, Dubin finds himself doubly married. It is a neat irony, one that suggests life is more telling than art, and that writing about Lawrence is, finally, less at the heart of the matter than living with Kitty/Fanny. Thus, we watch Dubin as comic complications turn him into the "subject" of a biography masquerading as a novel, or perhaps of a novel masquerading as a biography. In any event Dubin becomes the schlemiel-as-biographer, the man whose life reduplicates in miniature what he had once writ large. That the patterns—mythic, seasonal, inextricably tied to the "lives" he had formerly written about—suggest a partial return to Malamud's first novel (*The Natural*, 1952) is true enough, but the final notes struck in *Dubin's Lives*—like the somewhat darker ones in *Pictures of Fidelman*—speak to love, to commitment, to a man's responsibility. As Shimon Susskind puts it to Fidelman, "Tell the truth. Don't cheat. If it's easy it don't mean it's good. Be kind, specially to those that they got less than you."[14] In the lonely prisons of their respective comedies, Malamud's protagonists discover both the truth and the terrible cost of Susskind's instruction. Such quests may turn a character into a moral bungler, but, I would add, they can also turn him into a mensch.

Saul Bellow's *Seize the Day*

To be sure, Malamud was hardly alone in understanding that comic undercutting could coexist with moral vision, or that the two were more often inextricably combined than separated. Although chapter 6 discusses Saul Bellow's fiction in some detail, no account of sensitive flops would be complete without mention of Tommy Wilhelm and *Seize the Day* (1956), the remarkable novella in which he appears. In many respects Tommy Wilhelm is an Augie March grown old and slightly paunchy, his chances quickly running out. Here bounce and endurance are commodities of the fathers, and in the aging world of *Seize the Day* it is a father, rather than his son, who has the real staying power. In sheer economic terms Tommy may well be the greatest failure in Bellow's failure-ridden canon. But that said, let me hasten to point out that Tommy suffers from the same rage to be loved that afflicts other Bellow protagonists, and hence his collective failures are more emotional than financial. Like Willy Loman, Tommy believes that the "well-liked" never want, although the maxim works as poorly for him as it did for those caught in the tragic web of Arthur Miller's *Death of a Salesman*. Already in his midforties, Tommy has been a solid failure on a variety of fronts: as actor, as salesman, as father, and, perhaps most galling of all, as son. Instead of the oppressive heat and Dostoyevskian apartment that closed in on Leventhal, Tommy lives out his empty days in the comparative luxury of the Hotel Gloriana. There one's physical needs receive prompt and expensively courteous attention.

Life, however, is not all cigars, Coca-Cola, and Unicaps. More than anything else, Tommy had "wanted to start out with the blessings of his family, but they were never given."[15] Tommy remains—regardless of his age—one who could, as his father put it, "charm a bird out of a tree" (*SD*, 6). Tommy's situation, however, is not merely the reluctance of every father to see his son suddenly independent and a man. As Daniel Weiss suggests in his psychoanalytic study of the novel,

It is, I suppose, in those situations where life turns back on itself and breaks where it should begin that the tragic historical significance of the father-son relationship occurs. One thing seems fairly certain—that literature abounds more in those situations in which David destroys Absolom and Rustum, Schrab than those in which Theseus succeeds Aegeus and Prince Hal, King Henry—and more often than not defies the biological truism of youth succeeding age. It represents instead the efforts of an innately hostile father, who, by force of sheer vitality, or by the inertia of his established position, reverses the flow of progress and overshadows his son.[16]

Dr. Adler, Tommy's father, not only is capable of overshadowing his son or projecting such a standard of capital-*S* Success that Tommy is reduced to a capital-*F* Failure but also is so strong, so domineering, that his son has difficulty talking to him, much less oedipally arranging for his murder. Tommy's retreat into rationalization and the interior of the mind therefore comes as no great surprise:

Another father might have appreciated how difficult this was—so much bad luck, weariness, weakness, and failure. Wilhelm had tried to copy the old man's tone and make himself sound gentlemanly, low-voiced, tasteful. He didn't allow his voice to tremble; he made no stupid gesture. But the doctor had no answer. He only nodded. You might have told him that Seattle was near Puget Sound or that the Giants and the Dodgers were playing a night game, so little was he moved from his expression of handsome, good-natured old age. He behaved toward his son as he had formerly done toward his patients, and soon it was a great grief to Wilhelm; was almost too great to bear. (*SD*, 11)

What Tommy demands, of course, is that his father be more the Hebrew patriarch (giving blessings, hands on shoulders, etc.), and less the Jewish doctor. The real issue is not so much "assistance" as it is *love*: for Tommy, as for Leventhal, feelings count in ways that others cannot—or will not—take into account: "It isn't the money [Tommy tries to explain], but only the assistance; not even the assistance, but just the feeling. . . . Feeling got me in dutch at Rojax. I had the feeling that I belonged to the firm, and my *feelings* were hurt when they put Gerber in over me. . . . If [my father] was poor, I could care for him and show it. The way I *could* care, too. If I only had a chance. He'd see how much love and respect I had in me. It would make him a different man, too. He'd put his hands on me and give me his blessing" (*SD*, 56–57). The vacuum Tommy feels is soon filled by Tamkin, who dispenses stock tips instead of biblical blessings, quack psychology rather than medical advice. Tamkin is simultaneously a charlatan and a charmer, a character of exotic mystery to those who live at the Hotel Gloriana and a standard fixture in subsequent Bellow novels. He is also the schnorrer who lets Tommy keep him company at lunch only to stick him with the tab, and the *luftmensch* whose manipulations are more "in the air" than they are on the Stock Board.

For Tommy, however, Tamkin represents the last, desperate straw, and he stays with his speculations in rye and lard until the last dime. Tamkin's foolproof system and the various machines that never allow one to plunge into debt have failed; Tommy seized the day and found it bone dry. He does, however, manage to achieve a catharsis of sorts in the novella's closing lines. Unblocked at the funeral home into which he stumbles as he chases after Tamkin, Tommy, at last, cries. His tears suggest, in Bellow's cadenced but ambiguous prose, the "consummation of his heart's ultimate need"—presumably visible tokens of his realizations that death is the fate of everyone (his dead and unmourned mother, his lost father, himself) and that an unpacked heart (one might even say a *Jewish* heart) is the only path to Tommy's authentic self.

Tommy's failure is not so much a matter of playing his money on the wrong commodity or even of falling in with bad company as it is a disposition that makes life on the middle ground impossible. Like Bellow's other protagonists, Tommy is irritable and impatient. There is a sense in which he itches to get moving—even if that means there are risks involved. In short, Tommy has been pinning his hopes on avatars of Tamkin all his life. That he ends his speculative career with a Tamkin suggests, I think, a way of externalizing what have been constant but lower-keyed anxieties. And his ability to shed tears must be seen as a sign of health, however much the gesture is misinterpreted by the other mourners.

In our own time, of course, it is Woody Allen who has done the most to popularize the sensitive flop, to convince us that his bespectacled, anxious countenance speaks directly to a zeitgeist in which antiheroes often seem to be the only "heroes" left. And if one can raise questions about the "Jewishness" of Allen's humor (it is easy enough, after all, to trace his comic roots to Robert Benchley, James Thurber, and other *New Yorker* writers), there is little doubt that his sensitive flops/saintly fools are not unlike those I have paraded through this chapter.

Chapter Five
Bashing the
Jewish-American Suburbs

Philip Roth's *Goodbye, Columbus*

It is not hard to think of writers whose first books brought them equal shares of attention, notoriety, and fame (indeed, the harder task would be to think of writers whose second, third, or fourth books were similarly spectacular). It *is* hard, though, to think of a contemporary American writer who burst onto the scene with a more intriguing voice or a more controversial agenda than Philip Roth, for *Goodbye, Columbus* (1959) not only won its 26-year-old author a prestigious National Book Award but also forever changed the ways in which contemporary Jewish-Americans would be envisioned and written about. If an older generation of Jewish-American writers had insisted, in Bernard Malamud's oft-quoted (and probably apocryphal) words, that "all men are Jews," Roth's fiction seemed dedicated to the proposition that all Jews were also men.

Granted, Roth was hardly the first Jewish-American writer to cross verbal swords with the official Jewish community. Artists, regardless of ethnic affiliation, rarely cultivate good public relations. Abraham Cahan had been charged with self-hatred and various infractions of un-representativeness as early as 1917, when *The Rise of David Levinsky* struck many as confirming anti-Semitic stereotypes, and there were those who were less than amused by the portraits of Jewish-American life provided later by the likes of Samuel Ornitz, Daniel Fuchs, and Michael Gold. But Roth's *Goodbye, Columbus* brought these long-standing antagonisms to a rapid boil. For one thing, this was social criticism directed at the meretricious Jewish-American suburbs rather than at fading memories of urban Jewish ghettos; for another, this was mainstream literature, originally published in such magazines as the *New Yorker* and read as widely by non-Jews as by those who found themselves unflatteringly skewered by Roth's satiric pen. No doubt there were those who preferred the easier resolutions served up in potboilers like Herman Wouk's *Marjorie Morningstar* (1955), but Roth was both a leaner and a tougher customer. His vision of the new Jewish affluence did not have the look of soap opera about it.

Nearly half the pages of *Goodbye, Columbus* are devoted to the title story, a novella that is at once an earnest look at an ill-fated love affair and a scathing indictment of those Jewish-American times and places in which the Neil Klugman–Brenda Patimkin relationship unfolded. The saga begins, as it seemingly must, at poolside. After all, upward mobility had replaced tenement squalor with suburban ranchers and the ritual bath with the kidney-shaped swimming pool. To continue to write as if the majority of American Jews were stuck in an endless depression was to deny both economic fact and cultural truth. If anything, so much psychic distance existed between the suburban 1950s and earlier decades of struggle that it was now possible to read about one's impoverished "roots" with a mixture of sentimentality, nostalgia, and pride. *Those* Jews—whether one encountered them in a Bernard Malamud short story like "The Magic Barrel" or in a Saul Bellow novel like *The Adventures of Augie March*—did not threaten. By contrast, Roth's Jews did.

"Goodbye, Columbus."   Consider, for example, the ostensible hero-protagonist of "Goodbye, Columbus"—the testy, social-climbing Neil Klugman. His alternating currents of attraction and repulsion for the ethos that produces the likes of a Brenda Patimkin are foreshadowed in the novella's opening scene. Brenda casually asks Neil to hold her glasses and dives, myopically, into the country club pool. Effectively reduced to the status of impromptu servant, Neil is nonetheless fascinated by "her head of short-clipped auburn hair held up, straight ahead of her, as though it were a rose on a long stem";[1] her svelte, athletic body; and the easy ways in which her hand extends up to retrieve the eyeglasses he has been breathlessly clutching. Brenda is simultaneously goddess and Jewish-American princess, one born to the manor as well as the "manner." She expects the pampered treatment life has taught her she will receive.

What Brenda will later come to call Neil's "nastiness" has to do with his awkward role as an initiate into the mysteries of Short Hills. In this sense "Goodbye, Columbus" is the Cinderella story turned upside down, with Neil, a son of Newark, playing Prince Charming while the scullery maiden enters the stage with glass slippers already donned. In the traditional terms of class conflict, Roth's tale pits the have-nots of Newark against the haves of suburbia, although Roth seems less sure about such rigid categorizations than writers in the 1930s did. Thus, Neil lugs his ambivalent, conflicted allegiances about Newark into a wasteland fashioned from conspicuous consumption, gastronomic detail, and virtually nonstop athletic competition. What Neil wants, of course, is an independence from *both* factions, one as pristine in its innocence as it is radical in its implications. In short, Neil sides with neither side, and presumably this gives him the edge a satiric persona requires. He can judge both worlds—the yoo-hooing Yiddishkeit of his Newark relatives as well as the nouveau riche one of the Patimkins—from the vantage point of semiobjective distance.

That said, however, it is hard to see how Neil differs from those who are the easy targets of his cheap shots. He works diligently—perhaps a bit *too* dilligently—at making a virtue of having no definable virtues. The result reduces every effort along the middle-class continuum to such grotesquerie that Neil cannot fail to seem attractive by comparison. After all, he is hipper, more with-it than his immigrant Newark relatives, and more sensitive than the vulgarly garish Patimkins. Put another way, Roth's own allegiances stack the cards in favor of youth and youthful sarcasm.

That Roth so successfully managed to bash the Jewish-American suburbs is partly a matter of timing (he was at the right place at the right moment) and partly one of sheer talent. Roth's strongest suits have always been a sense of naturalistic detail and an ear for the flavors of native speech. Both are in generous supply as Short Hills slips under the microscope and Brenda's family is fastened to the rack. At first Neil is overwhelmed by a world in which grueling tennis matches, rather than hard work, occasion sweat, but he is a quick study, a *klug* (wise) man, as well as a *wise*cracker. Short Hills is not quite the Eden it is cracked up to be, even though sport abounds—from the swimming pool to the driving range to the basketball court—along with the more literal fruits of the leisure class: cherries, plums, watermelons. Indeed, Roth uses food as an easy index separating the Patimkins from their less affluent counterparts. At Newark dinners Neil's Aunt Gladys wonders, in the fractured synatax of Jewish immigrant speech, if he is "going to pick the peas out is all? You tell me that, I wouldn't buy carrots" (*GC,* 22). By contrast, at the Patimkins' "fruit grew in their refrigerators and sporting goods dropped from their trees." For an author who could claim, in 1961, that "small matters aside—food preferences, a certain syntax, certain jokes—it is difficult for me to distinguish a Jewish style of life in our country,"[2] it is these "small matters" that loom large in the texture of "Goodbye, Columbus." Here people *are* what they eat.

Moreover, the naturalistic nuances (the food on people's tables, like the garbage in their pails, is revealing stuff) quickly escalate into heavy-handed satire. Consider, for example, the much ado Roth makes of the Patimkins' refrigerator. It is both a haunting reminder of their less prosperous days in Newark and a visible symbol, à la Thorstein Veblen, of their new suburban credentials, but the net effect strikes us as more appropriate to the world of Andrew Marvell's poem "The Garden" than to a game room in Short Hills. Not only does the quasi-epical catalog of luxuriant fruits ("There were greengage plums, black plums, red plums, apricots, nectarines, peaches, long horns of grapes, black, yellow, red, and cherries, cherries flowing out of boxes and staining everything scarlet" (*GC*, 30–31).) suggest Marvell's image of "nectarine and curious peach"; it also suggests the sheer lushness that ensnares and ultimately trips both protagonists.

Granted, Marvell brought his metaphysical imagination and its requisite conceits to bear on a solitary Adam; by contrast, Klugman finds himself in Brenda's clutches from the very beginning. Radcliffe women, I suspect, do not find the portrait of their "classmate" either flattering or accurate. For Brenda, a phrase like "stringed instruments" refers to squash or tennis rackets rather than to violins or bass fiddles. No doubt she can find her way around Bloomingdale's, but not, one imagines, through the card catalog at the library where Neil works. In short, Brenda is a coed in the tradition of William Faulkner's Temple Drake—all parties, palaver, and a liberal arts education reduced to that easiest-of-all "liberations," a swinging flipness yoked to a shallow sophistication.

If life with Aunt Gladys and Uncle Max is too confining, too ethnically "Jewish," the Patimkins sound the same "responsible" notes in another key. Neil, of course, seeks a personal freedom as elusive as it is romantically impossible. In the process he confuses selfishness with integrity. That he is beginning to *look* like Brenda and that he might one day *act* like her brother Ron fills him with justifiable horror. After all, Ron is an unabashed glutton at the Patimkin dinner table, a "crew-cut Proteus rising from the sea," and, worst of all, the lover of recordings by André Kostelanetz. Neil may be something of an elitist snob, but then again, Ron more than deserves the condescension. One suspects he will follow his father's game plan into the world of Patimkin sinks and bathtubs as faithfully as he had obeyed his coaches at Ohio State.

Neil, on the other hand, finds his job at the public library a joyless business at best. The bureaucratic stink is, alas, everywhere. His fellow librarians are infected with the functionaries' mentality: as cautious as they are petty, as regulation-ridden as they are mean-spirited. Surrounded by these tyrannical wielders of small power, Neil derives a measure of solace in an alter ego of his own choosing: a small black boy who makes daily pilgrimages to look at what he calls "heart" books. The misnomer—for "art"—is in larger ways a Freudian slip, one that strikes Neil as charming (one wonders if he would have reacted the same way had his Aunt Gladys been similarly confused). In any event the young boy is a perfect candidate for a partner in some bookish secret sharing. The boy discovers Gauguin, and Neil finds himself protecting both the boy and the expensive reproductions from unworthy adults who might check the volume out. The shy boy thus serves as a point of reference when the garish world of the Patimkins threatens to become unbearable. Moreover, his alternating bravado and uneasiness at the library are a mirror image of Klugman's own behavior in the alien, suburban world of Short Hills.

Indeed, the fusion is achieved symbolically in Neil's mythopoeic dream filled with echoes of Leslie Fiedler's *Love and Death in the American Novel*:

The dream had unsettled me: it had taken place on a ship, an old sailing ship like those you see in pirate movies. With me on the ship was the little colored kid from the library—I was the captain and he my mate, and we were the only crew members. For a while it was a pleasant dream; we were anchored in the harbor of an island in the Pacific and it was very sunny. Up on the beach there were beautiful bare-skinned Negresses, and none of them moved; but suddenly *we* were moving, our ship, out of the harbor, and the Negresses moved slowly down to the shore and began to throw leis at us and say "Goodbye, Columbus . . . goodbye, Columbus . . . goodbye. (*GC,* 74)

A number of critics have pointed out that the Yiddish word *klug* means "wise," although Irving Howe insists Neil Klugman is neither very wise nor much of a man. And given the resonances of the novella's title, one is reminded of the Yiddish curse *"A klug af Columbus!"* (A curse on Columbus!), which was a bitterly ironic comment on the

Lower East Side's nongolden streets and the disappointments many Jewish immigrants experienced in America. Beyond a handful of obscenities, Roth pleads ignorance where most matters of Yiddish are concerned, but "new worlds" abound in *Goodbye, Columbus* all the same—from Ron Patimkin's schmaltzy phonograph record about Columbus, Ohio, to Neil's mythical dream about exotic islands and old-style explorers.

What Neil eventually bids a scornful farewell to, Ron embraces with not so much as a *first* thought. And in a tale that risks becoming vulgar—as well as being "about" vulgarity—Roth takes a special pleasure in piling up the cheap shots. At one point Mrs. Patimkin gives Neil the third degree about his synagogue affiliation, refusing to be sidetracked when he mumbles something about Martin Buber: "Is he *reformed?*" At another point Neil notices that among the gallery of photographs devoted to Brenda and Ron (on horseback, palming a basketball), there is not a single one of Mr. Patimkin. But the infamous wedding of Ron and Harriet allows Roth to pull out all the stops: "The husbands [of Mrs. Patimkin's twin sisters], named Earl Klein and Manny Kartzman, sat next to each other during the ceremony, then at dinner, and once, in fact, while the band was playing between courses, they rose, Klein and Kartzman, as though to dance, but instead walked to the far end of the hall where together they paced off the width of the floor. Earl, I learned later, was in the carpet business, and apparently was trying to figure out how much money he would make if the Hotel Pierre favored him with a sale" (*GC,* 106–7). In short, *Goodbye, Columbus* is filled with easy stereotypical targets, all too easily hit. Roth merely transferred the clannishness, boorishness, provinciality, and materialism to the hinterlands of suburbia. What remained constant, however, was the revulsion (the self-hatred?) he felt about things "Jewish."

But sophomoric swipes aside, it was the ersatz psychology of *Goodbye, Columbus* that finally reduced Roth's vision to the glib. As a post-Freudian, he vacillates somewhere between the half-serious and the self-consciously playful. The result ensures a certain amount of "victory" in advance: read the story's resolution through orthodox Freudian prisms and you miss the satiric point; defy the implications of "accident" and you miss even more.

Yet for all the straining Roth does in behalf of shocking middle-class sensibilities (e.g., Brenda and Neil playing musical beds under the senior Patimkins' very noses, or hide-the-diaphragm in Cambridge), the story now seems dated, even quaintly old-fashioned. For one thing, rewriting the saga of a rebellious protagonist who swaps a possessive woman for an ill-defined freedom puts Roth in very good, if very "traditional," company. American literature is, after all, filled with countless protagonists who head West rather than be "sivilized" by hoopskirts and the specter of domestic responsibility. But for all the charges and countercharges (Brenda's "forgetfulness" is more than matched by Neil's relief that the affair is, at last, over), "Goodbye, Columbus" transcends its conventional plot as a summer romance marooned on the rocks of autumn. For the moment, at least, Neil's floating anxieties have found an anchor worthy of his undivided contempt—and when he bids Brenda a dry-eyed farewell, he kisses off not only a single Jewish-American princess but also all the Patimkins gathered around their suburban living rooms: "I . . . took a train that got me into Newark just as the sun was rising on the first day of the Jewish New Year. I was back in plenty of time for work" (*GC,* 136). In one deft stroke the "sun also rises" for hard-boiled Jewish boys who have learned to mimic the tough, uncompromising talk of Jake Barnes rather than to suffer along with Robert Cohn.

The Other Stories in *Goodbye, Columbus*. Granted, not *all* the stories collected between *Goodbye, Columbus*'s hard covers were set in the suburbs. Some, such as "Defender of the Faith," played out on army bases the pulls and tugs of Jewish ambivalence and moral rectitude. But Roth seemed drawn to situations in which acculturation so blurred with assimilation that it was nearly impossible to tell the difference. The suburbs were an ideal locale for such investigations, of which none was more pointed—more paradigmatic, if you will—than "Eli, the Fanatic." Eli Peck, the story's protagonist, lives in the stifling safety of an affluent suburb. For the citizenry of Woodenton, New York, only that which is "different" constitutes a threat to the hard-won gains conformity has made. In a community built from virtually interchangeable parts, the old animosities between Jew and gentile, between immigrant and longstanding "American," are at last disappearing.

Enter the ultra-Orthodox Rabbi Tzuref, along with his motley band of yeshiva *bochers* (Talmud students), and the result is what the Yiddishspeaking world called *tsoris*. As a solid Woodenton citizen—and, more important, a lawyer who can cite chapter and verse of the municipal code—Peck is caught between his anxious clients ("Tell this Tzuref where we stand, Eli. This is a modern community." *GC,* 180) and a growing realization that there are "laws" and Laws, zoning ordinances and what exile teaches people like Tzuref. Tzuref, of course, is *meant* to

be protean, hard to pin down via points of jurisprudence, but his purposes speak to values the Jews of Woodenton have long ago forgotten:
"'The law is the law,' Tzuref said . . . 'And then of course'—Tzuref
made a pair of scales in the air with his hands—'the law is not the law.
When is the law that is the law not the law?' He jiggled the scales.
'And vice versa'" (*GC*, 251). The image of tipping scales is a useful
synecdoche for the story as a whole. Justice, both poetic and legalistic,
ultimately involves a balancing of empathy, a sharing of alternative
life-styles, even a switching of clothes.

By contrast, Eli Peck is committed to the ability—indeed the *necessity*—of minority groups melting anonymously into the fabric of mainstream America. Granted, city *streets* may promote anonymity, but
more often than not urban "neighborhoods" reinforce ethnic patterns
and identities. On the other hand, the suburbs encourage the camaraderie of a very different set of values: wide, well-tended lawns; ranch-
style homes; patios and charcoal grills; station wagons and whole
networks of social programming, from PTA meetings to Little League
games. As Peck's carefully argued letter to Tzuref puts it, "It is only
since the war that Jews have been able to buy property here, and for
Jews and Gentiles to live beside each other in amity. For this adjustment to be made, both Jews and Gentiles alike have had to give up
some of their extreme practices in order not to threaten or offend the
other" (*GC*, 262). Peck's argument makes sense in much the same way
as "the law is the law." Consensus reality is on his side; the Old World
yeshiva of Tzuref seems out of time, out of place.

Ironically enough, that is exactly the premise Roth's story tests.
Consensus authorities aside, it is Peck rather than Tzuref who suffers
an identity crisis. The tension pits a vaguely Hasidic mysticism against
a sanitized Freudian psychology. Surrounded by lives lived with what
Thoreau called "quiet desperation"—and occasionally with its noisier
manifestations ("I had a sort of Oedipal experience with the baby today," Peck's wife relays in a note)—Peck soon finds himself on the edge
of a nervous breakdown. Cocktail chatter about neuroses may be the
stuff of suburban chic, but it is deeply unsatisfying for the individual
neurotic. In Woodenton even a mildly examined life turns out to be
not worth the living.

Tzuref's old-fashioned Orthodoxy catapults Peck out of secular
time—out of a house filled with TV dinners, sling chairs, and floating
anxieties. In sacred time there is only the eternality of Sinai and the
Commandments divinely revealed there. Peck may be inarticulate about

their appeal and certainly unable to list what exactly the ordinances are, but he would swap his torts for Tzuref's Torah nonetheless.

Interestingly enough, the characteristic posture of the Jewish-American writer has been one of flight from the Hasid and all he represents. The reasons may have varied widely, but the end result was the same. The tightly drawn ideological lines that had once pitted Orthodox fathers against freethinking sons gave way to half-disguised folktales and irrational superstition as convenient indicators of the "religious." If the Hasid—with his disdain for American mores—was considered at first an unsavory "greenhorn," in the decades that followed he became a political reactionary. Rather than the Yahweh of biblical memory, it was the newfound trinity of Freud-Darwin-Marx that the young carried into battle against more modern philistines. In short, the Hasid came to symbolize that last, nagging barrier to sexual freedom, socioeconomic progress, and full credentials as an American. There was no room for the tribe of Tzuref at the suburban inn. Everything about them, from their earlocks and long black coats to their Yiddish accents and general otherworldiness, smacked of *threat*. As one of Peck's constituents puts it, "There's going to be no pogroms in Woodenton, Right? 'Cause there's no fanatics, crazy people— . . . Just people who respect each other, and leave each other be. Common sense is the ruling thing, Eli. I'm for common sense. Moderation" (*GC,* 277–78).

And yet for all its initial difficulties, the battle for assimilation was a relatively short skirmish. The harder task of assessing the "victory" fell to contemporary Jewish-American writers like Philip Roth. In this sense the stories in *Goodbye, Columbus* pit the Jews of stereotype against the more human ones we meet, and are. And if Roth could be—and indeed was—accused of knowing little about the broad sweep of Jewish history and even less about the intricacies of Jewish thought, he knew the Jewish suburbs in ways that shocked his more conventional Jewish-American readers.

Consider, for example, "Epstein," a mean-spirited affair out to deflate the going myth that Jewish husbands are as faithful as they are hardworking. "Why all the *schmutz?*" Theodore Solotaroff once asked Roth. "The story is the *schmutz,*" Roth replied. He was never more correct, for *schmutz*—literally, "dirt" in Yiddish but also suggesting the unsavory in general—is at the very heart of this sadly funny story. That Epstein "cheats" with Ida Kaufman is the last thing Jewish-American readers expected of a 59-year-old man. Maybe in an I. B. Singer story about European immigrants, but not in a tale about a solid suburban householder. While his wife, Goldie, continues to divide all of humanity into "poor" and "nice" eaters ("Recipes she dreams while the world zips," [*GC,* 149] Epstein muses ruefully), Ida turns out to be good for a much-needed laugh. Unfortunately, she also seems to have been good for a "rash," and the resulting "inspection scene" between the naked Goldie and the embarrassed Epstein is Roth at his unmerciful best.

Epstein's comic rash, like the sad comedy of Epstein's life, is hardly the stuff of tragedy. He may have had an affair with Ida, but he is not, as it turns out, afflicted with venereal disease because of it. Justice and guilt feelings remain very far removed; Epstein, in short, is no Job. And through it all, Roth has a good laugh at the expense of middle-aged flesh.

It is, however, a smart-alecky, cruel laughter. Epstein suffers a heart attack, and Roth's readers suffer through an ambulance reconciliation: "You have something that will cure what else's he's got—this rash? Goldie pleads. "So it'll never come back," the doctor replies. (*GC,* 165) But somehow we couldn't care less—either for "Epstein" the story or for Epstein the character. Even the satirically drawn Patimkins earn more of our sympathy and concern. Which is to say, "Epstein" is indeed a "dirty story"—not because it does dirt on sex but because it fulfills Lawrence's definition of the pornographic by doing dirt on life.

Portnoy's Complaint

Taken together, the stories of *Goodbye, Columbus* constituted an indictment against suburban Jewry. But as the old vaudevillians liked to put it, affluent Jewish-Americans hadn't seen nothin' yet. Parts of a new Roth novel had appeared in the *New American Review,* the *Partisan Review,* and *Esquire.* Publicity about it had appeared everywhere: on talk shows, in newspapers, and, of course, among the indignant congregants of synagogues. The advance sales were staggering; rumors about what Hollywood was willing to pay for the screen rights dazzled serious writers and critics alike. It was 1969, and Roth's newest assault was a sure bet to end the decade with a literary bang. The novel was, of course, *Portnoy's Complaint.*

Such a novel is by definition hard to pin down. Indeed, its very *title* works on at least three levels: (a) as a "complaint"—in the legalistic sense of an indictment—handed down against those cultural forces which have so crippled, so unmanned Alexander Portnoy; (b) as a "complaint" in the old-fashioned sense of illness, one that Dr. Speilvogel comically describes in clinical language as "a distortion in which strongly-felt ethical and altruistic impulses are perpetually warring with extreme sexual longings, often of a perverse nature";[3] and (c) as a "complaint" in its common usage as an expression of pain, dissatisfaction, or resentment.

Alexander Portnoy, a 33-year-old mama's boy and New York City's assistant commissioner of human opportunity, has come to the end of his psychological tether as the novel opens. That his age is the same as Christ's when crucified, that he protects the sacredness of every human opportunity (except, of course, his own), and that he rails against injustice, bigotry, and the body's fears make for intriguing mythopoeic possibilities—but that, to me, is precisely the critical point: *Portnoy's Complaint* is as filled with "possibilities" as it is riddled with interior "contradictions." No doubt Portnoy would insist that, like the speaker of Walt Whitman's "Song of Myself," he is large enough to contain multitudes. The difference, of course, is that Whitman's epical poem has aspirations that go well beyond his hairy-chested celebration of a cosmic, largely imagined selfhood; by contrast, Portnoy's systematic contradictions have the look and feel of a case study, however much he insists they are part of a larger cultural condition.

After all, it is Portnoy's voice—alternately boasting and pleading, *kvetching* and self-justifying—that we hear from cover to cover. He retains a relentless grip on the novel's point of view. For him, the analyst's couch functions in roughly the same way center stage did for the Barrymores—excess comes with the territory. Other characters are reduced to bit players, relegated to walk-ons in the fractured chronology of Portnoy's shifting memories.

But that said, one begins to suspect that Portnoy complaineth a bit *too* much, that there is another side to his psychologically crippled coin. I raise this caveat to those who were quick to identify with Portnoy and to shout, "Portnoy *c'est moi!*" while they gleefully compared the indignities of *their* childhoods with those of Portnoy, as well as to those who pointed out, correctly enough, that the whole Jewish mama–Jewish son business was neither ethnically indigenous nor particularly unique, that Italian mothers or Irish mothers or whatever share many of the same characteristics.

What both the overly sympathetic and the overly offended tend to miss, of course, is the novel's humor. As Portnoy puts it,

What was it with these Jewish parents—because I am not in this boat alone, oh no, I am on the biggest troop ship afloat . . . only look in through the portholes and see us there, stacked to the bulkheads in our bunks, moaning and groaning with such pity for ourselves, the sad and watery-eyed sons of Jewish parents, sick to the gills from rolling through these heavy seas of guilt—so I sometimes envision us, me and my fellow wailers, melancholics, and wise guys, still in steerage, like our forebears—and oh sick, sick as dogs, we cry out intermittently, one of us or another, "Poppa, how could you?" "Momma, why did you?" and the stories we tell, as the big ship pitches and rolls, the vying we do—who had the most castrating mother, who the most benighted father, I can match you, you bastard, humiliation for humiliation, shame for shame (*PC,* 117–18).

In a very real sense *Portnoy's Complaint* is a collection of the "stories we tell," an account of a castrating mother and a benighted father and the humiliations and shames they caused. But it is also a prolonged boast—not, to be sure, in the tradition of such ring-tailed roarers as Nimrod Wildfire and Davy Crockett (who took enormous pride in the fact they could outrun, outshoot, and outfight anybody in ol' Kentuck) but, rather, in the antiheroic tradition of a Leopold Bloom. Portnoy's tall tales make it clear that he is more anxious, more guilt-ridden—in a word, more screwed up—than anybody in Newark's suburbs.

Granted, Portnoy contributes mightily to the *tsoris* and the *tumel*. If his life is a series of comic accidents, many of them are of his own making. Take, for example, masturbation. The adolescent Portnoy, for all the vivid memories about how much he practiced "whacking off" and about the powerful gratifications doing so provided, had as little luck with his phallus as Chaplin's Little Tramp had with machines:

Then came adolescence—half my waking life spent locked behind the bathroom door, firing my wad down the toilet bowl, or into the soiled clothes in the laundry hamper, or *splat,* up against the medicine-chest mirror, before which I stood in my dropped drawers so I could see how it looked coming out. Or else I was doubled over my flying fist, eyes pressed closed but mouth wide open to take that sticky sauce of buttermilk and Clorox on my own tongue and teeth—though not infrequently, in my blindness and ecstasy, I got it all in the pompadour, like a blast of Wildroot Cream Oil. (*PC,* 16)

But for all the elaborate ways and means of his frenetic, compulsive masturbation, Portnoy is a bust at being bad. Indeed, that's the real struggle in *Portnoy's Complaint*: "to be bad—and to enjoy it! . . . But what my conscience, so-called, has done to my sexuality, my spontaneity, my courage! Never mind some of the things I try so hard to get away with—because the fact remains, *I don't*. I am marked like a road map from head to toe with my repressions" (*PC,* 123).

Others, apparently, have an easier time with sin. Smolka, Portnoy's freewheeling boyhood chum, "lives on Hostess cupcakes and his own wits"—ingesting the junk food of our junk culture without undue worries about either civilization or its discontents. By contrast, Portnoy hoards his guilty memories like a miser: in his days as an adolescent onanist, he had spilled his seed into empty Mounds-bar wrappers, into empty milk bottles, into cored apples, and, once, into a piece of liver that was later served up at the Portnoy family dinner table.

What he remembers most about these masturbatory binges, however, are his darkly comic failures. In this regard none is more spectacular than his disastrous episode with Bubbles Girardi. She has "agreed"—if that is the proper word for her listless, halfhearted resignation—to jerk off one of Smolka's buddies. But there are strict conditions—the lucky stiff must keep his pants on, and *she* will count the strokes: 50, and not a single one more. As fate would have it, Portnoy (who is a quick study when it comes to fantasy, but something of a flop in "real-life" situations) wins, and the result is an escalating series of comic disasters:

At long last, not a cored apple, not an empty milk bottle greased with vaseline, but a girl in a slip, with two tits and a cunt—and a mustache, but who am I to be picky? . . . I will forget that the fist tearing away at me belongs to Bubbles—I'll pretend it's my own! So, fixedly I stare at the dark ceiling, and instead of making believe that I am getting laid, as I ordinarily do while jerking off, I make believe that I am jerking off.

And it begins instantly to take effect. Unfortunately, however, I get just about where I want to be when Bubbles' workday comes to an end.

"Okay, that's it," she says, "fifty," *and stops*!

"No!" I cry. "More!"

"Look, I already ironed two hours, you know, before you guys even got here—"

"JUST ONE MORE! I BEG OF YOU! TWO MORE! PLEASE!"

"N-O!"

Whereupon, unable (as always) to stand the frustration—the deprivation and disappointment—I reach down and grab it, and POW!

Only right in my eye. With a single whiplike stroke of the master's hand, the lather comes rising out of me. I ask you, who jerks me off as well as I do it myself? Only, reclining as I am, the jet leaves my joint on the horizontal, rides back the length of my torso, and lands with a thick wet burning splash right in my own eye. (*PC,* 178–79)

In short, Portnoy's sexual antics are the stuff of which Borscht Belt stand-up humor is made, but as he keeps insisting, this is no Jewish joke, no *shpritz* (machine-gun spray of comic material) about lime Jell-O being heavy goyish and pumpernickel being *echt* Jewish, but, rather, his *life,* where the "hoit," pain, and humiliation are all too real. That Portnoy can talk so glibly about masturbation, about perversions (both real and imagined), suggests the difference between this book and those of such modernist masters as Lawrence and Joyce. What they took with high seriousness Roth reduces to the anxiously flip. The cunning of history is partly to blame here; when Portnoy shouts, "LET'S PUT THE ID BACK IN YID!" the effect dovetails a domesticated Freudianism into the jazzy stuff of popular culture.

In this sense what *Portnoy's Complaint* provides is an encyclopedia of moments drawn from a Jewish-American ethos in its cultural death throes. And as such, one axiom is worth recalling: that at the very moment a tradition begins to question itself, to mount elaborate campaigns in behalf of retrenchment, that tradition—whether it calls itself puritanism or transcendentalism or American Yiddishkeit—is in the long arc of its decline.

Exercises in nostalgia are certain to follow, as are increasingly self-conscious efforts by way of denial. Roth specialized in the latter. What he saw, of course, was the possibility of liberating himself from the tribal fears that were his Jewish immigrant legacy and the smothering Jewish-American suburbs that was its current environment.

As he explains in *Reading Myself and Others,* his book of self-conscious "explanation": "I was strongly influenced by a sit-down comic named Franz Kafka and a very funny bit he does called 'The Metamorphosis.' . . . Not until I had got hold of guilt, you see, as a comic idea, did I begin to feel myself lifting free and clear of my last book and my old concerns."[4] What Roth *doesn't* tell us—indeed, what he could not have realized in 1969—is just how long, protracted, and impossible this struggle was likely to be. Whatever else *Portnoy's Complaint* may be in terms of an effort—at once desperate and heroic, foolhardy and comic—to *enjoy* being bad, the novel itself is all prolegomenon.

The proudest boast of Whitman's persona is that he chants his "barbaric yawp" over the rooftops of the world—*untranslatable,* utterly

unique, and forever unavailable to those who prefer their poetry polite
and neatly captured on the page. Touch *these* "leaves," he insists, and
you've touched a man! By contrast, Alexander Portnoy is the crown
prince of whiners, a man with enough *tsoris* to beat all comers in a
misery contest. Roth, I would argue, never quite recovered from the
"surprises" (as he called them) that the extraordinary success of *Portnoy's
Complaint* brought.

Granted, he had *never* set himself up as a patient Griselda, and even
in the "old days"—that is, the days before a Jacqueline Susann could
crack up the "Tonight Show" crowd by telling Johnny Carson that she
thought Roth was a good writer but preferred not to shake hands with
him—he tried to silence his critics by writing essays full of explanatory
sound and justifying fury. Nonetheless, from *My Life as a Man* (1974)
onward Roth's novels began to glance uneasily over their shoulders at
who or what might be gaining on them and, perhaps more important,
became increasingly self-conscious about both the very act of writing
fiction and fictionality itself.

Tales of Nathan Zuckerman

In *Portnoy's Complaint* Alexander *kvetches,* and then *kvetches* some
more—all with the hope that *"kvetching* for me [might be] a form of
truth."* In *My Life as a Man* Peter Tarnopol tells his story, and tells it,
and *tells* it—all in the desperate hope that he will one day see the figure
in his carpet, that the disparate pieces of his abortive marriage will fall
magically into an aesthetic whole and at last make sense. To that end,
he creates Nathan Zuckerman, a countervoice who provides the distanc-
ing that art requires. Of Zuckerman we will hear much—indeed, sometimes more than we would prefer—but Tarnopol disappears, apparently
forever, with *My Life as a Man*'s final page.

As Amy Bellette puts it in *The Ghost Writer* (1979), the master—
E. I. Lonoff—is "counter-suggestable"; one manipulates him via reverse psychology in much the same manner as, say, Poe's cerebral de-
tectives match their wits against those of master criminals. Much the
same thing might be said of the young Nathan Zuckerman, who finds
that his latest story—an exposé of family greed entitled "Higher Education"—can have surprising, even wounding consequences. The
"games" that result are both subtle and stylistically dazzling. To be
sure, Nathan Zuckerman *dreams* many of the complications—for example, that Amy Bellette is *the* Anne Frank, an Anne Frank who survived,

who "got away," and that her extraordinary book exacts a silence, an ostensible death, in short, the shadowy life as a ghostwriter, if it is to retain its raw emotional power—but this countertext, if you will, is also an extended exercise in defending, justifying, and, I would add, deconstructing the knotty question of an artist's responsibility.

For Doc Zuckerman, the consequences of art are as clear and undeniable as the Jewish nose on Nathan's face: "from a lifetime of experience I happen to know what ordinary people will think when they read something like this story ["Higher Education"]. And you don't. You can't. . . . But I will tell you. They don't think about how it's a great work of art. They don't know about art. . . . But that's my point. People don't read art—they read about *people*. And they judge them as such. And how do you think they will judge the people in your story, what conclusions do you think they will reach? Have you thought about that?"[5] The young Nathan Zuckerman, surprised by his father's surprise, hurt by his father's hurt, thinks about loftier matters: the shape and ring of individual sentences, the rise and resolution of dramatic tensions, in short, about aesthetic considerations far removed from those messy interferences which now travel under the banner of "reader response" but that, in suburban Newark, boil down to the existential business of what is or is not good for the Jews. Read *this* way, Nathan's story strikes his father as an accident waiting to happen; it confirms, from one of their own no less and in public print to boot, what anti-Semites have long suspected—namely, that Jews squabble over money, that they are, in a word, kikes.

Small wonder, then, that Nathan seeks the "sponsorship," the surrogate fatherhood, of E. I. Lonoff. As a consummate Jewish-American fictionist, *he* will be able to extend the welcoming hand that Nathan's own father has refused. What Nathan discovers, however, is a man so committed to "fantasy" that the slightest hint of life has been rigorously, systematically crowded out. "I turn sentences around," Lonoff declares. "That's my life. I write a sentence and then I turn it around. Then I look at it and I turn it around again. Then I have lunch" (*GW*, 124). Although Lonoff tells his writing students that "there is no life without patience," he has little patience with the "deep thinkers" who are attracted to his work, and no doubt he would have even less patience with a deconstructive reading of his working habits.

By contrast, Zuckerman's aesthetic feeds on turbulence, on mounting tensions, on a world where sentences are shouted across a kitchen table and end in exclamation points. "You are not somebody who writes this kind of story," Doc Zuckerman insists, "and then pretends it's the truth" (*GW*, 95). But Nathan *did* write such a story; moreover, he *is* precisely "the kind of person who writes this kind of story!" For Lonoff, such truths are as much a part of the artistic landscape as the regimen of daily reading and obsessive scribbling. Zuckerman may be a nice polite boy when invited into somebody's home, but he is not likely to be so politic when he writes up the report of his visit. With a pen in his hand, Nathan becomes a different person, and if Lonoff's "blessing" is anywhere in the text, it is in his understanding, accepting wish that Nathan continue to be this "different" person when he sets about composing the novel we know as *The Ghost Writer*.

For those who would brand him as self-hating, as an enemy of his people, nothing short of his marrying Anne Frank will suffice. And indeed Zuckerman imagines exactly this triumph as a logical consequence of his imaginative rescue. Not only would he who had been misunderstood now be forgiven, but his father would utter the very words Nathan most wants to hear: "Anne, says my father—the Anne? Oh, how I have misunderstood my son. How mistaken we have been!" (*GW*, 159).

To be sure, the Anne Frank Nathan resurrects—the impassioned little sister of Kafka who lived out in Amsterdam the indictments, hidden attics, and camouflaged doors he had dreamed about in Prague—is a psychological ringer for Nathan himself: both exact their rebellions against family, synagogue, and state in the pages of their respective works; both suffer the loss of fathers for their art; and, interestingly enough, *neither* could answer Judge Wapter's questions (number 3, for example, asks: "Do you practice Judaism? If so, how? If not, what credentials qualify you for writing about Jewish life for national magazines?"; *GW*, 103) in ways that he would find satisfactory.

The Ghost Writer is, of course, a version of the modernist bildungsroman as reflected through the lens of a Nathan Zukerman some 20 years old and presumably light-years sadder and wiser about the "madness of art" and the human costs that come with landscaping a fictional territory. For better or worse, Nathan's congenial turf turns out to be the Jews. Unfortunately, what he discovers—after publishing a scandalously successful exposé entitled *Carnovsky*—is that no analogues to his modernist precursors will wash. Try as he might, the mantle of exile that slipped so easily and convincingly around James Joyce's shoulders will not quite fit. Granted, there are no end of attacks, no end of those who would add Zuckerman to the list of Hamen and Hitler—names that deserve being blotted out—but the Zuckerman of *Zuckerman Un-bound* (1981) craves approval rather than martyrdom. Deep down, he really cannot believe his antagonists are as angry as they claim to be or that they would stay mad if he just had a chance to explain himself:

Not everybody was delighted by this book that was making Zuckerman a fortune. Plenty of people had already written to tell him off. "For depicting Jews in a peep-show atmosphere of total perversion, for depicting Jews in acts of adultery, exhibitionism, masturbation, sodomy, fetishism, and whoremongery," somebody with letterhead stationery as impressive as the President's had even suggested that he "ought to be shot." And in the spring of 1969 this was no longer just an expression. . . . Oh, Madam, if only you knew the real me! Don't shoot! I am a serious writer as well as one of the boys![6]

Zuckerman goes on to argue that his readers "had mistaken impersonation for confession," but mostly he protests too much—about the assorted difficulties that come with being rich and famous, about his misunderstood high-mindedness, about his essential goodness, and most of all about his bad luck. After all, other writers—the modernist giants, for example—had it easier: "What would Joseph Conrad do? Leo Tolstoy? Anton Chekhov? When first starting out as a young writer in college he was always putting things to himself that way" (*ZU*, 109–10). The rub, of course, is that none of these writers grew up Jewish in Newark, had a Jewish mother pestered by reporters in Miami ("I am very proud of my son and that's all I have to say. Thank you so much and goodbye"; *ZU*, 63) and a dying father who kept faith with the conviction that "Tzena, Tzena" is going to "win more hearts to the Jewish cause than anything before in the history of the world" (*ZU*, 116).

Granted, there is much about Zuckerman's *tsoris* that has a familiar ring—in terms of not only Roth's canon (those who tsk-tsk about his candor; the shaky marriage sacrificed to the house of fiction; such grotesques as Alvin Pepler, the Jewish marine who won a bundle on a quiz show, only to be betrayed and then disgraced) but also the longer tradition of Jewish-American letters. Zuckerman is guilt-ridden about the money that crashes in as copies of *Carnovsky* roll off the presses. Side-walk superintendents shower him with free advice: "You should buy a helicopter. That's how I'd do it. Rent the landing rights up on apartment buildings and fly straight over the dog-poop" (*ZU*, 4). After all, true is true: "Gone were the days when Zuckerman had only to worry about Zuckerman making money: henceforth he would have to worry

about his money making money" (*ZU,* 4). In Abraham Cahan's scathing portrait of the Alrightnik—*The Rise of David Levinsky* (1917)—success is synonymous with an ashy taste. Some 60 years later Roth gives
the garment-district scenario a literary twist; now high art, rather than
the spring line, can make one wealthy and estranged. Which is to
say that although the addresses and income levels of the offended may
have changed, their charges—and the consequences—remain much the
same.

Roth, of course, has long been regarded as the prime basher of the
Jewish-American suburbs, but others have also pitched their tents on
its rich, manicured soil. For all her romantic rebelliousness (and intimations of Brenda Patimkin), Marjorie Morningstar (née Morganstern)
ends up in suburbia as the thoroughly dull Mrs. Schwartz in Herman
Wouk's best-selling 1955 novel. And later Bruce Jay Friedman would
follow Roth's lead in darkly comic novels underscoring that the suburbs
were anti-Semitic, terrifying, and decidedly *not* for nice Jewish schlemiels (*Stern,* 1962) or that mothers were smothering, oppressive, and
oedipally threatening (*A Mother's Kisses,* 1965). Roth, however, worked
this material harder, and in ways that were at once more comic and
more mean-spirited.

Joseph Heller's *Good as Gold*

The novel that tried hardest, though, to outdo Roth in comically
dismantling the Jewish-American family, in counting up the costs of
assimilation and the griefs of suburban Jewish-American life, was
Joseph Heller's *Good as Gold* (1979). And perhaps the first thing to say
about the novel is that, despite the title, it *wasn't.* But for those exas-
perated by the lack of plot and the confusing chronologies of *Catch-22*
and *Something Happened,* at least *Good as Gold* had the look of a conventional novel. Granted, the book was thick (perhaps overly thick), and
it wasn't at all clear how its apparently disparate "stories"—about the
squabbles within a contemporary Jewish-American family, about ambitious academic types, about the internecine warfare and plotting
among Washington, D.C., politicos—merged into a satisfactory
"novel"; nonetheless, there were whole scenes that struck Heller's fans
as "pure Heller," complete with the dark, absurdist humor and biting
satiric energy that have been his trademarks.

Bruce Gold, a teacher and writer, "had been asked many times to write about the Jewish experience in America."[7] Given his talent and track record, that is perhaps not unusual (writers are never at a loss for people willing to give them suggestions about where to turn their energies). But in this case Heller's choice of opening gambit says a good deal about both the literary atmosphere in 1979 and where Heller imagined his own place might be. In short, Bruce Gold was not the only one who had been asked—or who had wondered—if there might be a book in "the Jewish experience in America." The rub, of course, is that the Jewish-American literary landscape was already a crowded scene, filled with such heavy-hitting competitors as Bernard Malamud (from whose work Heller takes one of the novel's epigraphs), Saul Bellow, and Philip Roth, as well as countless Sammy-come-lately's and ever-paler carbon copies of the Real Thing.

In both *Catch-22* and *Something Happened* Heller had taken considerable pains to make his protagonists *non*-Jewish. Arthur Miller had made a similar decision about Willie Loman, the doomed salesman and failed father of his play *Death of a Salesman*. That is, Miller didn't want to so emphasize Loman's "Jewishness" that it would detract from the *American* tragedy he was trying to write. Nonetheless, Willie's (Miller's?) speech patterns betray him at every turn, and despite Miller's efforts there are those who continue to see *Death of a Salesman* as a play very much about the "Jewish-American experience." Roughly the same thing is true for *Catch-22*'s John Yossarian, try as Heller might to give his protagonist a nondescript first name and an "Assyrian" last one; Yossarian, the quintessential outsider, is also—in the minds of many— a distinctively "Jewish" character. And even *Something Happened*'s Robert Slocum—who lives the corporate life in all its external trappings and interior horrors—strikes many as less the creation of, say, a WASP writer like John Cheever than somebody one might meet in a novel by a Jewish-American writer like Bruce Jay Friedman.

Thus, Heller may well have realized that his efforts to beat back the rhythms and wisecracks of his Coney Island upbringing were in vain. He may not have given much attention to his Jewishness as a child, as a teenager, or as a young adult—after all, the "Jewish experience" was all around him, as natural and as unconscious as the air one breathed. But its effects, its earmarks, were there nonetheless; they suffused the very posture and gestures he brought to experience. As Gold puts it, in ways that in the most important biographical respects speak as well for Heller,

How can I write about the Jewish experience . . . when I don't even know what it is? I haven't the faintest idea what to write. What in the world for me was the Jewish experience? I don't think I've ever run into an effective anti-Semite. When I grew up in Coney Island, everyone I knew was Jewish. I never realized I was Jewish until I was practically grown up. Or rather, I used to feel that everybody in the world was Jewish, which amounts to the same thing. Just about the only exceptions were the Italian families living at the other end of Coney Island and the two or three living close enough to us to send their children to the same school. We had an Irish family on our block with a German surname and there were always a couple of Italians or Scandinavians in my class who had to come to school on Jewish holidays and looked perse-cuted. I used to feel sorry for them because *they* were the minority. The Irish family had a dog—no Jews had dogs then—and raised chickens in their back yard. Even in high school just about all the boys and girls I hung around with were Jewish, and virtually all of the teachers were. And the same was true at college. It was not until I went to Wisconsin for a summer session that I found myself among gentiles for the first time. But that was merely different, not unpleasant. And then I came back to Columbia for my degree and doctorate and felt right at home again. My closest friends were also Jewish: Lieberman, Pomoroy, Rosenblatt. Ralph Newsome was the only exception, but I felt no different with him than with anyone else, and he seemed perfectly at ease with me. I wouldn't know how to begin. (*GG*, 11–12)

It was time, perhaps, for Heller to come clean—and to do it in a novel (*Good as Gold*) that is, at least in part, about how he came to write a book on the "Jewish experience in America." Moreover, to do this Heller would view his protagonist through two very different prisms: the first as the ridiculed Jewish son caught in the oedipal grip of a large (and largely assimilated) Jewish-American family and the second as the Jewish-American intellectual caught in slippery folds of governmental doublespeak. In both cases, however, the crossed purposes and missed communications of *Catch-22* are very much in evidence. Here, for example, is how Bruce Gold remembers his first encounter with his stepmother, a meeting that could match the zaniest of Yossarian's run-in's frustration for frustration, absurdity for absurdity, dark comedy for dark comedy:

Sid had flown to Florida for the wedding and returned with her and his father for a reception at his home in Great Neck. There was an uncomfortable silence after the introduction when no one seemed sure what to say next. Gold stepped forward with a gallant try at putting everyone at ease.

"And what," he said in his most courtly manner, "would you like us to call you?"

"I would like you to treat me as my own children do," Gussie Gold replied
with graciousness equal to his own. "I would like to think of you as my very
own children. Please call me Mother."

"Very well, Mother," Gold agreed. "Welcome to the family."

"I'm not your mother," she snapped.

Gold was the only one who laughed. Perhaps the others had perceived
immediately what he had missed. She was insane. (*GG*, 27)

Heller's brand of sociology links family life with the dinner table,
and it is precisely this equation that Bruce Gold looks on with dread:
his aunts will exasperate him; his older brother, Sid, will continue his
lifelong habit of unfairly one-upping him; he will be positioned at the
table so that his knees bang into one of the legs; and no doubt he will,
yet once again, find himself the target of his father's tyrranical abuse:

Ashes, Gold grieved wildly, chewing away at his mouthful of mashed potatoes and bread more vigorously than he realized. The food! In my mouth to
ashes the food is turning! It has been this way with my father almost all my
life.

From the beginning Gold ruminated now. When I said I was thinking of
going into business, he told me to stay in school. When I decided to stay in
school, he told me to go into business. "Dope. Why waste time? It's not what
you know. It's who you know." Some father! If I said wet, he'd say dry. When
I said dry, he said wet. If I said black, he said white. If I said white, he
said . . . niggers, they're ruining the neighborhood, one and all, and that's it.
Fartig [Finished]. That was when he was in real estate. Far back, that peremp-
tory cry of *Fartig* would instantly create an obedient silence that everybody in
the family would be in horror of breaking, including Gold's mother.

It was no secret to anyone that his father considered Gold a *schmuck*. It
would be unfair to say his father was disappointed in him, for he had always
considered Gold a *schmuck*. (*GG*, 33)

Indeed, Julius Gold has a perverse genius for deflating his son's ego and
destroying any vestiges of his self-confidence. Once when Gold was visiting
in Florida, "his father drew him across the street just to meet some friends
and introduced him by saying, 'This is my son's brother. The one that never
amounted to much.'" And Alexander Portnoy thought he had complaints!
The senior Gold's *fartig* is every bit as threatening, as castrating, as Sophie
Portnoy's overprotective love is smothering. It signals the "end" of
communication—to any further debate, discussion, or even conversation.
Thou shalt not commit adultery, sayeth the Lord; Golds do not divorce.

Fartig. Thus announceth the latter-day patriarch, Julius Gold. Writing about Heller's *God Knows* in 1984, Leon Wieseltier makes the following observations about the techniques and targets of Jewish-American humor: "America, as is well known, was where Jewish humor fantastically flourished. It has become perhaps the most well-known product of American Jewish culture. But something happened to Jewish humor in America. It shrank in its scope. Its metaphysical commentary, its interest in the collective fate, the dimension of desperation that had made it an essential instrument of the healing heart, all disappeared. As the jokes have gone from Yiddish to English, they have gone from God to parents."[8] In attempting to explain—and then dismiss—the humor that undergirds *God Knows.* Wieseltier reveals a good deal more about what is both limited and delimiting in *Good as Gold.*

There are, of course, not a few ironies in the scorn Mr. Gold heaps on his son, ironies that a serious-minded sort like Wieseltier might miss, for if truth be told, Julius Gold is as much the *luftmensch*—that is, a study in illusion, self-deception, and failure—as he is a Freudian bully:

"I owned factories," Gold's father maintained. "I built gun turrets in the war for the Bendix people. I was in defense." He slowed, nodding. "They gave me once a small citation for efficiency because I had a small factory. I had a coat business and was in real estate. I had a leather business from which I was able to retire with an income. Ask Sid. Long ago I was in furs, spices, ships, import and export." His look grew distant and he seemed to be meandering. "Once I owned a fine apartment house in a bad neighborhood, but the banks took it back from me. I owned tailor shops, always the same one, but it was hard to make a go, so I kept closed. I was ahead of my time with my supermarket. Once I owned a store with surgical appliances for people with operations, and I knew how to talk—believe me. I knew what to say to people when it came to selling. 'Have I got an arm for you!' I would say to one. 'Who sold you that eye? I would ask another. I was the best in the whole world, but I couldn't make a living so I went into finance and was a commission man on Wall Street in the Depression when no one could sell a single share of stock, not even me. I was in building, but no one was building." (*GG,* 104)

Generally speaking, Jewish mothers steal the thunder in contemporary Jewish-American fiction. One thinks, for example, of Sophie Portnoy, rather than of her forever-constipated husband, as having the most memorably chilling lines and the most unforgettable scenes in Philip Roth's novel/indictment of the Jewish-American experience, *Portnoy's*

Complaint. But even those who would argue that Jake Portnoy is *more* than the history of his constipation realize that he is at best a minor character in the titanic, oedipal conflict that forever binds Sophie Portnoy to her son. By contrast, the volatile Julius Gold dominates not only the domestic landscape but also the world of old movies as beamed into the living room via television. It is a deftly accurate touch, one that combines Julius Gold's delight in somebody else's obituary with the family's intimations of his mortality:

> Gold's father would move after dinner to the television set in whatever home he had decided to be driven to that evening and begin watching old movies with the energetic vigilance of a custodian of dead souls. The movies themselves made no difference. The responsibility for keeping score was only his.
>
> "That one's gone," he would shout elatedly like the grim reaper himself, as though collaring another trophy for his collection. "A hundred years ago. Old age did him in. Remember that lawyer for the defense? *Geshtorben.* Heart attack. Gone in an instant. Look at that big guy there pushing everyone around. You know where he is today?" (*GG*, 42)

Julius Gold fears only one thing more than death: the word *condominium.* And while there were critics who would make a case for the Golds as emblematic of close-knit Jewish families, even for the values of Jewish Orthodoxy as opposed to the sleazy world of contemporary politics, the novel will hardly support such sentimental readings. Indeed, there are more similarities to *King Lear*—especially as the children conspire to unceremoniously dump their father in Miami—than to *Fiddler on the Roof.* Here, for example, is what happens at a Gold family dinner—this one held in a Chinese restaurant amid the wonton soup and pork spareribs that have become the bill of fare for assimilated American Jews. The trouble starts when Gold

> used the intermission [between orders of pork and their arrival] to escape his predicament. "Never mind my Niles," he put it bluntly. "What about your condominium?"
>
> His father was taken off guard. His jaw dropped and his cheeks quivered.
>
> "Yes," said Sid, joining forces with Gold.
>
> "Why can't I stay here?" asked Gold's father, and added winningly, "I'm no trouble."
>
> "Pa, I want you to buy that condominium."
>
> For one moment the old man glanced wildly about in hectic disorientation.

Blood rushed alarmingly to his whole face, and he choked with such anger and violent confusion that he seemed to be fighting for each mouthful of air. . . .

"*Vehr Gehargit!*" the old man roared. . . . "I don't want no condominium! I live here, not there! It's for a vacation I go!" (*GG,* 180)

And thus scores are kept and evenings with the family pass. Small wonder that Gold is more interested in making promises and collecting advances than he is in doing "research" for his study of the Jewish-American experience. Surrounded by his "family," Gold finds that his buttons get pushed, that he loses his cool, and, worst of all, that he curses in an ersatz Yiddish not unlike his father's. Could this capacity of sons to reduplicate fathers—despite the obvious gains posted by acculturation—end up as a chapter in his book? And what of the loves that may or may not be buried beneath his hatreds—for Julius, for his crazy stepmother, for his wacky aunts, for Sid? Does that possibility too have to be taken into account?

Heller "hints" at such possibilities but does not adequately explore them. Rather, the novel takes on other agendas—the bureaucratic, double-shuffling world of Washington politics and what can only be seen as a personal, white-hot vendetta against Henry Kissinger. Meanwhile, the "Jewish-American experience"—with its affluent suburbs, messy family relations, and contradictory attractions and repulsions—remains a subject that has been often attempted but not, I would argue, satisfactorily captured.

Chapter Six
Saul Bellow, Norman Mailer, and John Updike

Major American Writers and Jewish-American Material

A chapter that links Bellow, Mailer, and Updike deserves more than a few words of explanation, not because their status as major American writers is in question but because it is not clear what, if anything, Messrs. Mailer and Updike have to do with the achievement of the Jewish-American novel. Let me begin with the controversial case surrounding the controversial Mr. Mailer. In much the same way critics of modern literature tend to separate themselves into two opposing camps—those who feel Joyce is the defining modernist giant versus those who argue Lawrence is—nothing divides contemporary critics more than the bickering that separates Mailer devotees from Bellow enthusiasts. This is especially true if the context is a meeting of the Modern Language Association and the discussion turns to which fictionist is *the* reigning American writer.

Norman Mailer and the Jewish-American Past

Granted, Bellow has not been especially happy about being lumped with others (usually Bernard Malamud and Philip Roth) as one-third of a Jewish-American triumvirate, but Mailer, being Mailer, goes considerably further. As he once put it, being branded as "the nice Jewish boy from Brooklyn" is the one personality he found "absolutely unsupportable,"[1] and it would not be hard to argue that his entire career has been characterized by one increasingly desperate effort after another to put as much distance as possible between himself and his Jewish-American past.

That some critics have seen his efforts to be maler-than-thou, to affect the cocky postures of radical self-reliance, independence, and opposition as evidence of what Andrew Gordon calls "a conservative, moral, proselytizing (one might even say rabbinical) streak" (Gordon, 156), is not surprising. But neither is the ingenuity extended in behalf of a "Jewish" Mailer convincing, for the simple fact remains—despite the anthologies of Jewish-American literature that make heroic efforts to slip "Mailer, Norman" between "Lewisohn, Ludwig" and "Mala-mud, Bernard"—that Mailer's fictional landscape has little to do with Jewish-American characters, and nothing whatsoever to do with Jewish-American ideas. As he once put it, in a "confession" that smacks suspiciously of a boast, "My knowledge of Jewish culture is exception-ally spotty."

In fact, "spotty" may well be an exercise in gilding the lily, for Mailer's intellectual pursuits have taken him in every possible direction (existential, Reichism, versions of radical politics, even Egyptology) except those remotely associated with Jewish culture. And one need go no further than the nominally Jewish characters of *The Naked and the Dead* (1948) for exhibit A. I say this not to denigrate the considerable achievement of Mailer's first novel—indeed, there is every reason to believe, as the Big Book he keeps promising looks more and more unlikely, that his saga of soldiers under the pressures of battle in the Pacific campaign will remain the book on which his reputation as a fictionalist will finally rest—but, rather, to suggest that creations like Goldstein and Roth are fashioned from slim Jewish-American cloth.

Granted, *The Naked and the Dead* reduces other characters to cultural stereotype and cartoon; one thinks, for example, of the equally one-dimensional portraits of Texans, of the Boston Irish, and of Mexican-Americans. But there is little question, I think, that Mailer takes a special delight in reducing his Jewish soldiers—Goldstein and Roth—to caricature. Consider, for example, the following exchange, as Gold-stein ponders the laughter that had broken out when a truck driver "with a brutal red face" announced that F company is where "they stick the goddam Jewboys."[2] Why are they like that? Goldstein wonders, only to discover that Roth sees history, God, and most of all Jewish vulnerability very differently:

> "The Anti-Semiten. Why don't they ever learn? Why does God permit it?" Roth sneered. "God is a luxury I don't give myself."
> Goldstein struck the palm of his hand with his fist. "No, I just don't understand it. How can God look down on it and permit it? We're supposed to be the chosen people." He snorted. "Chosen! Chosen for *tsoris!*"
> "Personally, I'm an agnostic," Roth said.

For a time Goldstein stared at his hands, and then he smiled sadly. The lines deepened about his mouth, and he had a sarcastic indrawn look on his lips. "When the time comes," he said solemnly, "they won't ask you what kind of Jew you are."

"I think you worry too much about those things," Roth said. Why was it, he asked himself, that so many Jews were filled with all kinds of wives' tales? His parents at least were modern, but Goldstein was like an old grandfather full of mutterings and curses, certain he would die a violent death. "The Jews worry too much about themselves," Roth said. He rubbed his long sad nose. Goldstein was an odd fellow, he told himself; he was enthusiastic about almost everything to the point of being a moron, and yet just start talking about politics or economics or about anything that was current affairs, and like all Jews he would turn the conversation to the same topic. *(ND, 56)*

Mailer himself makes no bones about his sympathies; he identified— at least initially—with the liberal Left Lieutenant Hearn, the character most akin to Mailer himself. But it is also clear that his deeper affections are for those with a taste for violence (e.g., Croft). And indeed it is his obsession with violence (nurtured in its early stages by the raw naturalism of Theodore Dreiser and James T. Farrell, and later in the French existentialists he encountered in Paris) that has been Mailer's most identifiable trademark ever since. Rather than labored efforts to squeeze the square peg of Mailer's radicalism into the round hole of a Jewish prophetic tradition, I think it easier, wiser, and truer to see him as not only celebrating the fist and the knife but, more important, arguing for the necessity of using them in a decisive moment of defining truth.

Small wonder, then, that Mailer's fantasy hero of his projected eight-novel epic is named Sergius O'Shaugnessy, or that Sam Slovoda, the failed artist of "The Man Who Studied Yoga," is a Jewish-American. And small wonder too that the same Mailer who began his career by "taking on" fascism in *The Naked and the Dead* and by standing four-square against what he sees as a wide variety of its American incarnations should have surprisingly little to say about the Holocaust, for the Holocaust, after all, was fascism's "war against the Jews," and to confront its implications is to confront the Jewishness in himself. This Mailer has steadfastly refused to do. When he dreams, it is not rabbis or even New York Jewish intellectuals he sees but, rather, visions of ruddy Irish brawlers. To be sure, Sergius O'Shaugnessy's real name is Nick Adams, and as every student of American literature knows, the real name of Hemingway's prototypical protagonist is Adam. Which is to say that there is something just a touch ingenuous about Mailer's self-styled bravado. At the very least, it is hardly an example of what Ezra Pound meant when he counseled writers to make it *new*. Mailer's wide violent streak is in truth nearly as old as American literature itself; what is new about it is that the rage should leap from the pen of a nice Jewish boy from Brooklyn.

At the same time, however, it is not difficult—as Mark Shechner points out—to spot

the therapeutic agenda behind such a performance [he is speaking here about *Advertisements for Myself,* but the point applies to the whole of Mailer's oeuvre]. Like Freud, Mailer had done an analysis of himself without any aid save that of drugs (Freud had used cocaine) and had come away with a burning awareness of his own needs, ambitions, and terrors. As with Freud, the self-analysis was prelude to a burst of creativity and a new direction. And while the precise revelations that set them on their new courses have never been disclosed, we can, in Mailer's case, reconstruct their major themes with confidence, since they have dominated his writing ever since: courage, manliness, combat, God, and sex.[3]

Consider, for example, "The White Negro" (1957), in its day a seminal essay and, as Shechner puts it, the "insignia piece" of *Advertisements for Myself.* My hunch, however, is that Irving Howe has had occasion to regret the initial enthusiasm that caused him to print Mailer's essay in the pages of *Dissent.* No doubt there are those who would argue with Shechner about its dazzling social criticism/philosophy—Mailer, when he is not a "charmer" or our oldest enfant terrible, is something of a professional dazzler—but my complaint has less to do with how dusty, intellectually threadbare, and pretentious the airy talk about "hipsterism" seems now than with how glibly dangerous is the argument at its core:

The psychopath murders—if he has the courage—not out of the necessity to purge his violence, for if he cannot empty out his hatred then he cannot love, his being is frozen with implacable self-hatred for his cowardice. (It can of course be suggested that it takes little courage for two strong eighteen-year-old hoodlums, let us say, to beat in the brains of a candy-store keeper, and indeed the act—even by the logic of the psychopath—is not likely to prove very therapeutic, for the victim is not an immediate equal. Still, courage of a sort is necessary, for one murders not only a weak fifty-year-old man but an institution as well.[4]

Courage, of course, is one of those words that tend to get used in slippery ways, and that give to hindsight the whole show. My hunch is that Mailer does not feel the same giddy inclination to wax philosophical—in a mishmash of existentialism and half-digested Hemingway—since the Jack Abbot affair, and I feel even more confident that Howe, realizing the high probability that this "fifty-year-old candy-store keeper" was Jewish, would probably not give his editorial endorsement to a similar piece submitted today.

Even Leslie Fiedler, who makes a specialty of tweaking his nose at the Jewish-American establishment and its penchant for safety, for good PR with the gentiles, had his problems with *Ancient Evenings* (1983), a long-winded, creaky affair about the reincarnated lives of Menehetet I. As Fiedler saw it, Mailer's self-conscious return to Egypt constitutes nothing less than "a deliberate inversion of the myth of the exodus—in which he is able to project once more his lifelong fantasy of becoming the 'Golden Goy'" (Gordon, 165). But that said, let me hasten to add that *Ancient Evenings* is hardly a spear-and-sandal epic of the old school, and that Mailer's effort to write about a world before there were Jews is at best only half the story, for this latest attempt to pull off the Big Novel is merely the very old wine of sex, violence, and power, of homosexual rape and extrasensory perception, poured into what seemed like a new bottle.

How shall a bad man, son of Whitman and Hemingway, live? That is perhaps the central question Mailer's work poses. And while the specifics may change over the years, the answer, at bottom, strikes me as decidedly not as a Jew. From his excesses have come a certain number of valuable books—*The Naked and the Dead* (1955), *Advertisements for Myself* (1959), *An American Dream* (1965), *The Armies of the Night* (1968), *The Executioner's Song* (1979)—but none that add one jot to the story of Jewish-American fiction, except as an aberration, and perhaps as a cautionary tale.

John Updike's Bech Tales

John Updike, of course, is neither a writer who happens to be Jewish nor a Jew who happens to be a writer. In this sense Mailer would probably count him lucky. After all, he avoided the whole business: Jewish parents, Hebrew school, rabbis, Brooklyn. But if it is true that Mailer has been fascinated by gentiles (especially if they were quick with their fists), Updike has had moments when he was equally fascinated by Jews, especially if they were Jewish-American writers and much ballyhooed in the newspapers. From such curiosities came the character of Henry Bech, the protagonist of a *New Yorker* story that spawned two collections about his subsequent comic misadventures. As Saul Bellow once pointed out, "Writers are often unhappy and distracted. They have never been examined so earnestly before."[5] For Bellow, *distraction* is a term charged with special meaning and fraught with peril. Its networks of paralysis include the welter of information, the large public noise, that bombards us all but is especially harmful for the contemplative writer; ironically enough, those networks also include the distractions of prolonged solitude that can be equally damaging. Torn between grand declarations of power ("Poets are the unacknowledged legislators of the world") and characters afflicted by impotence (e.g., Oblomov, Moreau, John Marcher, Leopold Bloom), creative souls suffer from what the title of Bellow's essay identifies as "The Distractions of the Fiction Writer"—namely, the uneasy feeling that "the dread is great, the soul is small, man might be godlike, but he is wretched; the heart should be open but it is sealed by fear." ("Distractions," 369).

One could argue that John Updike's Bech books are a study in precisely this sort of "distraction," indeed, that Henry Bech is *the* distracted writer writ large, Jewish, and befuddled. After all, what do his picaresque adventures, furtive travels, and sexual entanglements add up to if not a life made up of—nay, sacrificed to—distractions? As Bellow puts it, "You can't build a business on inspirations," and that, apparently, is what Bech has tried to do during his protracted bout with writer's block and his ever-deeper entanglements with the distractions offered by invitations "to lecture at college, to represent American culture at diplomatic watering holes around the globe, and to be honored for the accomplishments of his past."[6]

But that said, distinctions must be made between the dreamy Bellow protagonist temporarily derailed from his writing desk and Updike's Henry Bech. For one thing, Updike is out to satirize the very sociological conditions that Bellow regards with an ever-increasing grimness; more to the point, Updike means to talk about the comic landscape that serious fictionists traverse at their peril by transmogrifying himself into the emblematic figure of those times and places—namely, the Jewish-American writer. As he put it in a review of *The Letters of James Agee to Father Flye,* "In the present apocalyptic atmosphere, the loudest sinner is most likely to be saved: Fitzgerald's crack-up is his ticket to heaven, Salinger's silence his claim on our devotion. The study of literature threatens to become a kind of paleontology of failure, and criticism a supercilious psychoanalysis of authors. . . . Authors *should* be honored only for their works."[7]

No doubt curiosity and a dash of healthy competitiveness account for at least part of Updike's fascination. If the heyday of Jewish-American writing was the 1950s, the following decade was characterized by the trappings of literary success: critical attention, literary prizes, public recognition. Indeed, there were those whose giddy enthusiasm for the phenomenon they dubbed the "Jewish-American renaissance" knew no bounds; there were also those who watched the proceedings from the sidelines, often with clenched teeth.

Generally speaking, Updike is a generous reviewer, as collections like *Hugging the Shore* will attest, and if he is driven by the demons of rancor and plain jealousy, he keeps his rages under wraps. Still, it must have galled him to see the lavish attention paid to ethnicity in general—and to Jewish-American writers in particular—especially since the popular press took such delight in what can only be called WASP-bashing. In Updike's case this was yet another instance of ironies piled atop ironies, for he found himself in the uncomfortable position of being touted as the WASP novel's last, best hope when in fact he had been raised unfashionably as a Lutheran in a small, rather déclassé Pennsylvania town.

Symbolically significant *real* WASPs are fashioned from sturdier stock. They do not drink boilermakers in neighborhood taverns, follow the Phillies, or listen to Reverend Kruppenbach's uncompromising sermons about sin and its terrible, eternal costs; they are power brokers. At the same time, however, Updike resisted the tack taken by, say, the poet Robert Lowell, who made so much of his "Jewish blood"—presumably passed through his deep blue bloodlines via his grandmother—that some Jewish-American poets grew first suspicious and then worried. No, Updike was, for better or worse, a writer who took his Christianity seriously—which meant not only that he knew his Karl Barth but also that his characteristic vision so intertwined sexuality with efforts at transcendence that the two became virtually identical. Indeed, not since D. H. Lawrence has a writer been so insistent about the holiness and potential sinfulness of sex, and not since D. H. Lawrence has a writer been more misunderstood on these grounds.

My hunch is that Henry Bech provided Updike with a vehicle for talking about the current literary scene from the safe distance a persona provides. In Bech's skin, as it were, Updike could take some well-deserved swipes at literary politics—the way it makes or breaks reputations, arranges junkets, and hands out its prizes. That the literary life has been something of a racket has hardly been a closely guarded secret, but most of the time we hear about its seamier side from sore losers, and in what might be called *very* "little magazines." Given Updike's long and mutually beneficial relationship with the *New Yorker,* rancor about the establishment probably has better—or at least angrier—spokespersons elsewhere.

Nonetheless, Bech was Updike's chance to tongue a vaguely aching tooth and, better yet, to do so in somebody else's mouth. It also provided a springboard to extended fantasy, not unlike the one that sent Rabbit Angstrom scampering through the last decades of our darkening century. Granted, there are important differences, for if, as I strongly suspect, Rabbit is a profile of what Updike might have become, had he stayed in Shillington, Pennsylvania, married a local girl, and lived out his life as dozens of his high school classmates did, Bech is fashioned from more vicarious observations: an outsider's sense of those times and places which characterized the *Partisan Review* crowd; a contemporary writer's amalgamation of Bellow, Malamud, Roth, and others; and a literary sociologist's dependence on what Cynthia Ozick calls an "Appropriate Reference Machine."[8]

Ozick refuses to be taken in by Updike's foray into "Jewishness." As Bech himself points out in the foreword to *Bech: A Book,* despite the bows to the "gentlemanly" Norman Mailer and the "gallant, glamorous" Bellow, the "whiff" of Malamud in the book's city breezes, and the extended fascination with the "more or less noble renunciations of H. Roth, D. Fuchs, and J. D. Salinger," Ozick nonetheless insists that there is "something Waspish, theological, scared, and insulatingly ironical [about the book] that derives, my wild surmise is, from you" (*AA,* v). Coy, yes, but not so coy as to fool Ozick. After all, writers from Vladimir Nabokov (*Pale Fire*) to Philip Roth (*The Facts*) have pulled much the same reflexive stunt, and in more elaborate ways. Besides, she knows that Bech is at bottom simply Updike in Jewish-American drag—complete with his omnipresent theological/sexual preoccupations and penchant for overheated lyricism: "Bech-as-Jew has no existence, is not *there,* because he has not been imagined. Bech-as-Jew is a switch on a literary computer. What passes for Bech-as-Jew is an Appropriate Reference Machine, cranked on whenever Updike reminds himself that he is obligated to produce a sociological symptom: *crank, gnash,* and out flies an inverted sentence. Not from Bech's impeccably acculturated lips, of course, but out of the vulgar mouth ('Mother don't be vulgar,' Bech says in boyhood) of a tough Jewish mother lifted, still in her original wrap, straight out of [Bruce Jay Friedman's] *A Mother's Kisses*" (*AA*, 115). As Ozick would have it, Bech is a compendium of a soi-disant Jewish novel, one fashioned from adjectives like *zaftig,* nouns like *shiksa* and *putz,* and generous sprinklings of exclamations like *ai.* That the habit puts Updike "about even with most indifferent disaffected de-Judaized Jewish novelists of his generation" is a fact Ozick acknowledges, but the *fact* does not make Bech an authentically Jewish character: "[B]ecause Bech has no Jewish memory, he emerges with less than a fourth-grade grasp of where he is. . . . In your uncle's back rooms in Williamsburg you learned zero; despite your Jewish nose and hair, you are—as Jew—an imbecile to the core. Pardon: I see, thanks to the power of Yuletide, you've heard of Hanukkah" (*AA*, 117).

Thus, Updike sociologizes his Jewish character but does not *theologize* him, and that, for Ozick, is where the Bech books go wrong: "It is not that Updike has fallen into any large-scale gaucherie or perilous failures-of-tone. It is not that Updike's American Jew is false. It it that he is not false enough. By which I mean made up, imagined, mythically brought up into truthfulness." Bech is, in a word, "all sociology" (*AA*, 121–22). And not surprisingly, in discussing the flaws in Updike's vision Ozick tells us a good deal about hopes for her own. After all, the charged words that stand as the title of Ozick's first collection of essays—*Art and Ardor* (1983)—are much bruited about in *Bech: A Book.* Hectored that he must learn to "replace ardor with art," Bech replies, "Art *is* ardor" (*BAB*, 164). Given the *and* that links the same terms in Ozick's collection and the ways in which these concerns both shape and identify her thinking, to see them bandied about as so much "small talk" must have given her pause. Indeed, one has the feeling that Ozick, like Queen Victoria, was not amused.

More important, however, is Ozick's insistence that the same Updike who continues to explore the ramifications of Christian theology in an age given to wholly secular preoccupations exhibits such little interest in how aspects of divinity operate for Jews. For Ozick, what matters is less Jewish "whatness" than Jewish *being*: "Being a Jew (like being a Christian) is something more than *what is.* Being a Jew is something more than being an alienated marginal sensibility with kinky hair. Simply: to be a Jew is to be convenanted; or, if not committed so far, to be at least aware of the possibility of becoming cove-

nanted; or, at the very minimum, to be aware of the Covenant itself"
(*AA*, 123). By Ozick's benchmark—important not only to her but also
to a whole range of Jewish-American writers such as Hugh Nissenson,
Arthur A. Cohen, Norma Rosen, and Nessa Rappaport—Bech is a
wholly American, rather than Jewish-American, phenomenon.

Such accusations, however, badly miss the point and strike me as
similar to the heated expressions of outrage from black critics about
Styron "stealing" their Nat which accompanied the 1967 publication
of *The Confessions of Nat Turner,* or to the anger among certain Jewish-
American critics when Styron had the audacity to "imagine" the Holocaust in *Sophie's Choice* (1979). What ought to matter is *not* ethnic rights
to certain material but, rather, how well an individual author has exe-
cuted his or her vision—and in this sense, and this alone, serious questions can legitimately be raised about both of Styron's novels.

Updike's donnée is clearly *not* Ozick's, but once that is made clear,
what profit is there in elaborating the differences? For better or worse,
Updike is as ill-equipped to answer Ozick's theological indictments as
he is to defend his portrait of Skeeter in *Rabbit Redux* (1971). Blacks
and Jews are blind spots in his considerable fictional arsenal, places
where renderings of the "other" rely far more on stereotype than mythical structure, and on preserving "distance" much more than vicarious
transformation.

Granted, Updike's Bech is hardly intended to stand for *the* Jew
(whatever that might be) in the ways that Skeeter, in a novel out to
mythologize the 1960s, represents the militant American black. Instead, the Bech books are of, by, and perhaps even *for* those with a
special interest in contemporary America's literary scene. And it is
about this rather circumscribed territory that Updike bears the bad
news about Jewish-American writing—not only that its heyday has
long passed but, more crushing still, that its richest accomplishments
were *never* on the printed page. As Bech himself puts it: "His own
writing had sought to reach out from the ghetto of his heart across the
Hudson; the artistic triumph of American Jewry lay, he thought, not
in the novels of the fifties but in the movies of the thirties, those
gargantuan, crass contraptions whereby Jewish brains project Gentile
stars upon a Gentile nation and out of their own immigrant joy gave a
formless land dreams and even a kind of conscience" (*BAB*, 5–6). In
Russia—where Bech finds himself "on tour" and, for the first time in
his life, flush with more rubles than he can possibly spend—he is

thankful that his host, Skip Reynolds, "pointedly" (diplomatically?) avoids talking about Jewishness in general or about Bech's "Jewishness" in particular. It is a subject "Bech was happy to ignore" (*BAB*, 5). But, of course, it is also a subject he cannot avoid—either across oceans or in his grim apartment on Riverside Drive—for Bech, as Updike envisions him, is the New York Jewish intellectual writ large: guilt-ridden, ironic, half-formed by literary modernism and the *Partisan Review,* half the captive of traumatic childhood memory. In a word, he is *alienated,* ill at ease in the larger America he wrote about in *Travel Light* (a book in the *On the Road/Easy Rider* mold, but written entirely from secondary sources while Bech remained holed up in his shabby Manhattan apartment) and equally uncomfortable with ethnic roots. A young Irving Howe, clearly speaking about himself, once described such characters this way: "Usually born into an immigrant Jewish family, he teeters between an origin he can no longer accept and a desired status he cannot attain. He has largely lost his sense of Jewishness, of belonging to a people with a meaningful tradition, and he has not succeeded in finding a place for himself in the American scene or the American tradition" (Howe 1946, 141). Updike means to number Bech among those who, as Mark Shechner puts it, saw life " 'without dogma and without hope' as their fate and, making a virtue of necessity, their refuge as well.' "[9] Nevertheless, Bech is but a pale, often-unconvincing carbon copy of middle-generation writers like Isaac Rosenfeld, Delmore Schwartz, and Irving Howe. If their careers were marked by a feeling that they had arrived too late—too late to experience firsthand the cohesiveness of Yiddish culture in the Lower East Side in the early 1900s, too late to participate in the triumphs of literary modernism that characterized Paris in the 1920s—they made up for *temps perdu* by bringing generous measures of restless brilliance to the literary essay. Bech's miscellany— *When the Saints* (1958)—is filled with examples of the assorted articles, book reviews, and picked-up pieces one might expect of a writer who, early in his career, was allowed to "use a desk" at *Commentary*'s office: "The Vanishing Wisecrack," "Graffiti," "Sunsets over New Jersey."

Now it is hardly a secret that Updike's work tends to get rough treatment in *Commentary*'s pages and that the Bech bibliography appended to *Bech: A Book* is, in Updike's own words, a way of "working off various grudges."[10] The result is a means both of keeping a protagonist at a healthy remove from its author and of establishing a representative literary history for the Jewish-American writer. As Updike would have it, the latter "began as a kind of war correspondent, a soldier who wrote stories with gung-ho titles for magazines like *Liberty* and *Collier's*. He was intellectualized in New York in the post-war period. And now he has fallen into silence. There are careers like this. Salinger? Irwin Shaw?" (*PUP*, 507).

The operative word in this imagined collective history is, of course, *silence*, a phenomenon that Bech presumably explored in a 1964 *Hudson Review* article entitled "Silence" and that stands, in Updike's mind, for the used-upness, the sheer "exhaustion," of Jewish-American writing itself. To be sure, Bech is the latter condition writ large; after the publication of his *The Chosen* 1963—a novel that not only garnered uniformly bad reviews and generated minuscule sales but also was usually confused with Potok's potboiler about Hasidic life in Brooklyn—he became the sort of "writer" revered much more for past works than for works in progress. Updike/Bech's swipe at Potok's popularity—one with which I heartily concur—draws a sharp if somewhat mean-spirited line between authentic Jewish-American writing and that, like Potok's, which is longer on realistic detail than on essential rhythm.

At times Bech's condition generates satiric one-liners that are as delicious as they are wicked—for example, when Bech (who made no secret of his admiration for Melville but could never quite make it through *Pierre*) is awarded the Melville Medal for the "most meaningful silence" or when he turns a discussion of "fascist *manqués*" into one of his much-celebrated quips: "*Manqué* see, *manqué* do" (*BAB*, 90).

And so it is that distractions from life, rather than life itself, begin to define Bech. Granted, he keeps faith with "those saints of formalism—Eliot, Valéry, Joyce—whose humble supplicant Bech had been" (*BAB*, 73), but more as a way of contrasting himself from the untutored than as a current practitioner. Indeed, what Bech does, at least for one spring term at Columbia, is to "give himself over—it amounted to little more than that—to the remarkably uninhibited conversations of fifteen undergraduates and to read their distressingly untidy manuscripts" (*BAB*, 73). In short, Bech becomes a *teacher*.

My hunch is that Updike is drawing here on the central conflict of Malamud's *The Tenants* (1971), in which a blocked but disciplined and altogether-knowledgeable Jewish-American novelist is paired with and pitted against an angry, impatient black counterpart. Thus, Lesser, the Jewish character, represents the craft that genuine art requires, while Spearmint, the black character, stands for the passion, the fire, that is equally essential. To be sure, Updike alters the formula in ways that lighten Malamud's tragic tone; rather than a battle to the death between literary Jews and literary blacks, we have in "Bech Takes Pot Luck" the stuff of early 1970s satire: "Languid and clever, these young people had lacked not only patriotism and faith but even the coarse morality competitiveness imposes, living off fathers they despised, systematically attracted to the outrageous, they seemed ripe for Fascism. Their politics burlesqued the liberal beliefs dear to Bech; their literary tastes ran to chaotic second-raters like Miller and Tolkien" (*BAB*, 73). Again and again Updike's saga stresses that Bech is an anachronism, a writer living in a thin cultural moment, and, as such, standing for that larger group of New York Jewish intellectuals who hector the young and cling to the belief that History itself will end when they do. But the Bech books are also Updike's "dream" that Jewish-American writing will end and that, in another country, as it were, his own "Rabbit" books will continue to roll on. Updike, of course, has proved himself right about the latter; however, with regard to the former I suspect that Cynthia Ozick will not be the only voice responding to Updike's comic elegy for Jewish-American fiction with a confident, even combative "We'll see about that!"

The Progress of Saul Bellow

Which brings me at long last to Saul Bellow, a writer of considerable achievement and, I would add, of considerable Jewish-American achievement. If Bernard Malamud's relationship to Jewish material has been primarily distanced—fabulist/fantastic (e.g., *The Magic Barrel*), symbolic (e.g., *The Assistant*), or allegorical (e.g., *The Fixer*)—the Jewish "matter" in Saul Bellow's fiction has always seemed more personal and immediate. As he puts it in his widely reprinted introduction to the Dell paperback collection entitled *Great Jewish Stories*, "For the last generation of East European Jews, daily life without stories would have been inconceivable. My father would say, whenever I asked him to explain any matter, 'The thing is like this. There was a man who lived . . .' 'There was once a scholar . . .' 'There was a widow with one son . . .' 'A teamster was driving on a lonely road. . . .'"[11] In many respects Bellow's progress has been a matter of integrating such material with the fabric of American literature, of blending the feel for Yiddish prose rhythms that resulted in his dazzling translation of I. B.

Singer's "Gimpel the Fool" with an ear for literary parody that made *Henderson the Rain King* a comic version of Conrad's "Heart of Darkness."

With the possible exception of *The Adventures of Augie March*—a novel longer on picaresque adventure and exuberant bounce than on brooding and moral consequence—Bellow's protagonists solve their respective problems within the context of fairly restricted societies, delicately balancing an inner life with increasing commitments to an outer world. It may have been fashionable for the Harvard undergraduate of Eliot's day to sail for England—thereby renouncing the America Ezra Pound thought of as a "half-savage country"—but that solution seems both dated and altogether self-conscious by now. In fact, the easy gesture of drawing thumb to nose is complicated endlessly in Bellow's novels by reservations that would never have occurred to a Stephen Dedalus or a Hugh Selwyn Mauberly. Herzog, for example, dangles between the two poles Marcus Klein describes as alienation and accommodation: he is a lover of highbrow literature and a sucker for *mammeloshen* (the mother tongue of Yiddish), a student of Heidegger as well as a product of *der heim* (the home), a synthesizer of Big Ideas and a regular mensch (human being).

But that said, the movement from a J. Alfred Prufrock to a Moses Herzog takes more than Yiddishkeit (Yiddish Culture), important though that concept may be in the formation of Herzog's character. Nor is it enough to say that nowadays the Robert Cohns *teach* at Princeton, in an age in which "acceptance" has something to do with journals and editorial judgment but very little to do with people like Jake Barnes and Bill Gorton.

Dangling Man

For Bellow, the transition I've been alluding to begins with a novel designed to take the edge off the neurosis created by World War II. In this sense *Dangling Man* (1944) became the novel Bellow had to write if he were to clear the air sufficiently to continue. Joseph, *Dangling Man*'s protagonist, lives in an ill-defined middle: he has been classified 1–A but has not yet been drafted; he is unemployed but unable to use his leisuretime productively; he is, ironically enough, free from responsibility but denied a context in which the term might be meaningful.

And so he dangles—opposing both the traditional involvement/disillusionment syndrome of the standard World War I novel and the hard-boiled Hemingway response that was its enduring legacy. That *Dangling Man* is written in the form of a diary—the first entry on 15 December 1942, the last on 9 April 1943—suggests not only its parallels to *Notes from Underground* but also the interior nature of Joseph's problems. Shut up in an urban apartment, Joseph has no convenient rivers into which he can plunge, thus effecting his "separate peace" from the war. Indeed, if *A Farewell to Arms* sounded the death knell to abstract words like *courage, honor,* and *bravery, Dangling Man* shifted the ground until the possibilities of the inner life—complicated now, to be sure, by the social institutions that inevitably cluster about it—seemed a more appropriate response to the condition of the 1950s.

Indeed, Joseph's first entry seems to insist that this will be a contemporary novel stripped of the masculine hysterics usually associated with the cult of the tough and tight-lipped:

> Today, the code of the athlete, of the tough boy—an American inheritance, I believe, from the English gentleman—that curious blending of striving, asceticism, and rigor, the origins of which some trace back to Alexander the Great—is stronger than ever. Do you have feelings? There are correct and incorrect ways of indicating them. Do you have an inner life? It is nobody's business but your own. Do you have emotions? Strangle them. To a degree, everyone obeys this code. . . . But in the truest candor, it has an inhibitory effect. Most serious matters are closed to the hard-boiled. They are unpracticed in introspection, and therefore badly equipped to deal with opponents whom they cannot shoot like big game or outdo in daring.[12]

Adherents of the code may be unpracticed in introspection, but Joseph seems to "practice" it all too much. Instead of the grand compensations available to the hard-boiled ("They fly planes or fight bull or catch tarpon"), the dangling man is circumscribed by his narrow room and the "minor crises of the day"—the "maid's knock, the appearance of the postman, programs on the radio, and the sure, cyclical distress of certain thoughts" (DM, 12).

Yet like other Bellow protagonists to follow, Joseph is impatient, eager to get things moving. He is, finally, neither Dostoyevski nor Goethe. For all his pretenses about the sedentary, scholarly life, Joseph finds it difficult to enjoy as a "dangling man" those things which will be simply impossible in the army: "About a year ago, I ambitiously began several essays, mainly biographical, on the philosophers of the Enlightenment. I was in the midst of one on Diderot when I stopped.

But it was vaguely understood, when I began to dangle, that I was to continue with them" (*DM,* 11–12). Given his circumstances, we are hardly surprised when Joseph's good intentions lack sticking power, and he soon discovers himself "unable to read." Books no longer either hold his interest or seem relevant to his new "dangling" condition: "After two or three pages or, as it sometimes happens, paragraphs, I simply cannot go on" (*DM,* 10).

The result is a deep-seated hostility that seeks outlets for repressed anger at the same time it continues to profess philosophies of accommodation. In this sense Joseph is a preview of such coming attractions as Asa Leventhal, Tommy Wilhelm, and Moses Herzog. James Hall shrewdly points out that Bellow's characters tend to be compulsive "leaners," seeking support and confirmation wherever they can find them, but that they also tend to push things over, to confuse angry sentiment with the pieces of china that inevitably get broken in Bellow's novels. [13]

Caught in what he calls the "craters of the spirit," Joseph vacillates between aggression as a strategy to preserve one's identity (his version of the Cartesian equation reads, "I hit; therefore I am") and speculation about the relative virtues of alienation versus accommodation. In one of the many lonely hours he spends with "The Spirit of Alternatives," Joseph rejects the solace of an easy, relatively painless alienation: "You have gone to [the world's] schools and seen its movies, listened to its radios, read its magazines. What if you declare you are alienated, you *say* you reject the soap opera, the cheap thriller. The very denial implicates you" (*DM,* 137). On the other hand, Joseph is all too aware that "alternatives, and particularly desirable alternatives, grow only on imaginary trees." Therefore, he resolves to make no protest: "[W]hen I am called I shall go. . . . Somehow I cannot regard it as a wrong against myself" (*DM,* 84).

As Joseph's diary moves inexorably toward spring and the rhythms of resurrection it traditionally connotes, he moves beyond an embrace of alternatives to a realization that all quests and "alternatives" are, finally, "one and the same": "All the striving is for one end. . . . It seems to me that its final end is the desire for pure freedom" (*DM,* 115). In what Leslie Fiedler calls "the purest of ironies," Joseph leaves for camp, concluding his diary with the following entry: "Hurrah for regular hours! And for the supervision of the spirit! Long live regimentation!" (*DM,* 191). The lines echo Stephen Dedalus's final entry in *A Portrait of the Artist as a Young Man,* but with all the terms turned upside down. Like other of Bellow's claustrophobic protagonists, Joseph strikes us as a Miniver Cheevy set down in the world of the contemporary American novel. He had dangled as he "thought and thought. And thought about it" in ways that threaten to make resolution impossible. Whatever else Bellow might be, he is not Kafka, and his novels, unlike Kafka's, have a way of suggesting that simple mechanisms (in this case, writing a letter to one's draft board) can push one out of the spirit's crater with great haste.

The Victim

In *The Victim* (1947) Bellow continues to exploit many of the same themes that had given substance to *Dangling Man*. Although one would not want to talk about Joseph's curiously introspective world as a bastion of good cheer, it does seem to me that the energy and health generated by his last remarks suggest—at least sotto voce—the life-affirming resiliency we warm to in *The Adventures of Augie March*. Granted, Augie's energy thrives without complication or borders; whatever else he might be, Augie is neither attuned to the claustrophobic nor given to whining. He is, in short, the larky picaresque hero whose lot it is to primarily "experience," and then to move on, encumbered by neither consequences nor second thoughts, to still more experiences.

By contrast, Asa Leventhal is the "victim" in ways that force him to see failure as a problem of the psyche and responsibility as a consequence of misdirected anger. Even more so than with Joseph, Leventhal lives in a world filled to the bursting point with "other people," most of whom seem intent on crowding into the same subway car. When Asa pushes back, however, his aggressiveness creates a rash of complications. Most of Leventhal's anxious, aggressive edge is reserved for the business of getting and spending in the great megapolis. His persistent fears about a blacklist are complicated enough (Do such lists exist, or are they paranoid delusions?), but the situation gets even stickier when one adds to the equation the specialized nature of Leventhal's job. After all, there are only so many trade journals to go around—a sobering thought indeed for the Leventhal who remembers his former civil service job (tenured, absolutely secure) with a mixture of anxiety and regret. Most of all, however, Leventhal is nagged by the growing realization that he is the sort of person who allows anger and outrage to spoil his chances.

The first anxious days of his search for a new job are a good example. Leventhal quickly discovers a "spirit of utter hopelessness" and embraces it like an old friend: "The small trade papers simply turned him away. The larger ones gave him applications to fill out; occasionally he spent a few minutes with a personnel manager and had the opportunity to shake someone's hand. Gradually he became peculiarly aggressive and, avoiding the receptionists, he would make his way into an inner office, stop anyone who appeared to have authority, with coldness and with anger. He often grew angry with himself."[14]

It is, however, not so much a generalized, free-floating aggressiveness as it is a moment of genuine aggression that eventually becomes the center of Asa's dilemma. In Allbee (his very name suggesting allegorical properties), Leventhal confronts a situation remarkably similar to Joseph's angry psychological encounter with Etta—although this time the tension it produces stretches out over the entire novel.

Too many readers, I think, have reacted to Allbee and to his systematic persecution of Leventhal in easy, predictable ways. For them, clear lines of distinction separate victim and victimizer. The result turns *The Victim* into a sentimental, and sentimentalizing, exposé of anti-Semitism along the lines of, say, Laura Z. Hobson's *Gentlemen's Agreement.* Bellow's novel, I would submit, is much more subtle and, in its own way, much more disturbing. To begin at the beginning, the incident that triggers Allbee's anti-Semitic outburst and forces Leventhal to confront both his Jewishness and, perhaps more important, himself is so buried in the past that the novel's epigraph—an anecdote about the consequences of tossing date pits over one's shoulder and striking the innocent—seems more evidence of Leventhal's "guilt" than the narrative provides. In an effort to help the badly floundering Leventhal, Allbee sets up a job interview with his boss, a man named Rudiger. Unfortunately but not surprisingly, the interview is a disaster, and Leventhal makes an already-unpleasant situation worse by screaming at his potential employer. Years later, Allbee—now a solid down-and-outer—returns to accuse Leventhal of deliberately insulting Rudiger, thus linking Asa's revenge with Allbee's unemployment. Leventhal, of course, denies all responsibility and promises himself that "'if he follows me now I'll punch him in the jaw. I'll knock him down.' he thought. 'I swear I'll throw him down and smash his ribs for him!'" (*Victim,* 39).

But the barrage of Allbee's accusations preys on Leventhal in ways that "hitting" cannot solve. For more traditional writers, such as

Robert Penn Warren, the point about the past is that it *is* retrievable—moreover, that it is essential to retrieve it if one is to understand the present moment and move beyond it into the future. But that said, Asa Leventhal is not akin to the Jack Burden of *All the King's Men,* and for him there is no way of looking at the scene in Rudiger's office through either the diligence of historical research or the miracle of instant re-play. Rather, Leventhal is forced to do what Bellow's characters do best—rationalize and *lean*:

[Allbee] must have brooded over the affair for years, until he convinced himself that Rudiger had fired him because of that interview. Of course, it was true enough that Rudiger had a rotten temper, probably was born bad-tempered, but not even he would fire an employee, not for what the man himself had done but because of someone he had recommended. "How could he?" Leventhal asked himself. "Not a good worker; never." It was absurd. Allbee must have been fired for drunkenness. When could you get a drinking man to acknowledge that he had gotten into trouble through drinking, especially when he was far gone? And this Allbee was far gone. (*TV,* 36–37)

In Leventhal's case, however, rationalizations have a nasty habit of turning on themselves. A "good worker" never gets fired, but that is exactly what Leventhal himself is worrying about when he takes an afternoon off—complicated, of course, by the specter of an industry-wide blacklist. Allbee in effect presses at the nerve of Asa's deepest fears and quickly becomes the objectification of his angst, the secret sharer of his fate.

In this case even "leaning" has its darker side, as Asa's friends never quite give him the support, the assurance, he had hoped for. After the Rudiger incident, Leventhal began to worry about the possible conse-quences of his action: *Was* there a blacklist? *Could* Rudiger ruin his career? Granted, his friend Harkavy assures him that "there isn't a thing [Rudiger] can do to you. Whatever you do, don't get ideas like that into your head. He can't persecute you. Now be careful. You have that tendency, boy, do you know that?" (*TV,* 46). Leventhal, of course, has precisely that sort of "tendency," but hearing about it secondhand, as it were, is hardly what he was angling for when he unpacked his heart to Harkavy.

A mind operating this way finds itself drawn much more to an Allbee than to a Harkavy. What Leventhal demands is a world that singles him out for special attention—indeed, that is why he takes such a perverse pleasure in imagining Rudiger manipulating secret empires to effect his destruction—and Allbee answers this need in bold relief. Initially Leventhal tolerates his outrageous accusations because even an enemy is better than nobody at all. Besides, Allbee, unlike Harkavy, confirms Leventhal's sense of the world as a risky business wherein one slip can have lifelong consequences.

For the dangling man, there was a modicum of joy in "anticipating the minor crises of the day," among which was the maid's knock. Leventhal too feels this keen sense of loneliness. Thus, when Allbee finally does make his presence known, Leventhal is so hungry for human contact that even "trouble" is preferable to tedium. Put another way, tensions (even those which are anxiety-producing and not a little neurotic) are surefire adrenaline producers, proof positive that one is fully alive. And as the full impact of his victim-victimizer relationship unfolds, Leventhal finds himself living on both sides of what turns out to be a very slippery coin.

Granted, Leventhal means to "clear" himself and in this regard goes first to Harkavy and then to his friend Williston; however, what he collects only muddies the ethical waters. Leventhal ostensibly wants his friends to say the obvious—namely, that he is right and Allbee wrong. Instead, they shower him with versions of what Moses Herzog contemptuously calls "reality instruction"—advice that sounds as sensible as Ann Landers's but in fact is laced with brutal reality's harsher truths. Harkavy, for example, tells him, "You want the whole world to like you. There're bound to be some people who don't think well of you. As I do, for instance. Why isn't it enough for you that some do?" (TV, 88).

The systematic movement toward Allbee is carefully documented: Allbee accepts Leventhal's money, moves into his apartment, and even dons his bathrobe. And Leventhal, not to be outdone, gets drunk at Harkavy's birthday party, effecting an identification with his alcoholic antagonist. In short, their fates intertwine in what Kenneth Burke calls "symbolic overlap."

But just when it looks as if Mary will never return and that Allbee will never leave, Leventhal simply throws Allbee out and suddenly things look very much improved: Mary, his long-absent wife, not only returns but soon becomes pregnant. Leventhal lands an excellent position with *Antique Horizons*; "his health was better"; and the newly reconstituted Leventhals can even afford a night out at the theater.

To be sure, the old, irritable Leventhal is never out of the picture entirely. After returning the $10 Williston had given him for Allbee, he waits for a reply—already prepared to assume the worst: "But no reply came from Williston, and Leventhal was too proud to write a second letter; that would be too much like pleading. Perhaps Williston felt that he had kept the money from Allbee out of malice. . . . At first he was deeply annoyed; later he prepared some things to say to Williston if they should meet. But the opportunity never came" (*TV*, 286–87).

As for Allbee, Leventhal continued to hear rumors about "some journalist, from New England originally, who hit the bottle," but he preferred to believe that "he had continued to go down. By now he was in an institution, perhaps, in some hospital, or even already lying in Potter's Field" (*TV*, 287). While such ignoble fates might be the logical conclusion of a naturalistic novel—one thinks of, say, Hurstwood's slow, agonizingly downward spiral in Dreiser's *Sister Carrie*—this is not the case in *The Victim*. Indeed, Allbee is not only alive but from all appearances doing quite well for himself, thank you. Moreover, the old irritations, the old anxieties, lurk just beneath their respective surfaces: Allbee claims that he isn't the sort who "runs things," which, not surprisingly, leads to Leventhal's defensive "Who do you think does?"

Granted, what I've been describing is at best only half of Bellow's loaf. His novels tend to alternate between studies of psychological stasis and exercises in exuberant celebration. In such novels as *Dangling Man* and *The Victim*, there are usually both a claustrophobic setting (nights as hot as Bangkok, subways stuffed with other people, tiny rooms in which people scratch away in their diaries) and a pitched battle between the forces of sensibility and those of the will. Both Joseph and Asa are creatures with their fingers always poised at the pulse, ready to report at every instance exactly how they feel, but they are also men on the edge of anger. At times the bottled-up rage gives way to an action of sorts (generally a clumsy, ineffective shove); nonetheless, each is quick to speculate about the consequences. Granted, Asa strikes us as a good deal more active than Joseph, for Asa rides to Staten Island and derives some measure of good health from hitting Allbee.

Herzog

With *Herzog* (1964) Bellow began to suggest some directions out of the intellectual wastelands and the irritations that had afflicted his more aggressive protagonists. Indeed, during the period between *Herzog* and

Humboldt's Gift (1975) center stage was monopolized by the protago-
nist-as-historian, rather than by the traditional concerns of the historical novel. As Bellow himself has suggested, "People don't realize how
much they are in the grip of ideas. We live among ideas much more
than we live in nature. . . . People's lives are already filled with mental
design of one sort or another" (Pinsker, 14). In this regard *Herzog, Mr.
Sammler's Planet* (1970), and *Humboldt's Gift* form a loose trilogy, one
concerned with the impress of ideas on the fabric of contemporary culture and with the comic interaction between a culture's notion of ideas
and Bellow's embattled spokesmen. Unlike the whining Tommy Wilhelm of *Seize the Day* (1956), these are protagonists more likely to utter
ironic, urban prayers ("Lead me not into Penn Station," quips Moses
Herzog) than to flood the world in tears, more prone to trade wisecracks
on the street than to hide, like Joseph, between the pages of a solipsistic
journal. In an age that pays both lip service and hard cash to the special
importance of intellect, such protagonists grow to expect the gingerly
treatment afforded an endangered species. Moses Herzog, for example,
earns his way from grant to grant as a bona fide egghead—no small
task, given a literary tradition that prefers to outshoot its antagonists
and to restrict its reading to the labels of whiskey bottles.

Granted, life as the academy's darling is a decidedly mixed blessing.
People respond to Herzog with nearly equal doses of admiration and
thinly veiled condescension. As the Unwashed would have it, old saws
like "If you're so smart, why aren't you rich?" become the unspoken
"And if you were really so smart, how come your wife kicked you out?"
This is bad enough, but those who appoint themselves as Herzog's
instructors into the Nature of the Real are even worse. They elbow into
his life with teeth bared and a stomach for the worst brutalities quotidian life can offer.

Herzog is peculiarly unequipped to deal with the hard edges of a
reality seemingly cut off from time and wrenched from better, more
humanistic continuities. What we need, he half-playfully insists, is a
"good five-cent synthesis," one that would provide "a new angle on the
modern condition, showing how life could be lived by renewing universal connections; overturning the last of the Romantic errors about
the uniqueness of the Self; revising the old Western Faustian ideology;
investigating the social meaning of Nothingness."[15] It is a grand, won-
derfully nutty dream, the stuff that makes protagonists like Artur
Sammler (*Mr. Sammler's Planet*), Charlie Citrine (*Humboldt's Gift*), and
the Benn Crader of *More Die of Heartbreak* tick. Bellow's urban come-

dians are more likely to be men of moral vision than accountants of hard fact. Their respective sagas are chapters in what Citrine calls "the intellectual Comedy of the modern mind." In Herzog's case, everything militates against him making good on his early promise as a scholar: the sleazy cultural moment, Reality Instructors, Potato Lovers, nearly *any* woman, and, of course, Herzog himself.

One shorthand way of putting this might be to say that victimhood finally meets its comic match. More than any other Bellow character thus far, Herzog is a saintly fool with solid credentials: he is both cuckold and "suffering joker," the architect of his misfortune as well as a man perfectly capable of turning irony inward. What he refuses to be, however, is a *victim*. Indeed, the sweep of *Herzog* works—often laboriously—toward justification: "Late in Spring, Herzog had been overcome by the need to explain, to have it out, to justify, to put in perspective, to clarify, to make amends" (*H*, 3). For a Milton, *Paradise Lost* is an epic attempt to justify the ways of God to man, and in certain respects *Herzog* is its equivalent in our time—albeit with human interactions getting the major focus and Herzog's mental letters providing a ready soapbox for both the novel's protagonist and its author.

But that said, let me hasten to add that the letters form not only the core of Herzog's—and often Bellow's—wide-ranging ideas but also the novel's sense of urgency, of having it out once and for all with cultural naysayers. Such an epistolary novel may have its historical roots in eighteenth-century novels like *Pamela* and *Humphrey Clinker,* but Herzog's letters—with their divided streams of elegant argument and psychological breakdown—suggest a distinctively modern variant.

Moreover, if the letters per se are the stuff of monologue, Herzog's truncated responses to them—as the world pulls him back into its quotidian grip—often suggests the flavor of an interior dialogue. Eliot's J. Alfred Prufrock's associative stream of consciousness makes something of the same comic point: that spontaneity often dies a quick, ignominious death amid the clutter of tea and cakes and ices. Indeed, at times the parallels between Prufrock and Herzog are as striking as their final adjustments are different. For example, Herzog, like Prufrock, "was losing his hair." But rather than worrying about whether or not he should "part it behind" (as Prufrock does), Herzog "read the ads of the Thomas Scalp Specialists with the exaggerated skepticism of a man whose craving to believe was deep, desperate. Scalp experts! So . . . he was a formerly handsome man" (*H*, 3). Both Herzog and Prufrock are formed by the great tradition of Western ideas, but the uses to which they put their allusive powers differ markedly. Prufrock uses the past as an index of how far we—and *he*—have fallen; Herzog keeps insisting that Herzogean innocence and the Herzog heart may yet carry the day. To be sure, both commodities are under heavy attack. The recurrent nursery rhyme "I love little pussy"—implying "If you don't hurt her, she'll do you no harm"—is continually undercut by a Madeleine who hurts him anyway.

In addition, Herzog, unlike Prufrock, can bring a rich past to bear on his messy present. And very often it is this abiding sense of life at its richest (e.g., the warmth of Napolean Street covering him like a blanket) that Herzog remembers when he frames his own "overwhelming questions": "Dear Doktor Professor Heidigger, I should like to know what you mean by the expression 'the fall into the quotidian.' When did this fall occur? Where were we standing when it happened?" (*H*, 49).

Granted, such questions reflect a comic spirit more directly than Prufrock's hyperserious balancing of "Do I dare disturb the universe?" with "Do I dare to eat a peach?" Prufrock, of course, is afraid to take any action at all—fearful that he might be misunderstood ("That is not what I meant at all!"); fearful that he may be inadequate ("I am no Prince Hamlet, nor was meant to be"); fearful that the mermaids are singing to somebody else. By contrast, Herzog's personal life has been filled with commitments, but they are rapidly falling apart. When in his letters he speaks about his cuckoldry, Herzog raises the age-old suspicion that schlemiels create their own misfortunes. For the Talmudic rabbis, seductions came when one was swaying over a thick volume at the House of Study; for Herzog, they occur when men like Gersbach throw around ideas as casually as they toss off their clothing: "I'm sure you know the views of Buber. It is wrong to turn a man (a subject) into a thing (an object). By means of a spiritual dialogue, the I-It relationship becomes an I-Thou relationship. God comes and goes in men's souls. And men come and go in each other's souls. Sometimes they come and go in each other's bed, too. You have a dialogue with a man. You have intercourse with his wife" (*H*, 64).

Even more important, however, Herzog has dared to step beyond the clichés of modernist alienation and its standard line about the impossibility of communication. Part of the irony in Prufrock's "love song" is that it is entirely interior—not a love song in the ordinary sense at all. At best Prufrock may be saying something vital to his readers, but what he is saying, it seems to me, is that all of us live in a rather unfortunate time. Marvell has enough energy to "seize the day"; Hamlet had a tragic stature; but all poor Prufrock has is a balding head and concerns about how he looks at parties. Herzog has more than his fair share of troubles, but they have a value of their own; there is no need to dress them up with elaborate citations to the library stacks. "He was in no mood," he writes the pedantic Shapiro, "for Joachim de Floris and the hidden destiny of Man. Nothing seemed especially hidden—it was all painfully clear" (*H,* 74).

When Prufrock finds himself so disenchanted with modern man—the disappointing product of biological evolution and social progress—he dreams of reversing the process until he becomes "a pair of ragged claws, scuttling across the floors of silent seas." Yet even after the horrors of Auschwitz, Herzog can still ask if "all the traditions [have been] used up, the beliefs done for, the consciousness of the masses not yet ready for the next development? Is this the full crisis of dissolution? Has the filthy moment come when all moral feeling dies, conscience disintegrates, and respect for liberty, law, public decency, all the rest, collapses in cowardice, decadence, blood?" (*H,* 74). These post-Holocaust questions, I would submit, are the shivery, overwhelming ones for our time and, interestingly enough, precisely those which, say, Mailer has either assiduously avoided (despite his sustained encounter with fascism in *The Naked and the Dead*) or "celebrated" in ways that made him part of the problem rather than the solution.

By contrast, beginning with *Herzog* Bellow's protagonists have greeted these same questions about the breakdown of civilization with their respective "No's, in thunder!" Granted, the elderly Artur Sammler of *Mr. Sammler's Planet* is spared both sexual grief and comic suffering; Charles Citrine (*Humboldt's Gift*) spends his time speculating about the tragicomic career of Humboldt von Fleisher; Albert Corde, the dean of *The Dean's December* (1982), meditates away on his nonfiction article about Chicago; and, most recently, the eggheads of *More Die of Heartbreak* (1988)—this time a world-renowned scientist and his secret-sharing nephew—add their names to the roll of those who also find themselves stumped by Freud's (in)famous question, *Was will das Weib?* (What does woman want?).

In short, the beat that Herzog began goes on, albeit without Herzog's charm, without his Jewish wit, and without his brand of schlemielhood. Which is to say that Bellow's latest protagonists—like Bellow himself—do not suffer fools gladly; nor do they expect to encounter them as they shave. Rather, they insist that we pay attention as they pontificate. To be sure, Herzog also drags us along as he works out the fine points of his "grand synthesis," but if we are impressed by the occasional flashes of brilliance we are equally convinced they will never make their way between hard covers. Herzog's life is too messy, and the man too distracted.

Nonetheless, Herzog manages to shore up what may have been ruined to preserve what may still be left. The fall from innocence—both as comment on the nation's past and as synopsis of his own history— suggests the ways in which his question to Heidigger, his nursery rhyme to Madeleine, and his historical study, *Romanticism and Christianity,* are all related. Modernism molded such materials into gloomy portraits and even grimmer prognoses. By contrast, Herzog rejects "the canned sauerkraut of Spengler's 'Prussian Socialism,' the commonplaces of the Wasteland outlook, the cheap mental stimulants of Alienation, the cant and rant of pipsqueaks about Authenticity and Forlornness. I can't accept this foolish dreariness" (*H,* 74–75). When he writes to his colleague Professor Mermelstein (the man who has been systematically scooping his best ideas), he again reaffirms his faith that "we must get it out of our heads that this is a doomed time, that we are waiting for the end, and the rest of it, mere junk from fashionable magazines" (*H,* 316–17).

Both Prufrock and Herzog emerge as intellectual indexes of their respective decades. But that said, Prufrock's elegantly rendered pathos strikes us now as less the stuff of "confession" than a posture of comfortable inadequacy, while Herzog—after much resistance—abandons the field of self-definition altogether. As Herzog imagines writing to Mermelstein, "I am even willing to leave the more or less [of what Herzog "is"] in your hands. You may decide about me. You have a taste for metaphors" (*H,* 317).

His solution is the Herzog heart. It is an extension of his name (the German *hertz* meaning "heart") but, more important, is the result of a distinctively Jewish vision. As a certified academic Herzog may have thought his way out of the wasteland, but on more emotional levels he simply refuses to indulge in orgies of despair. Indeed, he is more likely to wave his hands to illustrate a joke than to wring them to demonstrate how bad things are. As Himmelstein puts it: "You're not one of those university phonies. You're a *mensch."* And in this case Himmelstein is probably more correct than he imagines.

But the lower-brow case for Herzog does not end there. For all his trenchant criticism of sentimentality's darker sides, Herzog cannot obliterate that part of him which is an inveterate "potato lover." Despite his embattled situation and his understandable bitterness, versions of potato love ooze out—for his brothers, for his children, and finally for life itself. Herzog is, in short, the lovable bumbler, the comically distracted professor who had "once tucked [his] jacket into the back of [his] trousers, coming from the gentlemen's room and walked into class." His is the ironic, self-deprecating vision that cannot *not* see: absorbed in reading Kierkegaard's *Sickness unto Death,* only a Herzog—waist-high in *tsoris*—could note that this was "nice reading for a depressive!" and only a Herzog could answer an overly enthusiastic admirer's comment that "art is for Jews!" by quipping back, "It used to be usury!"

Although he is "sick with abstraction" (Madeleine's diagnosis of Herzog's problem), he can still turn his attention to "this planet in its galaxy of stars and worlds [going] from void to void, infinitesimal, aching with its unrelated significance" and then reverse fields—with "one of his Jewish shrugs"—and whisper, *"Nu, maile. . . .* Be that as it may." He is, finally, the American Jew: fully assimilated into its experiences and sharing its aspirations, teaching in its universities and flying off to its conferences, but able nevertheless to bring a special heritage of endurance to bear on its modern situations. To the knowledge of a Prufrock Bellow adds an aching Herzog heart and a ready Herzog quip. The result speaks to the *virtues* of assimilation reflected in Bellow's fiction, as the mingling of two heritages produces a new hybrid more rewardingly complex than either.

Mr. Sammler's Planet

Herzog's progress in the novel is, admittedly, a tiring one, both for Herzog and for its readers. By contrast, *Mr. Sammler's Planet* (1970) begins at a point well beyond Herzog's rage for a synthesizing book or even the exhaustion that stretches Moses across his pastoral hammock. Artur Sammler casts his "one good eye" on the junk of contemporary culture from the perspective of sobering experience and advanced age. In this sense Sammler is less an extension of the romantic Herzog than he is a variation of the themes in Yeats's "Sailing to Byzantium." Caught in a city that has added genital-bullying to our century's "mackeral-crowded" landscape, he also concludes, "That is no country for old men." It is also not the time or the place for further "explanations": "You had to be a crank to insist on being right. Being right was largely a matter of explanations. Intellectual man had become an explaining creature. Fathers to children, wives to husbands, lecturers to listeners, experts to laymen, colleagues to colleagues, doctors to patients, man to his own soul, explained."[16] Nonetheless, *Mr. Sammler's Planet* is composed of exactly these sorts of "explanations." If the subways were hot and overcrowded in *The Victim,* if the Africa of *Henderson the Rain King* (1959)—simultaneously a parody of Conrad's "Heart of Darkness" and "mental journey"—was filled with "tests," things have worsened steadily since. Sammler walks cautiously through "invariably dog-fouled" streets, no longer surprised that the counterculture's young look "autochtonous" or that one must search like Diogenes for a functioning telephone booth.

In *Mr. Sammler's Planet* the rage for a "charmed and *interesting* life" turns minor characters into menagerie of grotesques and the city itself into a theater of decadence. That much about Bellow's fiction has remained constant—in *More Die of Heartbreak,* in which Fishl Vilitzer, the local representative of a West Coast maharishi, cons potential investors into playing the market "from a spiritual base"; in those who surround Clara Velde, the protagonist of *A Theft* (1989); and, most recently, in the machinations that give rise to the Mnemosyne Institute in *The Bellarosa Connection* (1989). Sammler hectors nearly everyone as if he were an East European Gibbon and this was the decline and fall of New York City.

Bellow's earlier fiction was careful to keep such rancor at least half-hidden behind comic masks, but with Sammler, as well as those who follow in his increasingly neoconservative footsteps (e.g., Dean Albert Corde, Kenneth Trachtenberg, Teddy Regler, and the unnamed narrator of *The Bellarosa Connection*), enough sociopolitical *narishkeit* (foolishness) is apparently enough. Besides, Sammler *enjoys* his role as a self-styled Jeremiah among the unclean who care as little for authority as they do for Old World "culture." Not since the days of T. S. Eliot has there been such an eloquent and extended appeal in behalf of reestablishing that necessary relationship between tradition and individual talent: "Antiquity accepted models, the Middle Ages—I don't want to turn into a history book before your eyes—but modern man, perhaps because of collectivization, has a fever of originality" (*MSP*, 229).

Mr. Sammler's Planet is in effect a three-tiered world: on the naturalistic level, sexuality asserts a chaotic power, one expressed in bold relief by the elegant black pickpocket; Lal (whose manuscript is an Eastern version of Norman Mailer's *Fire on the Moon*) projects an overhanging lunar metaphor; and Sammler himself directs our attention to those depths wherein each of us can rediscover the terms of our human contract. Ironically enough, of the three possibilities it is the first that garners the largest amount of space. *Mr. Sammler's Planet* is as filled with urban oddballs as it is with realistic detail. It is, in short, a world that begins to look more and more like Shula-Slawa's shopping bags—crammed to the bursting point with all manner of eccentric goods. Although the book's minor characters tend to irritate the priggish Sammler, their follies are an index of his own strength. *He* can explain the mental designs that lie just behind the city's veneer of hustle and tough talk.

Humboldt's Gift

In similar ways, *Humboldt's Gift* (1975) is at once a prolonged, often painful meditation on the responsibilities of the living to the dead and a comic paean to Chicago, full of zany romps through its streets and buildings. The result is God's plenty, both of heady thought and urban savvy. The story of Charles Citrine is divided into two separate but unequal parts—backward glances at what Citrine calls his "significant dead" and the forward motions of a life growing increasingly cluttered. Von Humboldt Fleisher epitomizes the lyric poet *extraordinaire*. During the thirties his *Harlequin Ballads* was "an immediate hit," the stuff of which literary fame—and literary power—is fashioned. But an appetite like Humboldt's depends on a calculated restlessness, a fight to the finish between life as it is and what his poetry might make it become. If Goethe insisted, at the end, on "more light!" poor Humboldt required an even wider range of excesses: more enemies, more influences, more sex, more money, and so on. As Citrine puts it, "Humboldt wanted to drape the world in radiance, but he didn't have enough cloth."[17]

Humboldt haunts the novel both as an abiding presence and as a fearful reminder. Had I. B. Singer written the novel, Humboldt would surely have been an invading *dybbuk* (restless spirit of the dead); Bellow seems willing to settle for the dead poet as one of Citrine's more troublesome ghosts of the heart. Humboldt has spent his life "pondering what to do between *then* and *now*, between birth and death to satisfy certain great questions," and now Citrine must face the awful possibility that the costs have outstripped their accomplishments. For one thing, the centers of power have shifted, reducing Humboldt to an object America can "love," but need not take seriously, much less *fear*.

Humboldt is, of course, not the only casualty of America's unflinching toughness. Citrine's elegiac tone reveals as much about himself as it does about his poetic master. Humboldt's epical list of "sacred words" (*alienation, wasteland, the unconscious,* etc.) is a poignant reminder of those days when, as Lionel Abel once put it, New York was a very Russian city, a "metropolis yearning to belong to another country." Which is to say, Von Humboldt Fleisher was the Jewish-American renaissance in powerful miniature. By contrast, Citrine had been "too haughty to bother with Marxism, Freudianism, the avant-garde, or any of these things that Humboldt, as a culture Jew, took so much stock in" (HG, 158). Like Bellow himself, Citrine operates on the gut feeling that if 10 New York intellectuals embrace an idea, it could not possibly have much lasting value. Both author and character prefer the naturalistic turf of Chicago (where one is forced, in Citrine's words, to become "a connoisseur of the near-nothing") to the assorted isms that Humboldt's crowd generates. And yet Citrine finds himself uncomfortably famous as the graph of his success rises in something like direct proportion to Humboldt's decline.

To be sure, Citrine bears more than a little resemblance to Moses Herzog. He too has a grand book more in mind than on paper, and he too suffers all the pangs of a life "in great disorder." But the Humboldt-Citrine relationship is also a version of the psychological sharing Bellow had explored in *The Victim*. Humboldt's accusations, however loony or unfounded, cannot be dimissed out of hand. Citrine's meditations are filled with the suspicion that Humboldt may have been right after all. Has the intellectually competitive life turned him (however unintentionally, however unconsciously) into an "operator," an enemy of true Art?

Penance requires nothing less than an "inspired levitation" toward the truth, a project big enough to prevent the "leprosy of souls." It is a tall order, as tiring as it is impossible. And not surprisingly, carrying the weight of Western thought on his shoulders takes a comic toll. In short, Citrine becomes yet another architect of his own misfortune, a schlemiel whose moral reclamation projects are as large as his failures. In his case the result is a Charles Citrine ("Pulitzer Prize, Legion of Honor, father of Lish and Mary, husband of A, lover of B, a serious person and a card"; *HG,* 90) who tries valiantly to square the mystical pronouncements of Rudolph Steiner (*Knowledge of the Higher Worlds and Its Attainment*) with the concrete surfaces of Chicago.

Citrine gives the effort his all, but he ends in what his analyst calls "melancholia . . . interrupted by fits of humor" (*HG,* 164). Even the much-harried Artur Sammler had better luck plowing his way through Meister Eckhart. Citrine begins a Steinerian meditation only to find himself interrupted by angry knocks from the outside. In this case the "knocks" include those by Reality Instructors who hector him about his dreaminess; lovable con men with schemes for projected books or an African mine; racketeers who run the gamut from those who dress like gentlemen and play paddleball to those who batter expensive automobiles with baseball bats; quack spiritualists; sensuous women; and those ultimate heavies in Bellow's universe—lawyers representing an estranged wife. Citrine suffers them all—and himself—with comic grace.

After all, Citrine has long recognized that "in business Chicago, it was a true sign of love when people wanted to take you into money-making schemes" (*HG,* 176). But there are other, more *literary* reasons as well. Characters like Citrine require a thickly textured counterbalancing if the novel is to avoid spinning off into those "high worlds" Steiner writes about. Thus, the city provides a necessary comic grounding, a way of keeping a dreamer like Citrine under pressure and in what he calls his "Chicago state": "I infinitely lack something, my heart swells, I feel a tearing eagerness. The sentient part of the soul wants to express itself. There are some of the symptoms of an overdose of caffeine. At the same time I have a sense of being the instrument of external powers. They are using me either as an example of human error or as the mere shadow of desirable things to come" (*HG,* 66). I suspect that comes as close to a description of Bellow's own creative process as we are likely to get. In *More Die of Heartbreak* Kenneth Trachtenberg, the narrative voice out simultaneously to protect and justify his dreamy, distracted uncle, puts it this way:

My work was cut out for me: I was to help my dear uncle to defend himself. I didn't suppose that the Layamons meant him great harm; only they weren't likely to respect his magics or to have the notion of preserving him for the sake of his gifts. There was quite a lot at stake here. I can't continually be spelling it out [although, unfortunately, Kenneth does precisely that for long stretches of the novel]. As: the curse of human impoverishment as revealed to Admiral

Byrd in Antarctica; the sleep of love in human beings as referred to by Larkin; the search for excitements as the universal nostrum; the making of one's soul as the only project genuinely worthy of undertaking.[18]

Trachtenberg's last phrase is especially important because, as we learn earlier in the novel, "[t]he city is the expression of the human experience it embodies and this includes all personal history." The result is that if a Benn Crader, an Albert Corde, a Clara Velde, and the unnamed protagonist of *The Bellarosa Connection* are to make their respective souls, the smithy on which they will be forged is the city.

All of which brings my discussion of Bellow's sense of urban comedy full circle, back to his lovesick meditators and their efforts to bring a humane order to the chaos of contemporary culture. Not surprisingly, the anger, argumentation, "mental letters," and stump speeches generally end in silent acceptance, in a feeling that the values of the heart will, indeed *must*, prevail. At one point in *Herzog* Moses remembers how, when he was a small boy, his mother had taught him a lesson far outweighing any truth that armies of subsequent "reality instructors" have tried to pound into him. She had rubbed her palm until a small ball of dirt appeared—empirical proof that man was made of dust and is destined to return to it. As an adult, Herzog is no longer able to believe the story as a child believes, but in many respects *Herzog* is a novel that blends what Mama Herzog had known from a Jewish tradition with what her educated son had "learned" from an American one. In the last lines of the novel Herzog is at peace, just on the edge of telling his housekeeper, Mrs. Tuttle, not to make so much dust. And in a way, the novel itself has been out to dampen down some of the "dust" that Bellow's more irritable protagonists tend to stir up. *Herzog* ends with the letters stopped and a version of health virtually indistinguishable from sheer exhaustion. Thus, Moses Herzog leads himself, and us, out of the wasteland and into a country where if it doesn't hurt enough to cry, at least it doesn't ache too much to laugh.

Chapter Seven
New Directions

The nagging sense that Jewish-American fiction had played itself out, that there were only so many ways one could bash overprotective Jewish mothers, their benighted husbands, and their whining sons or pampered daughters, was hardly a secret when, writing in 1977, Irving Howe put the matter this way:

> My own view is that American Jewish fiction has probably moved past its high point. Insofar as this body of writing draws heavily from the immigrant experience, it must suffer a depletion of resources, a thinning out of materials and memories. Other than in books and sentiment, there just isn't enough left of that experience. Even some of the writers, men and women of middle age or beyond, who have themselves lived through the immigrant experience now seem to be finding that their recollections have run dry. Or, that in their stories and novels they have done about as much with those recollections as they can. The sense of an overpowering subject, the sense that this subject imposes itself upon their imaginations—this grows weaker, necessarily, with the passing of the years. There remains, to be sure, the problem of "Jewishness," and the rewards and difficulties of definition it may bring us. But this problem, though experienced as an urgent one by at least some people, does not yield a thick enough sediment of felt life to enable a new outburst of writing about American Jews. It is too much a matter of will, or nerves, and not enough of shared experience. Besides, not everything which concerns or interests us can be transmuted into imaginative literature. [1]

Nobody was eager to read, much less "review," yet another pale carbon copy of *Portnoy's Complaint,* and even those who disagreed with Howe about the centrality of the immigrant experience could only share his feeling that a literature that had lived by the sword of sociology was now destined to wither, if not perish, from it.

The Emergence of Cynthia Ozick

Not surprisingly, a generation of younger writers were hardly shy about raising their respective "objections," and of this group none was

more insistent—or more eloquent—than Cynthia Ozick. Her fiction
has radically changed the way we define Jewish-American writing, and,
more important, the way Jewish-American writing defines itself. With
certain notable exceptions (e.g., Frankie Alpine's tortured conversion
to Judaism during the final pages of *The Assistant*), Jewish-American characters—to say nothing of their creators—found themselves
attracted to and influenced by the dominant gentile culture swirling
everywhere around them. The writers who mattered were Sherwood
Anderson and Theodore Dreiser, James Joyce and Ernest Hemingway.
And while Ozick also spent a long, largely fruitless apprenticeship (in
her case worshiping at the shrine of Art as defined by the Jamesean
novel), from *Trust* (1966) onward she has made it something of her
trademark to insist on the essential *Jewishness* of Jewish-American literature. As she put it in a ringing manifesto entitled "Toward a New
Yiddish":

The fact is that nothing thought or written in Diaspora has ever been able to
last unless it has been centrally Jewish. . . . By "centrally Jewish" I mean, for
literature, whatever touches the liturgical. Obviously this does not refer only
to prayer. It refers to a type of literature and to a type of perception. There is
a critical difference between liturgy and a poem. Liturgy is in command of the
reciprocal moral imagination rather than of the isolated lyrical imagination. A
poem is a private flattery; it moves the private heart, but to no end other than
being moved. A poem is a decoration of the heart, an art of the instant. . . .
Liturgy is also a poem, but it is meant not to have only a private voice. Liturgy
has a choral voice, a command voice: the echo of the voice of the Lord of
History. Poetry shuns judgment and memory and seizes the moment. In all of
history the literature that has lasted for Jews has been liturgical. (AA, 168–69)

I suspect that I. B. Singer—surely an authentically "Jewish" writer in ways
that, say, the sociologically driven, Jewishly ignorant Philip Roth is
not—would demur. In the world of Singer's father's court, "Jewish writers"
were those who penned commentaries on the Holy Books—on Torah,
Talmud, *responsa*. They did *not*—as first his older brother, I. J. Singer, and
then Singer himself did—write "stories," including whatever liturgically
based stories might be. Nor would Singer be so quick to dismiss the power
of the imagination as the stuff of decoration. But Ozick was so insistent and
uncompromising—about history, memory, law, restraint, and about what
Jewishly *lasts* and what is Jewishly "important"—that she has been accused
(in the pages of *Commentary,* no less) of writing fictions that are "actually
Jewish assaults on fields of Gentile influence."

Until very recently Ozick worried not so much about "assaulting Gentile influence" (something that troubles her little) but, rather, about the creative act itself. In what ways—sometimes subtle, sometimes not—was the writer a usurper of God, a maker of idols? What the modernist giants took as both their mission and their elitist prerogative (e.g., Joyce's Stephen Dedalus pridefully declaring himself a "priest of the eternal imagination") Ozick turned into declarations of self-abnegation:

Imagination is more than make-believe, more than the power to invent. It is also the power to penetrate evil, to take on evil, to become evil, and in that guise it is the most frightening human faculty. Whoever writes a story that includes villainy enters into and becomes the villain. . . . The imagination, like Moloch, can take you nowhere except back to its own maw. And the writers who insist that literature is "about" the language it is made of are offering an idol: literature is for its own sake, for its own maw; not for the sake of humanity. (*AA*, 247)

It would, of course, have been easy enough to point out that Ozick, for all her quarrels with the "imagination"—with its frightening potential for evil, its lawlessness, its attraction to "magic" and indeed to everything she regarded as pagan, as gentile—continues to write stories. Even her insistence that literature is *not* language seemed curious given her reservations about writing in English and her hopes about something she called "New Yiddish":

There are no major works of Jewish imaginative genius written in any Gentile language, sprung out of any Gentile culture.
. . . .
Like the old Yiddish, New Yiddish will be the language of a culture that is centrally Jewish in its concerns and thereby liturgical in nature. Like the old Yiddish before its massacre by Hitler, New Yiddish will be the language of multitudes of Jews: spoken to Jews by Jews, written by Jews for Jews. (*AA*, 167, 174)

And yet press this matter too hard—suggest, for example, that Ozick's ambivalence about the English language ("When I write in English," she points out, "I live in Christendom") disqualifies her for serious consideration as an American writer—and Ozick will wince. Overdo the "foreignness" of her sources, her allusions, and indeed her "vision" and she will squirm with obvious discomfort. "What do they think I am," she once asked me, "a visitor?"

In short, Ozick has become an inveterate explainer—of her own fiction and, perhaps more important, of a Jewish aesthetic that is shared in large measure by such writers as Hugh Nissenson, Arthur A. Cohen, and Norma Rosen. Together, they represent a willed movement away from the sociology that sustained Jewish-American fiction during its heyday in the 1950s and 1960s and toward something harder to define, something yet to be fully worked out but clearly more responsive to theological concerns and authentically Jewish sources.

Ozick's two collections of essays—*Art and Ardor* (1983) and *Metaphor and Memory* (1989)—suggest just how invigorating such a quest can be; indeed, Ozick's essays are so brilliant and so influential that they threaten to eclipse her talents as a fiction writer. Ozick has clearly been troubled by the implications. In her foreword to *Art and Ardor,* for example, she points out that she "never meant to write essays" (*AA,* ix), and later goes on to explain that "[e]ssays summarize. They do not invent. In undertaking the writing of an essay (or article, or 'piece', and most particularly in journalism), I know beforehand what I think. I see the end, it is all the while uncompromisingly, inflexibly, in sight, and my task is to traverse the space between. The risks are small. The way is predictable. . . . But in beginning a story I know nothing at all: surely not where I am going, and hardly at all how to get there. . . . Fiction is all discovery" (*AA,* x–xi). And in the "Forewarning" of *Metaphor and Memory* she complains about the special problems that crop up when one is a writer of both stories and essays:

The essays will too often be forced into a tailoring job for which they were never intended. The essays, like chalk marks, are used to take the measure of the stories. The essays become the stories' interpreters: their clues, or cues, or concordances, as if the premises of the essays were incontrovertibly the premises of the stories as well. As if the stories were "illustrations" of the essays; as if the essays expressed the ideational (or even at times the ideological) matrix of the stories. . . . in other words, if a writer of stories is also a writer of essays, the essays ought not to be seized as a rod to beat the writer's stories with; or as a frame into which to squeeze the writer's stories; or, collectively, as a "philosophy" into which to pen the writer's outlook.[2]

A critic can sympathize with Ozick's position and still point out that it is hard to think of another Jewish-American writer—including the endlessly self-justifying Philip Roth of *Reading Myself and Others*—whose essays have been more insistent about Jewish literature in general or more germane to her own fiction in particular. Indeed, there are those who feel, with some justification, that Ozick is far more interesting as an essayist than as a fiction writer.

Granted, disputes of this sort do not resolve themselves easily, but let me suggest that a close look at a representative Ozick story may help. I have chosen "The Pagan Rabbi" partly because it lends itself to precisely the kind of confusion between essay and story that Ozick complains about and partly because it is a superb example of the "new directions" in Jewish-American fiction that this chapter means to explore.

"The Pagan Rabbi"

"The Pagan Rabbi" (1971) begins with a riveting sentence—to my mind, one of the most evocative in all of contemporary American literature: "When I heard that Isaac Kornfeld, a man of piety and brains, had hanged himself in the public park, I put a token in the subway stile and journeyed out to see the tree."[3] Like the narrator, we are curious to find out more about Kornfield (whose name, by the way, turns out to be highly suggestive—the Isaac hinting at the story's wider themes of father-son tension and of oedipal sacrifice, the Kornfield pointing toward nature and the park where the "pagan rabbi" meets his tragic destiny); "The Pagan Rabbi" is an attempt to explain, perhaps justify, or at any rate fill in the gaps that Kornfield's sudden suicide left. It is also a case—like Conrad's "Heart of Darkness" or Fitzgerald's *The Great Gatsby*—in which a narrator looms as more important than the enigmatic character he tries to understand.

In "The Pagan Rabbi" the motion of fathers and sons has the precision of a Morris dance. The sons—Isaac Kornfeld and (again) the unnamed narrator—"had been classmates in the rabbinical seminary ("Pagan," 3)." Not surprisingly, Isaac was the more brilliant; indeed, it is his restless brilliance, his Faustian energy, if you will, that drives him beyond the "fences" of the law, that turns him into a "pagan."

By contrast, the narrator becomes an atheist, withdraws in his second year at the seminary, and marries outside the faith. The respective fathers—both of them rabbis and mutual friends/enemies who "vie with one another in demonstrations of charitableness, in the captious glitter of their scholia, in the number of their adherents"—blame philosophy for ruining their children: "Neither man was philosophical in the slightest. It was the one thing they agreed on. 'Philosophy is an abomination,' Isaac's father used to say. 'The Greeks were philosophers, but they remained children playing with their dolls. Even Socrates, a monotheist, nevertheless sent money down to the temple to pay for incense to their doll'" ("Pagan," 3). The narrator, however, disagrees: "The trouble was not philosophy—I had none of Isaac's talent." Indeed, Isaac is the *chochem,* the wise son personified. As the narrator puts it, he was a "nincompoop and no *sitzfleish,*" while Isaac was another story altogether: "You could answer questions that weren't even invented yet. Then you invent them" ("Pagan," 6).

The diverging paths that lead Isaac to his paganism and the narrator to more mundane careers first as a furrier and then as a bookseller reduplicate the general outlines of Rabbi Nahman of Bratslav's famous story, "The Wise Man and the Simple Man." In that story a man of enormous talent and wide-ranging abilities leaves his village to find a challenge worthy of his gifts. His friend, a simpler, less ambitious soul, remains in the village and becomes a humble shoemaker. Years later the wise man returns. His powerful intellect, however, has brought him no happiness. Indeed, he came to doubt everything, including the existence of God. For Rabbi Nahman, whose stories are among the most revered in Hasidic literature, "The Wise Man and the Simple Man" is a cautionary tale, a warning against the very pursuits that ultimately consume Isaac Kornfield: "I noticed [the narrator remembers] that he read everything. Long ago he had inflamed my taste, but I could never keep up. No sooner did I catch his joy in Saadia Gaon than he had already sprung ahead to Yehudah Halevi. One day he was weeping with Dostoyevsky and the next leaping in the air over Thomas Mann. He introduced me to Hegel and Nietzsche while our fathers wailed. His mature reading was no more peaceable than those frenzies of his youth" ("Pagan," 9).

Granted, Jewish-American literature's "second generation" made a cottage industry of mythologizing those immigrant sons who devoured whole bookshelves in the reading rooms of public libraries and then went into the larger world to become its celebrated writers and professors. Indeed, that is what the story of the New York intellectuals from Alfred Kazin (*A Walker in the City*) and Irving Howe (*A Margin of Hope*) to Norman Podhoretz (*Making It*) and Saul Bellow (*Herzog*) is largely about. Rabbi Kornfield's saga, however, is a radical departure from these oft-told celebratory tales. Several weeks short of his thirty-sixth birthday, Kornfield hangs himself—and by his prayer shawl no less: "I . . . marveled [the narrator tells us] that all that holy genius and intellectual surprise should in the end be raised no higher than the next-to-lowest limb of a delicate young oak, with burly roots like the toes of a gryphon exposed in the wet ground" ("Pagan," 4). That the narrator makes his way to Trilham's Inlet (a "bay filled with sickly clams and a bad smell") to what we are accustomed to calling "the scene of the crime" suggests the outlines of a detective story. All that remains, though, are the "where" and the "how" of the tree; the "who" and the "why" are hidden elsewhere.

Ozick's narrator-protagonist finds versions of the latter in Kornfield's papers. Quotations from Leviticus and Deuteronomy are juxtaposed with snatches from Keats and Byron. The narrator finds himself "repelled by Isaac's Nature: it wore a capital letter, and smelled like my own Book Cellar." Significantly enough, Kornfield's notebook concludes with this entry: "Great Pan lives" ("Pagan," 17). The effect is akin to Marlow reading Kurtz's elegant report on the suppression of savage customs in Conrad's "Heart of Darkness." Marlow wants nothing more than to pluck the heart out of Kurtz's mystery, and nothing characterizes Kurtz's mystery more than his *voice*. Marlow hears it, in all its ringing eloquence, during the first paragraphs of the report, only to find himself disquieted by the shaky scrawl of Kurtz's final words: "Exterminate all the brutes!" That Rabbi Kornfield has abandoned his Jewish soul in an obsessive pursuit of the pagan body, that he has traded—quite literally, quite graphically—the beauty of Jewish Law for the flesh of Nature, is at the center of Ozick's story.

How is one to respond to such a scene—at once surrealistic and magical, grotesquely rendered and all too "real"—for Kornfield had "placed one hand (the other I kept around the tree's waist, as it were) in the bifurcation (disgustingly termed crotch) of that lowest limb and the elegant and devoutly firm torso, and caressed that miraculous juncture with a certain languor, which gradually changed to vigor" ("Pagan," 29)? Is the coital act that results meant to be dark humor, in something of the same spirit that caused Kafka to laugh uncontrollably when he read "The Metamorphosis" to a small circle of friends? Or is it to be read as moral fable, as a caution to those (perhaps including Ozick herself) who would become pagans, idolators, defilers of the Law?

Stories, of course, do not explain themselves. And *as story,* "The Pagan Rabbi" is able to divide its sympathies between the doomed Isaac Kornfield and his astonished narrator-friend, between an attraction to the lush vitality of "paganism" and an understanding—expressed by the Niad—that "It is not Nature they love so much as Death they fear."

What Kornfield finds at Trilham's Inlet is not the liberated soul he had imagined but, rather, his true, his "Jewish," soul: that of an old man forever hunched over a Talmud volume, forever separated from nature. After such knowledge, suicide is apparently the only forgiveness—that is, unless "forgiveness" comes in the muted form of the narrator's parting words to Kornfield's widow: "Your husband's soul is in that park. Consult it."

I would argue that "The Pagan Rabbi" is so *un*like any previous Jewish-American story one can think of that its central tension has become Ozick's signature. It is as if the old charges about Jewish writing—that everything not Torah is levity, that the wider cultural world is both pagan and utterly in conflict with the Jewish imagination, that the fiction writer is himself a species of the pagan—had been filtered through a consciousness at once thoroughly literary and uncompromisingly Jewish.

The bulk of Ozick's short stories (e.g., "The Dock Witch," "Usurpation," "Bloodshed," and "Puttermesser and Xanthippe") are variations on "The Pagan Rabbi"'s central conflict: Nature versus Law, ecstasy versus restraint, or, as Ozick likes to put it, Pan versus Moses. In addition, she has explored the nobler and nastier sides of the disappearing world of Yiddish; examined the ways in which "translation" simultaneously lures and irritates its writers (all this and a thinly veiled portrait of I. B. Singer as public charmer and deliciously imaginative genius are contained in "Envy, or Yiddish in America"); and created a devastating portrait, in *The Cannibal Galaxy,* of the cultural mishmash known as the "Dual Curriculum" that masquerades as Jewish education. The latter deserves extended analysis because it so clearly articulates the difference between Ozick's attitudes toward cultural assimilation and those which characterized most previous Jewish-American writers.

The Cannibal Galaxy

In *The Cannibal Galaxy* (1983) Joseph Brill, principal of a Jewish day school, is a satiric study in failed learning and failed teaching, in what happens when a life presumably devoted to visions—astronomical and otherwise—is revealed as a sham, an illusion, merely a mediocrity. Everything conspires to suggest the smug safety of a middling course, right down to the geography that surrounds Brill and the curious institution known as the Edmond Fleg Primary School: "The school was on a large lake in the breast-pocket of the continent, pouched in inwardness. It was as though it had a horror of coasts and margins; of edges and extremes of any sort. The school was of the middle and in the middle. Its three buildings were middling-high, flat-roofed, moderately modern."[4]

Nonetheless, Brill sees himself as a man "of almost sacral power": "*The world rests on the breath of the children in the schoolhouses*—this fragment of Talmud feathered his spirit like a frond from a tree in deep warmth" (*CG*, 4). To these children and to their school Brill brings an idea of education forged by French culture and the nightmare of the Holocaust: "François Villon danced through Joseph Brill's nostrils. Philanthropy, dutiful and ambitious, would bring a shadow of the Sorbonne into being in the middle of America: a children's Sorbonne dense with Hebrew melodies, a Sorbonne grown out of an exiled Eden. The waters of Shiloh springing from the head of Europe" (*CG*, 36). The result is a dual curriculum heavy with Brill's thumbprint: Chumash, Gemara, Social Studies, French. It would be, as Brill envisages it, "a school run according to the principle of twin nobilities, twin antiquities: "The fusion of scholarly Europe and burnished Jerusalem. The grace of Madame de Sévigné's flowery courtyard mated to the perfect serenity of a purified Sabbath. Corneille and Racine set beside Jonah and Koheleth. The combinations wheeled in his brain" (*CG*, 27). As Brill's no-nonsense father might have quipped, "*Nit ahin, nit aher*" ("Neither one thing nor the other").

More damning still, however, is the wide gap Ozick satirically explores between principle and principal, between the idea that energized a younger Brill and the middle-aged, shallow administrator he became:

Every spring he invaded the sixth-grade room to write on the blackboard
        Mais où sont les neiges d'antan?,
but he no longer seriously read. He never so much as yawned through the *Times,* not even on Sundays; he let lapse his dutiful subscription to *Le Monde;* instead, he bought the town paper with its quick news of burglaries and local funerals—he liked to see which cans of vegetables were on sale at the A&P. . . . [H]e dozed away nights in the shifting rays of lampless television, stupified by Lucy, by the tiny raspy-voiced figures of the Flintstones; by the panic-struck void. (*CG*, 40–41)

Meanwhile, class after class at the Edmund Fleg Primary School pass through thinning versions of the Dual Curriculum and receive their meaningless diplomas as the fifth-grade choir—totally unaware of either the respective contexts or the attendant ironies—sings *"The minstrel bo-o-oy to the wars is gone"* and then *"Chevaliers de la Table Ronde, goûtons voir si le vin est bon, goûtons voir, oui, oui, oui."*

As *The Cannibal Galaxy* dramatizes, Brill's dream makes not only for bad pedagogy but also for a diminished American Jewry. As the central image of the title makes clear, smaller bodies are consumed for larger ones, whether as concerns the stars or ethnic minorities. Thus, "cannibal galaxies" are "megalosaurian colonies of primordial gases . . . [that] devour small brother-galaxies—and when the meal is made, the victim continues to rotate like a Jonah-dervish inside the cannibal, while the sated ogre-galaxy, its gaseous belly stretched, soporific, never spins at all—motionless as digesting Death" *(CG, 69)*.

Granted, several generations of Jewish-American writers had toted up the costs of acculturation and some (e.g., Ludwig Lewisohn, in his 1922 book *Up Stream*) had raised strong objections. But perhaps nothing characterizes the new directions more than tone, a post-Holocaust consciousness, and a willingness on the part of contemporary Jewish-American writers to confront the nightmare of twentieth-century Jewish history. In this regard Ozick has been among the stronger, more imaginatively riveting voices. Not only do Holocaust survivors figure prominently in her stories (e.g., "Bloodshed," "Levitation"), but increasingly she has turned her fiction toward confronting the Holocaust itself.

The Messiah of Stockholm

A decade before the publication of *The Messiah of Stockholm* (1987) Ozick, in a review of *The Street of Crocodiles,* talked about Bruno Schulz and his importance to Jewish-American writers. Schulz, a 50-year-old high school art teacher was, in Ozick's words, "in command of the most original literary imaginations of modern Europe"; he was also gunned down by the Nazis in the small, otherwise-inconsequential town of Drohobycz, Galicia. For Ozick, what is being invented in Schulz's extraordinary novel is nothing short of religion itself: "What is being invented in the very drone of our passive literary expectations is Religion—not the taming of theology and morality, but the brute splendors of rite, gesture, phantasmagoric transfiguration, sacrifice, elevation, degradation, mortification, repugnance, terror, cult. The religion of animism, in fact, where everything comes alive with an unpredictable and spiteful spirit-force, where even living tissue contains ghosts, where there is no pity" (*AA,* 227). Ozick's review also mentions in passing that Schulz's final manuscript—a novel entitled *The Messiah*—"was carried for safekeeping to a friend; both friend and manuscript were swallowed up by the sacrificial fires of the Europe of 1942." Years later, when Ozick visited Sweden, stories about the lost manuscript kept surfacing, and kept pressing on her imagination. *The Messiah of Stockholm* is the result—at once a fabulation and a moral imperative, an account of what may or may not have been Schulz's lost manuscript. It is also yet another tale of art and obsession, of usurpations and betrayals, of angelic illusion and idolatrous reality. At its center is a book reviewer for a Stockholm newspaper.

The book reviewer—Lars Andemening—is a man in the throes of a peculiar "midlife crisis": "Lars Andemening believed himself to be an arrested soul: someone who had been pushed off the track. He belonged elsewhere. His name was his own fabrication. He had told almost no one . . . that he was the son of a murdered man, a man shot down in the streets over forty years ago, in Poland, while the son was still in the mother's womb. It was a thing he knew and kept buried. There was something dangerous in it, not only because it did not conform—he had been seized in infancy by an unnatural history—but because this father of his was a legend, a dream."[5]

As Andemening's obsession would have it, his father is none other than Bruno Schulz, the author of two brilliant, Kafka-like collections of short fiction (*The Street of Crocodiles* and *Sanatorium under the Sign of the Hourglass*) and of a lost manuscript called *The Messiah*. Orphaned in Poland during World War II, Andemening both hoards and suffers from "an orphan's terrifying freedom to choose." Among the things he has chosen is his own history. As a result, he cherishes, perhaps idolizes, Schulz's writing; he saturates himself in the Polish language; and he casts his lot, as a book reviewer, with the complicated fictions of Kis, Musil, Broch, Canetti, and Kundera. As one of Andemening's colleagues puts it, "I'll tell you what your trouble is, Lars, Central Europe, that's your trouble" (*MS,* 14).

Indeed, visions of *Mittel* Europe, of a world altered forever by the Holocaust, are never far from Andemening's imagination. By contrast, his fellow book reviewers on the *Morgontörn* are less esoteric souls. One of them loved "everything American, including their fake cheese; on his last trip to New York he had brought back six pounds of Velveeta as a present for his wife" (*MS,* 11); the other was "a kind of provocateur, particularly on the subject of [Swedish] flatbread. He was nasty to any cookbook that praised it. It was an instance, he said, of Swedish provincialism" (*MS,* 17). The effect of this "literary stewpot" is somewhat akin to the office of legal clerks Melville creates in "Bartleby the Scrivener," but with a comedic touch and a satiric sharpness we have come to identify with Ozick's best work.

In any event we are hardly surprised when Andemening's colleagues generate more controversy, receive more mail, and get better treatment than he does. Andemening has transmogrified himself into his father: "On account of this father Lars shrank himself. He felt he resembled his father; all the tales were about men shrinking more and more into the phantasmagoria of the mind" (*MS,* 5).

At this point a few more words about Bruno Schulz are in order. Schulz is usually compared with Kafka, not only because both were specialists in the grotesque, the surreal, but also because Schulz translated Kafka's *The Trial* into Polish. Nonetheless, there are important differences. Schulz spent his entire life in Drohobycz, outside the mainstream of literary or Jewish life. *His* father, unlike Kafka's, was more lovable, and loved, than he is tyrannical and terrifying. What Kafka and Schulz share is the capacity for strange, dark, uncompromisingly modernist dreams.

In *The Messiah of Stockholm* Ozick is a shrewd critic of Schulz's fiction, but the assessments apply equally to her own. One is reminded of, say, the "spirit-force" that operates so powerfully in such early stories as "The Pagan Rabbi" or of the reflexive, story-within-a-story aspect of "Usurpations." Indeed, Ozick's readers will find many echoes of her previous work transported to Andemening's Sweden. Here, for example, is a passage—yet another novel-within-the-larger-novel—that with an alteration here, a change of emphasis there, is a dead ringer for the essential themes in an earlier Ozick story entitled "Virility":

The novel was called *Illusion.* [Andemening] admired the plot, which was founded on the principle of ambush. A kind and modest elderly spinster—a self-taught painter—falls in love with a ne'er-do-well, a beautiful and clever young man. She has declined to show her paintings because she believes them to be of no merit. The young man is the first to see them; she had never had the courage to reveal them to anyone before. But the young man recognizes at once that she is a hidden genius; he will claim the paintings as his own and give them to the world. The scheme is a grand success. (*MS*, 84–85)

More important, however, is the way in which illusion spreads over everything from Andemening's attempt to "usurp" Bruno Schulz to the richly complicated tapestry of illusion/reality that surrounds what may or may not be the lost manuscript of *The Messiah*. Ozick is at what reviewers—even those who will recognize themselves in her satiric portrait of literary hacks—like to call "the top of her form."

And finally, there is, as always in Ozick's work, the problem of idolatry. The manuscript that is purported to be Schulz's *The Messiah* is a tale of Drohobycz drained of its citizenry and populated by hundreds of idols: "A few were contemptibly crude and ill-constructed, but most represented the inspired toil of armies of ingenious artisans, and there was actually a handful of masterworks. . . . The idols of Drohobycz were relatively passive and had no idea of how to go about rounding up their worshippers. . . . More and more frequently there were sacrificial bonfires all over Drohobycz. The taller and stronger idols began seizing the smaller and lesser idols and casting them into the flames. . . . The town was on fire, idols burning up idols in a frenzy of mutual admiration" (*MS*, 108). This imaginative world precedes the coming of a strange, dark, phoenixlike messiah: "It was a birth. The Messiah had given birth to a bird, and the moment the bird flew living out of the relentlessly wheeling contrivance that had been the Messiah, the thing—or organism—collapsed with the noise of vast crashings and crushings, cardboard like stone, cotton like bone, granite petal on brazen postulate: degraded and humiliated" (*MS*, 111).

This is the stuff over which Ozick's critics will break their heads in years to come. Ozick herself makes no bones about the essential Jewishness of her vision or about the Nazis who are the idolmakers of Drohobycz. But I suspect one will have to look deeper than the work of Bruno Schulz—just as one will have to look deeper than contemporary Jewish theology—to find appropriate analogues. Joseph Lowin's recent study *Cynthia Ozick* (1988) argues persuasively that the novel is a tale of "creation and redemption," a midrash (biblical commentary) on the story of Terach and Abraham, and, as such, is also "a rewriting of Bruno Schulz for didactic purposes. The first half of the story is inspired by Terach, and that is why the village of Drohobycz, which has been emptied of humanity, is now peopled exclusively by idols.

Where idolatry reigns there does death become a sacrament, even if it means the sacrifice of idols to each other."[6] My own hunch is that cabala explains much of the energy in *The Messiah of Stockholm*. In this sense Ozick's last novel is more akin to, say, Arthur A. Cohen's brilliant fusion of mysticism and theology in *The Days of Simon Stern* than it is to Schulz's *The Street of Crocodiles*.

About some mysteries I can be clearer: *The Messiah of Stockholm* is dedicated to Philip Roth. No doubt readers will wonder about this. Ozick has said that Roth presented her with a gift of some of Schulz's self-portraits, one of which is reproduced at the front of her book. I think the dedication is also a nod to Roth's energetic efforts in behalf of Central European writers like Kafka, Milan Kundera, and, not least, Bruno Schulz. Moreover, Roth's Nathan Zuckerman can imagine an Anne Frank in such meticulous detail and with such passionate, obsessive involvement that some readers of *The Ghost Writer* were no longer sure about the line dividing fact from fiction. Ozick engages in a similar effort at "rescue" with Lars Andemening's obsession with Bruno Schulz, and with the "found" manuscript she nearly convinces us is—was?—"read." The result haunts one long after Andemening's spirit is broken by a lost *Messiah* and he is propelled back to the normality—and the illusion—in which all of us live.

Coming to Terms with the Holocaust

That Jewish-American fictionists should feel uncomfortable writing about the Holocaust is understandable enough. After all, geography or good luck had spared them. Moreover, there was both eloquence and an undeniable truth to the assertions—by Elie Wiesel, Theodor Adorno, and others—that "Holocaust literature" was an oxymoron, a contradiction in terms that could only trivialize what demands our respectful silence. How, then, could they now presume, and how could they begin, to speak about the unspeakable?

At the same time, however, other voices were calling Jewish-American writers to account for their silence. As Robert Alter put it in a 1966 essay on Israeli Holocaust fiction, "With all the restless probing into the impliciations of the Holocaust that continues to go on in Jewish intellectual forums . . . it gives one pause to note how rarely American Jewish fiction has attempted to come to terms . . . with the European catastrophe."[7]

In the years since 1966, however, the situation has changed markedly, as S. Lillian Kremer persuasively demonstrates in her recent study *Witness through the Imagination* (1989). As she argues, "Tradition commands all Jews to consider themselves figuratively present at Sinai to receive the Torah. Contemporary Jews increasingly feel that, geography aside, they were present at Auschwitz. American Jews carry the psychological burden of Auschwitz and Chelmno and Dachau and Bergen-Belsen and Treblinka and all the other Nazi death factories where their relatives died brutal deaths."[8] Put another way, in the post-Holocaust universe the task of bearing witness takes on new dimensions and broader responsibilities.

Besides, as Ozick points out in an effort to explain how she came to write "The Shawl" (1980), stories write authors, rather than the other way around. My suspicion is that the same thing is true of Arthur Cohen's *In the Days of Simon Stern* (1973) and Leslie Epstein's *The King of the Jews* (1979). Kremer's study focuses on Bernard Malamud, Edward Louis Wallant (*The Pawnbroker*), Saul Bellow, George Steiner (*The Portage to San Crisobal of A.H.*), Leslie Epstein (*King of the Jews*), I. B. Singer (*Enemies, a Love Story*), Chaim Potok (*In the Beginning*), Richard Elman (*The Reckoning*), and Cynthia Ozick—and while there are moments that strain or do not entirely convince, there is little question, I think, that imaginative reflections on the Holocaust have become a significant new direction in Jewish-American fiction.

Another, of course, is Israel, although this direction has thus far produced slimmer results. On the one hand, there are the evocative, haunting stories of Hugh Nissenson's early collections—*A Pile of Stones* (1965) and *In the Reign of Peace* (1972); on the other, the "Judea" section of Philip Roth's *The Counterlife.* But the fact remains that—noteworthy exceptions like Tova Reich's recent novel, *The Return of the Master,* aside—Israel, the Hebrew language, and Israeli literature remain largely "foreign" entities to many Jewish-American writers. By contrast, Israeli novelists read their Jewish-American counterparts with interest, profit, and—let me simply say it—a certain amount of indignation. If there is even a particle of truth in the gloomy assessments about the thinning resources of the Jewish-American experience, about its increasing inability to sustain imaginative fiction, one would think the situation would be very different, and perhaps someday it will be.

Meanwhile, however, Jewish-American fiction continues apace and somehow manages to produce new young writers—one thinks of Max Apple (*The Oranging of America*), Steve Stern (*Lazar Malkin Enters Heaven*), Jerome Badanes (*The Final Opus of Leon Solomon*), Robert Cohn

(*The Organ Builder*), Rhoda Lerman (*God's Ear*), and Allegra Goodman (*Total Immersion*)—who strongly suggest that the full chronicle of Jewish-American literature's "achievement" has not yet been written. Nothing could please me more, both as the author of this interim report and as one who enjoys turning the pages of new Jewish-American fictions.

Notes and References

Preface

1. Rather than rehash the "American-Jewish" versus "Jewish-American" controversy—a debate critics fret about much more than writers—I am using this note to announce that, whenever necessary, I will use the phrase "Jewish-American" without apology or italics. Other critics apparently share my view because I have noticed a subtle shifting from studies of American-Jewish literature to those of Jewish-American literature in recent years.

2. Sanford Pinsker, *Conversations with Contemporary American Writers* (Amsterdam: Rodopi NV, 1985), 42; hereafter cited in text.

3. Writers bristle when they are lumped together in ways that suggest they have regular meetings, set a common agenda, and nominate—or blackball—new members. On the other hand, it should not be surprising that critics respond to the world and the vision that writers present. Thus, when Saul Bellow, for example, complains that nobody talks about him as a hockey fan, one need only point out that if his next novels deal exclusively with hockey, that is what the reviewers for *Sports Illustrated* will focus on. In point of fact, however, what Bellow writes about are Jews and Jewish-American life—and, as such, articles in such journals as *Commentary* and *Studies in American Jewish Literature* come with the territory.

4. Daniel Walden, "The American Yiddish Writer: From Cahan to Singer," in *Ethnic Liberations Since 1776: The Many Voices of America,* ed. W. T. Zyla and Wendell Aycok (Lubbock: Texas Tech Press, 1976), 603.

Chapter One

1. Irving Howe, *World of Our Fathers* (New York: Harcourt Brace Jovanovich, 1976), 517; hereafter cited in text.

2. Isaac Rosenfeld, "The Fall of David Levinsky," in *Preserving the Hunger: An Isaac Rosenfeld Reader,* ed. Mark Shechner, (Detroit: Wayne State University Press, 1988), 152; hereafter cited in text as "Fall."

3. Ibid., 524.

4. Abraham Cahan, *The Rise of David Levinsky* (New York: Harper & Row, 1960), 3; hereafter cited in text as *RDL.*

5. Leslie Fiedler, *The Jew in the American Novel* [pamphlet] (New York: Herzl Institute, 1959), 17.

6. Henry Roth, *Call It Sleep* (New York: Avon, 1964), 437; hereafter cited in text as *CIS.*

7. Cited in Bonnie Lyons, *Henry Roth: The Man and His Work* (New York:

Cooper Square, 1977), 152. Despite Ribalow's yeoman service in discovering Roth and then negotiating for the reissue of his novel, Roth himself grew resentful of the "finder's fee" that was subtracted from his subsequent royalties.

Chapter Two

1. Sol Liptzin, *The Jew in American Literature* (New York: Bloch, 1966), 2.

2. Mary Antin, *The Promised Land* (Boston: Houghton Mifflin, 1969), 364.

3. Michael Gold, *Jews without Money* (New York: Carroll & Graf, 1984), 7; hereafter cited in text as *JWM*.

4. Cited in Walter Allen, afterword to *Call It Sleep,* by Henry Roth (New York: Avon, 1964), 443.

5. Nathanael West, *A Cool Million* (New York: Covici Friede, 1934), 142.

6. Meyer Levin, *The Old Bunch* (New York: Viking, 1937), 23; hereafter cited in text as *OB*.

7. Allen Guttmann, *The Jewish Writer in America* (New York: Oxford University Press, 1971), 45.

8. Daniel Fuchs, *The Williamsburg Trilogy* (New York: Avon, 1934–37), 30.

Chapter Three

1. Irving Howe, *A Margin of Hope* (New York: Harcourt Brace Jovanovich, 1983), 187; hereafter cited in text.

2. Cited in Irving Howe, *World of Our Fathers*, 503.

3. Marian Janssen, *The Kenyon Review, 1939–1970* (Baton Rouge: Louisiana State University Press, 1990), 39.

4. Alan Wald, *The New York Intellectuals* (Chapel Hill: University of North Carolina Press, 1987), 6.

5. Saul Bellow, "Zetland: By a Character Witness," in *Him with His Foot in His Mouth* (New York: Harper & Row, 1984), 195; hereafter cited in text as *HWHF*.

6. Isaac Rosenfeld, "Adam and Eve on Delancey Street," in *Preserving the Hunger,* ed. Shechner, 150; hereafter cited in text as "Adam and Eve."

7. Isaac Rosenfeld, "King Solomon," in *Jewish-American Stories*, ed. Irving Howe (New York: New American Library, 1977), 70.

8. Joseph Heller, *God Knows* (New York: Alfred A. Knopf, 1984), 5.

9. Mark Shechner, "Introduction" to *Preserving the Hunger,* ed. Shechner, 28.

10. Isaac Rosenfeld, *Passage from Home* (New York: Markus Wiener, 1988), 239; hereafter cited in text as *PFH*.

11. Irving Howe, "The Lost Young Intellectual: A Marginal Man, Twice Alienated," *Commentary,* October 1946, 361; hereafter cited in text.

12. Delmore Schwartz, "In Dreams Begin Responsibilities," in *Jewish-American Stories*, ed. Howe, 186; hereafter cited in text as "Dreams."

Chapter Four

1. Y. L. Peretz, "Bontsha the Silent," in *A Treasury of Yiddish Stories*, ed. Irving Howe and Eliezer Greenberg (New York: Viking Press, 1954), 223; hereafter cited in text as "Bontsha."

2. I. B. Singer, "Gimpel the Fool," in *Gimpel the Fool and Other Stories* (New York: Noonday Press, 1957), 3; hereafter cited in text as "Gimpel."

3. Alvin Kernan, *The Cankered Muse* (New Haven, Conn.: Yale University Press, 1959), 11; hereafter cited in text.

4. Bernard Malamud, "The Magic Barrel," in *The Magic Barrel* (New York: Farrar, Straus & Cudahy, 1958), 187; hereafter cited in text as "Magic."

5. Bernard Malamud, *The Assistant* (New York: Farrar, Straus & Cudahy, 1961), 229; hereafter cited in text as *TA*.

6. Jonathan Baumbach, *The Landscape of Nightmare* (New York: New York University Press, 1965), 111.

7. Bernard Malamud, *A New Life* (New York: Farrar, Straus & Cudahy, 1961), 3; hereafter cited in text as *NL*.

8. Mark Goldman, "Bernard Malamud's Comic Vision and the Theme of Identity," *Critique* 7 (Winter 1964–65): 105; hereafter cited in text.

9. Ruth Mandel, "Bernard Malamud's *The Assistant* and *A New Life*: Ironic Affirmation," *Critique* 7 (Winter 1964–65): 105.

10. Robert Alter, "Malamud as Jewish Writer," *Commentary* 42 (September 1966): 72; hereafter cited in text.

11. Bernard Malamud, *The Fixer* (New York: Farrar, Straus & Giroux, 1966), 4; hereafter cited in text as *TF*.

12. Ruth Wisse, *The Schlemiel as Modern Hero* (Chicago: University of Chicago Press, 1971), 114–17.

13. Bernard Malamud, *Dubin's Lives* (New York: Farrar, Straus & Giroux, 1979), 9–10; hereafter cited in text as *DL*.

14. Bernard Malamud, *Pictures of Fidelman* (New York: Farrar, Straus & Giroux, 1967), 276.

15. Saul Bellow, *Seize the Day* (New York: Viking, 1956), 23; hereafter cited in text as *SD*.

16. Daniel Weiss, "Caliban on Prospero: A Psychoanalytic Study of the Novel *Seize the Day*, by Saul Bellow," *American Imago* 19 (Fall 1962): 115.

Chapter Five

1. Philip Roth, *Goodbye, Columbus* (Boston: Houghton Mifflin, 1959), 18; hereafter cited in text as *GC*.

2. Philip Roth, "Commentary Symposium," *Commentary* 31 (April 1961): 350.

3. Philip Roth, *Portnoy's Complaint* (New York: Random House, 1969), i; hereafter cited in text as *PC*.

4. Philip Roth, *Reading Myself and Others* (New York: Farrar, Straus & Giroux, 1975), 211.

5. Philip Roth, *The Ghost Writer* (New York: Farrar, Straus & Giroux, 1979), 91–92; hereafter cited in text as *GW*.

6. Philip Roth, *Zuckerman Unbound* (New York: Farrar, Straus & Giroux, 1981), 7–8; hereafter cited in text as *ZU*.

7. Joseph Heller, *Good as Gold* (New York: Simon & Schuster, 1979), 1; hereafter cited in text as *GG*.

8. Leon Wieseltier, "Shlock of Recognition," *New Republic*, 29 October 1984, 31.

Chapter Six

1. Cited in Andrew Gordon, "Norman Mailer," in *Twentieth-Century American-Jewish Writers*, ed. Daniel Walden (Detroit: Gale Research, 1984), 155; hereafter cited in text.

2. Norman Mailer, *The Naked and the Dead* (New York: Rinehart, 1948), 55; hereafter cited in text as *ND*.

3. Mark Shechner, *After the Revolution* (Detroit: Wayne State University Press, 1987), 173.

4. Norman Mailer, *The White Negro* (San Francisco: City Light Books, 1957), 38.

5. Saul Bellow, "Distractions of a Fiction Writer," in *Saul Bellow: "Herzog,"* ed. Irving Howe (New York: Viking Press, 1976), 369; hereafter cited in text as "Distractions."

6. John Updike, *Bech: A Book* (New York: Alfred A. Knopf, 1970), 164; hereafter cited in text as *BAB*.

7. John Updike, review of *The Letters of James Agee to Father Flye*, *New Republic*, 13 August 1962, 23.

8. Cynthia Ozick, "Literary Blacks and Jews," in *Art and Ardor* (New York: Alfred A. Knopf, 1983), 115; hereafter cited in text as *AA*.

9. Mark Shechner, foreword to *Passage from Home*, by Isaac Rosenfeld (New York: Markus Wiener, 1988), 1.

10. John Updike, *Picked-up Pieces* (New York: Alfred A. Knopf, 1975), 507; hereafter cited in text as *PUP*.

11. Saul Bellow, ed., *Great Jewish Stories* (New York: Dell, 1963), 11.

12. Saul Bellow, *Dangling Man* (New York: Vanguard, 1944), 9; hereafter cited in text as *DM*.

13. James Hall, *The Lunatic Giant in the Drawing Room* (Bloomington: Indiana University Press, 1968), 166.

14. Saul Bellow, *The Victim* (New York: Vanguard, 1947), 18–19; hereafter cited in text as *TV*.

15. Saul Bellow, *Herzog* (New York: Viking Press, 1964), 23; hereafter cited in text as *H*.

16. Saul Bellow, *Mr. Sammler's Planet* (New York: Viking Press, 1970), 3.

17. Saul Bellow, *Humboldt's Gift* (New York: Viking Press, 1975), 115; hereafter cited in text as *HG*.

18. Saul Bellow, *More Die of Heartbreak* (New York: William Morrow, 1988), 155.

Chapter Seven

1. Irving Howe, ed., *Jewish-American Stories* (New York: New American Library, 1977), 16.

2. Cynthia Ozick, "Forewarning," in *Metaphor and Memory* (New York: Alfred A. Knopf, 1989), ii.

3. Cynthia Ozick, "The Pagan Rabbi," in *The Pagan Rabbi and Other Stories* (New York: Alfred A. Knopf, 1971), 3; hereafter cited in text as "Pagan."

4. Cynthia Ozick, *The Cannibal Galaxy* (New York: Alfred A. Knopf, 1983), 3–4; hereafter cited in text as *CG*.

5. Cynthia Ozick, *The Messiah of Stockholm* (New York: Alfred A. Knopf, 1987), 4; hereafter cited in text as *MS*.

6. Joseph Lowin, *Cynthia Ozick* (Boston: Twayne, 1988), 159–60.

7. Robert Alter, "Confronting the Holocaust: Three Israeli Novels," *Commentary* 41 (March 1966), 67.

8. S. Lillian Kremer, *Witness through the Imagination: Jewish American Holocaust Literature* (Detroit: Wayne State University Press, 1989), 15.

Selected Bibliography

PRIMARY WORKS

Note: This listing is limited to *fiction* by the respective writers, even though many of them published numerous other books. In certain instances I have added works of nonfiction and autobiography where they have been important to the writer's reputation.

Bellow, Saul. *Dangling Man*. New York: Vanguard, 1944.
———. *The Victim*. New York:Vanguard, 1947.
———. *Seize the Day*. New York: Viking Press, 1956.
———. *Herzog*. New York: Viking Press, 1964.
———. *Mr. Sammler's Planet*. New York: Viking Press, 1970.
———. *Humboldt's Gift*. New York: Viking Press, 1975.
———. *To Jerusalem and Back* (nonfiction). New York: Viking Press, 1975.
———. *The Dean's December*. New York: Harper & Row, 1984.
———. *Him with His Foot in His Mouth and Other Stories*. New York: Harper & Row, 1984.
———. *More Die of Heartbreak*. New York: William Morrow, 1987.
———. *A Theft*. New York: Viking Penguin, 1989.
———. *The Bellarosa Connection*. New York: Viking Penguin, 1989.
Cahan, Abraham. *The Rise of David Levinsky*. New York: Harper, 1917.
Gold, Michael. *Jews without Money*. New York: Liveright, 1930.
Heller, Joseph. *Catch-22*. New York: Simon & Schuster, 1961.
———. *Something Happened*. New York: Alfred A. Knopf, 1974.
———. *Good as Gold*. New York: Simon & Schuster, 1979.
———. *God Knows*. New York: Alfred A. Knopf, 1984.
———. *No Laughing Matter* (memoir). New York: Putnam, 1986.
———. *Picture This*. New York: Putnam, 1988.
Mailer, Norman. *The Naked and the Dead*. New York: Rinehart, 1948.
———. *The White Negro*. San Francisco: City Lights Books, 1957.
———. *Advertisements for Myself*. New York: Putnam, 1959.
———. *An American Dream*. New York: Dial Press, 1965.
———. *Armies of the Night*. New York: New American Library, 1968.
———. *Ancient Evenings*. Boston: Little, Brown, 1983.
Malamud, Bernard. *The Assistant*. New York: Farrar, Straus & Cudahy, 1957.
———. *The Magic Barrel*. New York: Farrar, Straus & Cudahy, 1958.

————. *A New Life*. New York: Farrar, Straus & Cudahy, 1961.

————. *The Fixer*. New York: Farrar, Straus & Giroux. 1966.

————. *Pictures of Fidelman: An Exhibition*. New York: Farrar, Straus & Giroux, 1969.

————. *The Tenants*. New York: Farrar, Straus & Giroux, 1971.

————. *Rembrandt's Hat*. New York: Farrar, Straus & Giroux, 1973.

————. *Dubin's Lives*. New York: Farrar, Straus & Giroux, 1979.

————. *God's Grace*. New York: Farrar, Straus & Giroux, 1982.

————. *The Stories of Bernard Malamud*. New York: Farrar, Straus & Giroux, 1983.

————. *The People and Uncollected Stories*. New York: Farrar, Straus & Giroux, 1989.

Ozick, Cynthia. *Trust*. New York: E. P. Dutton, 1966.

————. *The Pagan Rabbi and Other Stories*. New York: Alfred A. Knopf, 1971.

————. *Bloodshed and Three Novellas*. New York: Alfred A. Knopf, 1976.

————. *Levitation: Five Fictions*. New York: Alfred A. Knopf, 1982.

————. *Art and Ardor,* New York: Alfred A. Knopf, 1983.

————. *The Cannibal Galaxy*. New York: Alfred A. Knopf, 1983.

————. *The Messiah of Stockholm*. New York: Alfred A. Knopf, 1987.

————. *Metaphor and Memory*. New York: Alfred A. Knopf, 1989.

Rosenfeld, Isaac. *Passage from Home*. New York: Markus Wiener, 1988.

————. *Alpha and Omega*. New York: Viking Press, 1966.

Roth, Henry. *Call It Sleep*. New York: Ballou, 1934.

Roth, Philip. *Goodbye, Columbus*. Boston: Houghton Mifflin, 1959.

————. *Letting Go*. New York: Random House, 1961.

————. *Portnoy's Complaint*. New York: Random House, 1969.

————. *My Life as a Man*. New York: Holt, Rinehart & Winston, 1974.

————. *The Ghost Writer*. New York: Farrar, Straus & Giroux, 1979.

————. *Zuckerman Unbound*. New York: Farrar, Straus & Giroux, 1981.

————. *The Anatomy Lesson*. New York: Farrar, Straus & Giroux, 1984.

————. *The Counterlife*. New York: Farrar, Straus & Giroux, 1987.

————. *The Facts* (autobiography). New York: Farrar, Straus & Giroux, 1988.

————. *Deception*. New York: Simon & Schuster, 1990.

————. *Patrimony* (memoir). New York: Simon & Schuster, 1991.

Schwartz, Delmore. *In Dreams Begin Responsibilities*. Norfolk, Conn.: New Directions, 1938.

Singer, Isaac Bashevis. *Gimpel the Fool and Other Stories*. New York: Noonday Press, 1957.

————. *The Magician of Lublin*. New York: Farrar, Straus & Giroux, 1957.

————. *The Slave*. New York: Farrar, Straus & Giroux, 1961.

————. *Short Friday and Other Stories*. New York: Farrar, Straus, & Giroux, 1965.

————. *In My Father's Court* (memoir). New York: Farrar, Straus & Giroux, 1967.

————. *The Seance and Other Stories.* New York: Farrar, Straus & Giroux, 1968.

————. *A Friend of Kafka and Other Stories.* New York: Farrar, Straus & Giroux, 1970.

————. *The Collected Stories of Isaac Bashevis Singer.* New York: Farrar, Straus & Giroux, 1982.

————. *Enemies: A Love Story.* New York: Farrar, Straus & Giroux, 1987.

————. *The Death of Methuselah and Other Stories.* New York: Farrar, Straus & Giroux, 1988.

————. *King of the Fields.* New York: Farrar, Straus & Giroux, 1988.

————. *Shoym.* New York: Farrar, Straus & Giroux, 1991.

West, Nathanael. *A Cool Million.* New York: Covici Friede, 1934.

————. *The Day of the Locust.* New York: Random House, 1939.

SECONDARY WORKS

This listing is of background and theoretical works; criticism on individual authors and their works can be found in the authors' respective guides, in *American Literary Scholarship, an Annual,* published by Duke University Press, and in special issues of *Studies in American-Jewish Literature* published by Kent State University Press.

Alter, Robert. *After the Tradition: Essays on Modern Jewish Writing.* New York: Dutton, 1969.

————. *Defenses of the Imagination: Jewish Writers and Modern Historical Crisis.* Philadelphia: Jewish Publication Society of America, 1977.

Baumgarten, Murray. *City Scriptures: Modern Jewish Writing.* Cambridge: Harvard University Press, 1982.

Berger, Alan. *Crisis and Covenant: The Holocaust in American Jewish Fiction.* Albany: SUNY Press, 1985.

Chametzky, Jules. *Our Decentralized Literature: Cultural Mediations in Selected Jewish and Southern Writers.* Amherst: University of Massachusetts Press, 1986.

Dembo, L.S. *The Monological Jew: A Literary Study.* Madison: University of Wisconsin Press, 1988.

Eisenberg, Azriel, ed. *The Golden Land: A Literary Portrait of American Jewry 1654 to the Present.* New York: Yoseloff, 1965.

Fiedler, Leslie. *The Jew in the American Novel.* New York: Herzl Institute Pamphlet, 1956.

Gittleman, Sol. *From Shtetl to Suburbia: The Family in Jewish Literary Imagination.* Boston: Beacon, 1978.

Guttmann, Allen. *The Jewish Writer in America: Assimilation and the Crisis of Identity.* New York: Oxford University Press, 1971.

Harap, Louis. *The Image of the Jew in American Literature from Early Republic to Mass Immigration.* Philadelphia: Jewish Publication Society of America, 1974.

———. *Creative Awakening: The Jewish Presence in Twentieth-Century American Literature.* Philadelphia: Jewish Publication Society of America, 1987.

Howe, Irving. *World of Our Fathers.* New York: Harcourt Brace Jovanovich, 1976.

Knopp, Josephine Z. *The Trial of Judaism in Contemporary Jewish Writing.* Urbana: University of Illinois Press, 1975.

Kremer, S. Lillian. *Witness Through the Imagination: Jewish American Holocaust Literature.* Detroit: Wayne State University Press, 1989.

Liptzin, Sol. *The Jew in American Literature.* New York: Bloch, 1966.

Malin, Irving. *Jews and Americans.* Carbondale: Southern Illinois University Press, 1965.

———, ed. *Contemporary American-Jewish Literature: Critical Essays.* Bloomington: Indiana University Press, 1973.

Pinsker, Sanford. *The Schlemiel as Metaphor: Studies in the Yiddish and American Jewish Novel.* Carbondale: Southern Illinois University Press, 1971. Enlarged and revised ed., 1991.

Schulz, Max. *Radical Sophistication: Studies in Contemporary Jewish-American Novelists.* Athens: Ohio University Press, 1969.

Shechner, Mark. *After the Revolution: Studies in the Contemporary Jewish-American Imagination.* Bloomington: Indiana University Press, 1987.

Wisse, Ruth. *The Schlemiel as Modern Hero.* Chicago: University of Chicago Press, 1971.

Index

The Author

Sanford Pinsker is Shadek Professor of English at Franklin and Marshall College. He is the author of *The Schlemiel as Metaphor* (1971), *The Comedy that "Hoits"; An Essay on the Fiction of Philip Roth* (1975), *The Languages of Joseph Conrad* (1978), *Between Two Worlds: The American Novel in the 1960s* (1978), *Philip Roth: Critical Essays* (1982), *Conversations with Contemporary American Writers* (1985), *Three Pacific Northwest Poets: Stafford, Hugo, and Wagoner* (1987), *The Uncompromising Fictions of Cynthia Ozick* (1987), *Bearing the Bad News* (1990), and *Understanding Joseph Heller* (1991). In addition, Professor Pinsker is a widely published poet and book reviewer.

The Editor

Warren French (Ph.D., University of Texas, Austin) retired from Indiana University in 1986 and is now an honorary professor associated with the Board of American Studies at the University College of Swansea, Wales. In 1985 Ohio University awarded him a doctor of humane letters. He has contributed volumes to Twayne's United States Authors Series on Jack Kerouac, Frank Norris, John Steinbeck, and J. D. Salinger. His most recent publication for Twayne is *The San Francisco Poetry Renaissance, 1955–1960*.